Praise for *Confessing Community: An Entryway to Theological Interpretation in North East India*

"What Taimaya Ragui brings to the fore in this book is the context of the confessing community—the one holy catholic church in its varied local expressions. What happens when the centrifugal force of contextual theology meets the centripetal force of catholicity? The great contribution of this book lies in its demonstration that there need be no final conflict between locality and catholicity: the confessing community, which is to say the local church as interpretive community, can be fully catholic and fully contextual—two natures, as it were, in one ecclesial body."

—*Kevin J. Vanhoozer*
Trinity Evangelical Divinity School
Deerfield, IL

"In this significant work, Taimaya Ragui brings together a unique conversation between theological interpretation of Scripture (TIS) and contextual theology. He does it in such a way that each can learn from the other. I highly recommend this book not only for its accurate accounting of TIS and tribal theology but also as a great example of doing theology."

—*Varughese John*
South Asia Institute of Advanced Christian Studies
Bangalore, India

"This North East Indian theologian examines a major problem in biblical interpretation: Should we aspire to be context-free (like in the West) or to be context-bound (like North East India)? Astutely diagnosing the resulting dangers and building on Kevin Vanhoozer, Taimaya Ragui brilliantly offers a clear way forward: a multi-contextual biblical-theological interpretation of Scripture. Enormously important for North East India and for interpreters of the Bible everywhere, *Confessing Community* is a clarion call for church and academy to refocus on and retrieve what God has said and done and is saying and doing in Jesus and the Spirit."

—*Ian Walter Payne*
Theologians Without Borders
Auckland, New Zealand

"Some do theology without the Bible. Others study the Bible without being aware of their theology. In this excellent book, Taimaya Ragui combines the Bible with theology in an insightful way that avoids both problems.

His theological interpretation of Scripture is a much-needed methodology to encounter the contextual realities facing majority world academia and churches."

—Nigel Ajay Kumar
theological education consultant
Bangalore, India

"Dr Ragui has given us an important book, engaging the theological interpretation of Scripture with a significant Asian context. Where so much of theology is written with a blind Western worldview, we need such a thoughtful and stimulating voice to expand our thinking and help contextualize our theological method more sharply. I thoroughly commend this book to a wide readership."

—Bishop Paul Barker
Anglican Diocese of Melbourne
Melbourne, Australia

Confessing Community

Confessing Community

An Entryway to Theological Interpretation in North East India

By

Taimaya Ragui

Foreword by

Kevin J. Vanhoozer

FORTRESS PRESS
MINNEAPOLIS

CONFESSING COMMUNITY
An Entryway to Theological Interpretation in North East India

Cover design and art by Savanah N. Landerholm

Print ISBN: 978-1-5064-8678-9
eBook ISBN: 978-1-5064-8679-6

CONTENTS

Acknowledgments ix

Foreword xi

Introduction 1

1. Modern Biblical Interpretation in the West: The Tension Between Biblical Studies and Theology and the Privileging of the Original Context 7

    Introduction 7

    Modern Biblical Interpretation 10

    Early Modern Period 13

        Authority and Reason 13

        Naturalists and Criticism 18

        Rationalism and Criticism 22

    High Modern Period 29

        Historicism and Criticism 30

        Hermeneutics and Criticism 32

        Historical Theology and Criticism 34

        "Believing Criticism" and Criticism 37

    Late Modern Period 42

        Postmodernism (Ideology) and Criticism (Exegesis) 44

        Church (Theology) and Criticism (Biblical Studies) 50

    Conclusion 55

2. Tribal Theology and Tribal Biblical Interpretation in North East India: The Tension Between Dominant Voice and Voices from the Margin and the Privileging of the Tribal Context 57

    Introduction 57

    Tribal Theology in North East India 58

    Early Tribal Discussions 59

Early Tribal Discussions in North East India 62
Emergence of Contextual Concerns 65
Distinctive Developments of Tribal Theology 67
Contemporary Concerns and Issues 70
Biblical Interpretation in North East India 74
Conclusion 80

3. Theological Interpretation of Scripture: The Tension Between Theological Disciplines Over Biblical Interpretation and the Privileging of Theology 81
Introduction 81
The Reemergence of Theological Interpretation of Scripture 82
Approaches of Theological Interpretation of Scripture 95
Biblical Studies and Systematic Theology 96
Biblical Theology and Systematic Theology 102
Theological Interpretation of Scripture: Kevin J. Vanhoozer 106
The Core Principle 107
The Canonical Principle 111
The Catholic Principle 113
The Contextual Principle 116
Observation and Conclusion 117

4. A Constructive Proposal of Theological Interpretation of Scripture with Catholic Sensibility and Contextual Sensitivity in North East India Tribal Context 121
Introduction 121
Theological Interpretation of Scripture and Contextual (Tribal) Theology: The Stage 123
Theological Interpretation of Scripture and Contextual Concerns 125
Tribal Theology and Theological Concerns 127
Theological Interpretation of Scripture and Contextual Theology: A Constructive Proposal 129

A Constructive Theoretical Framework: History, Theology, and Context 132
History 133
Theology 137
Context 140
A Constructive Theological Proposal: Biblical Theology and Contextual Theology 147
Biblical Studies/Theology and Contextual Theology 149
Biblical Theology and Contextual Theology 154
Conclusion 170
Conclusion 173
Bibliography 179
Index 197

ACKNOWLEDGMENTS

Writing this book came with the help, guidance, and wisdom of several individuals. Such providence came in the form of prayers, insights, and encouragement from my mentors, friends, family, and strangers. As a part of this project deals with the local-tribal confessing community, such community involvement was desirable.

I am thankful to God for God's presence, provision, and protection in this PhD journey. This journey was more than an intellectual pursuit. It was indeed a spiritual pilgrimage.

My gratitude goes out to Kevin J. Vanhoozer. He was kind enough to reply to my 2012 email, supervise my doctoral thesis, and write a foreword for this work. His prompt, insightful, critical, and *always* constructive response is much valued.

I am thankful to Nigel Ajay Kumar who began influencing me as a master's student. His ever-present openness to talking things through encouraged me to bravely finish my thesis on time.

I am very thankful to Anglican Evangelical Trust (Melbourne), which generously provided my tuition fees for PhD studies. I am thankful to Paul Barker, Drew Mellor, Alan Ashmore, and Neil Bach for their help.

As I struggled with financial constraints, my niece and nephew sent me their piggy bank savings throughout my studies. Along with them, occasional and timely provision came through Phungyo Baptist Church, Achei Ton, Awo Phaning, Luminao, Rakmi, Achon Rin, and Ayung. Their generosity helped me meet my needs during my doctoral studies.

English is my third language. And I needed to make my work more reader-friendly. Paul Barker and Themreichon Leisan were gracious enough to read through my dissertation.

In the initial stage of my work, I received critical comments and insights from Ian W. Payne and Aruthuckal Varughese John. I am thankful to them (and the SAIACS theology department) for their continual support and encouragement.

I am also thankful to the SAIACS and UTC library staff. My interaction with UTC students during my one-week stay at UTC was quite motivating.

Along this journey, moral support and encouragement come through friends and family members. Aton Hungyo helped me stay sane in the whole process. Ama, Papa, and other family members who unceasingly prayed for me. Intellectually stimulating conversation came through friends like Johnson, Worring, Stavan, Apam, Ngatar, and Meren.

I am thankful to the Tangkhul churches that gave me the privilege to be part of their pulpit ministry. Interaction with them assured me of why this research is needed, i.e., biblical interpretation should be local and catholic, like the church it serves.

FOREWORD

Can anything good come out of Tangkhul Nagas, a tribal group living in the borderlands of Burma and North East India? Philip's reply to Nathaniel's equally impertinent question about Nazareth serves as my answer too: "Come and see" (John 1:46)—or rather, take up and read.

It was my privilege to serve as Taimaya Ragui's doctoral dissertation supervisor under the auspices of the South Asia Institute for Advanced Christian Studies (SAIACS). I didn't need the work, nor did I "come and see"—in fact, Tai and I have never met—but I was intrigued by his thesis proposal: to relate (Western) theological interpretation of Scripture to (non-Western) contextual theology. This struck me as a task that was as heroic as it was Ricoeurrian in its ambition to mediate a seemingly intractable opposition ("Blessed are the peacemakers" [Matt 5:9]).

As Mikhail Bakhtin pointedly observed, none of us can see what is behind our backs; we need someone else's vantage point ("outsideness") to see what is behind us. Tai hails from North East India, and offers a valuable outsider's perspective on two fateful Western oppositions—between the academy and the church, between biblical and theological studies—charting the various twists and turns of these century-long developments. Tai not only sees behind but has our back. He is kind enough never to tar these long-standing Western conflicts with the rhetorical brush-off "tribal" (though he could arguably have done so).

Tai's description of how colonialism exported Western conflicts into his own context is equally of interest. However, what surprised me most was the realization that our respective churches, though separated by languages and oceans, cultures, and continents, are nevertheless not *worlds* apart, inasmuch as both Western and non-Western Christian churches struggle to interpret Scripture in ways that speak into their respective contexts.

Context is indeed the operative term. Tai rightly argues that the differences between the aims and interests of interpretive communities may be seen in the priorities that each gives to different contexts. For example, in the Western academy, modern biblical scholars tend to privilege the original historical context, whereas in the tribal theology of North East India, pride of interpretive place typically goes to the contemporary sociocultural context.

Tai's original contribution brings this conflict of interpretive interests into dialogue with the recent retrieval of older interpretive practices associated with the so-called "theological interpretation of Scripture." This latter approach lies somewhere between the academy and the church, *and* between the Majority and non-Western worlds inasmuch as it seeks to be catholic: to read with Christians everywhere and at all times.

What Tai therefore ends up meditating on, and mediating in, in this book are the various contexts—historical, literal, cultural, and *ecclesial*—that jockey for position, and pride of place, in biblical hermeneutics. What he eventually brings to the fore is the context of the confessing community—the one holy catholic church *in its varied local expressions.* What happens when the centrifugal force of contextual theology meets the centripetal force of catholicity? The great contribution of this book lies in its demonstration that there need be no final conflict between locality and catholicity: the confessing community—which is to say, the local church as interpretive community—can be fully catholic and fully contextual, two natures as it were in one ecclesial body.

Can anything good come out of Tangkhul Nagas? Yes! Perhaps the most noteworthy insight to emerge from the present book concerns the need to attend to multiple contexts—historical, canonical, contemporary, ecclesial—for this pertains to the nature of Christian theology everywhere, to anyone, and at all times. This central insight is every bit as relevant to the academy and local churches in North East India as those in North East Indiana. My hope is that more good yet will come from this proposal, and from the confessing Tangkhul communities, as they learn to read the *canonical* Scriptures with the one holy *catholic* church in their singular local *context*, and, in so doing, set an example for local churches (and academies) everywhere, not just in the West.

Kevin J. Vanhoozer
Research Professor of Systematic Theology
Trinity Evangelical Divinity School
Deerfield, IL

INTRODUCTION

One of the pressing concerns facing Christianity has to do with biblical interpretation, and consequently, the concerns of methods that are related to how history, theology, and context determine the meaning of the text for the church. Whether it is the modern or postmodern interpretation, it has not been able to provide viable solutions for the church. In fact, since the emergence of modern biblical criticism, there are perceived tensions,[1] crises,[2] or even turmoil[3] in biblical interpretation.

The problem facing biblical interpretation is threefold. One aspect of the problem is the tensions within biblical studies itself. With modern and postmodern pursuits, they are offering various ways to arrive at the meaning of the text. New approaches, especially with the literary turn in philosophy and interpretation, challenge historicism or historical interpretation.[4] Another aspect of the problem is the tension between biblical studies and theology. Here, the clash extends beyond methodology to the presuppositions and identities of the interpreters. In "theology" the use of doctrines to shape interpretation is a pushback against the "objective" focus, toward a recovery of classical (pre-modern) approaches to reading Scripture. On the other end, Majority World[5] scholars differ from their

---

1 Kevin J. Vanhoozer, "Introduction: What is Theological Interpretation of the Bible?" in *Dictionary for Theological Interpretation of the Bible*, ed. Kevin J. Vanhoozer (Grand Rapids: Baker, 2005), 19–25.

2 Garrett Green, *Theology, Hermeneutics, and Imagination: The Crisis of Interpretation at the End of Modernity* (Cambridge: CUP, 2000).

3 John Barton, "Introduction" in *The Cambridge Companion to Biblical Interpretation*. ed. Barton John (Cambridge: CUP, 1998), 1–6.

4 Barton, "Introduction" in *The Cambridge Companion to Biblical Interpretation*, 1–6.

5 As the term Western is not intended to be used as a negative, "Majority World" is not essentially positive. The "Majority World" is a terminology used in this study, in contrast with the "West," to refer to the regions of South America, Africa, and Asia, where most Christians live. Majority World scholars would thus refer to scholars from those regions.

Western[6] counterparts by offering radical rereadings of the text that challenge conventional interpretation. This affects the allegedly "context-free" and "context-bound" settings to interpret Scripture;[7] the context, in this case, refers to the current/local context. However, the most pressing aspect of the problem has to do with the growing divide between academics and the local church in biblical interpretation. There is an apparent gap between what is discussed and taught in the academy and what is preached and practiced in the church. Most of the discussions on theology or biblical interpretation are in the academy, while its teachings or discussions remain irrelevant to the church.

This is not to say that the church has no problems of its own. While emphasizing only on spiritual or devotional reading of the Bible, the church often neglects the basic skills of exegesis, or even lacks the ability to systematically bring the Bible and context through a theological vision. While the church may encourage its members to read the Bible, the congregation often must fend for itself when it comes to reading the Bible or interpreting difficult texts. Consequently, most of the church members are not equipped with even the basic skills of Bible reading. This is a failure on the part of the church. It is also to suggest that the church plays its part concerning the divide between the church and the academy in biblical interpretation. The academy may have ignored the concerns of the church, but the church itself seems to have neglected the need to stay relevant to its sociopolitical context, and to a certain extent, ignored its responsibility to teach and equip its members. Considering this reality, the church—in this case, tribal[8] churches—needs to own their responsibility to engage with their context/culture and equip its church members instead of operating with the assumption that the text will speak to the people on its own. Meaning or the message of the text is not yet settled. It is an ongoing task.

---

[6] I do not intend to mean "Western" in a negative sense, though some scholars I quote below may mean it as such. I use the "Western" terminology here in a qualified sense. I find the term useful as a shorthand reference to American and European contexts that influenced a lot of our theological thinking today, including biblical interpretation.

[7] I am indebted to Ian W. Payne, the former principal of SAIACS, for the use of the terms *context-free* and *context-bound* when used in reference to modern and postmodern/Majority World scholars/interpretation. Ian W. Payne, email to the author, January 23, 2018.

[8] Though the term *tribe* or *tribal* is problematic (i.e., it is derogatory), it is used with the awareness of the struggle of Indigenous people and their ongoing struggle to be freed from the captivity of dominant structure. Cf. R. L. Rocky, "Tribes and Tribal Studies in North East: Deconstructing the Politics of Colonial Methodology," *Journal of Tribal Intellectual Collective India*, 1.2 (2013): 25–37.

While all these issues are complex, one way to approach this tension is to focus on the idea of context. The historical, theological, and contextual concerns can be seen as problematic, especially when the interpreter prioritizes one context and reduces/ignores a focus on others. However, rather than offering a simplistic "multi-contextual" approach, one needs to understand the value of each context to then offer a methodology that holds the multiple contexts together, if indeed they are worthwhile to hold together. With this concern in mind, the current project poses (and answers) the question: Is a multi-contextual approach to reading the Bible desirable, or even possible? To put the question another way: How can we constructively engage in reading Scripture through historical, theological, and contextual contexts for the purpose of edifying the church?

To answer this question, I take a long and hard look at the *theological interpretation of Scripture* movement, called TIS. Over the past few decades, TIS has emerged as an academic movement (but with ecclesial concern) that has challenged biblical criticism and called for the integration of theology with biblical studies. This study focuses much of its attention on TIS, and how it addresses the need for theological thinking in biblical interpretation. In addition to TIS, this study looks at contextual theology, particularly *tribal theology*. Tribal theology, representing one end of theological method, tends to take theology and context seriously, but sometimes loses the value and rigor of biblical historical meaning. It is because of tribal theology that I see that simply rejecting biblical criticism cannot be the answer, but a consolidated approach is needed.

The above reality suggests that there are tensions in terms of the differing priorities readers give in various contexts (e.g., the original historical context vs. the contemporary context). There is a tendency for modern Western biblical studies to claim to be context-free, or at least to privilege the original historical context rather than the ecclesial context, and a tendency in Majority World theology to be context-bound, or at least to privilege the present-day contexts of various ethnic groups (see chapter 2). However, this tension, whether in the West or Majority World, has caused a divide between the church and the academy, i.e., there is a gap between what is preached in the church and what is discussed in the academy. This project investigates and addresses the divide between the church and the academy in biblical interpretation. While considering the importance of reading the Bible with multiple contexts in mind, it argues for ecclesial context—with particular attention to the emergence of the confessing community of Tangkhul Naga—as the location to do theology in the North East India tribal context.

This project is taken up from a twofold perspective. First, it will enter the theological discussion by examining the relationship between TIS and contextual theology. This is done by interfacing biblical theology with contextual theology that results in theological interpretation of Scripture in NEI tribal context. The task is carried out by adapting Kevin J. Vanhoozer's theodrama or theological method, which recognizes canon sense, catholic sensibility, and contextual sensitivity. His model of theodrama provides a framework to challenge the exclusive academic claim of modern and postmodern interpretation or Majority World Bible reading with pluralistic tendencies. What is differentiated from his work is the attention given to the historical particularities of *the emergence of the confessing community* of the Tangkhul Nagas. Second, it will enter the theological discussion in NEI with attention to ecclesial concern. Rather than privileging the tribal theological discussion in the academy, this project attempts to bring the tribal local church as the location to do theology, i.e., the local-tribal confessing community. When the terms *local context* or *local churches* are used, they refer to the Baptist church of the Tangkhul community in Ukhrul, Manipur. The given task will be done from an evangelical perspective by associating with but moving beyond the theological discussion and direction of the Asia Theological Association (hereafter, ATA), in the context of both the larger tribal theological discussion and development of tribal biblical interpretation in NEI.

This project is interested in bringing out a constructive account of theological interpretation of Scripture in NEI tribal context with canonical sense, catholic sensibility, and contextual sensitivity. As TIS dialogues with contextual theology, it seeks to provide a constructive theological-scriptural account of how and why catholicity and contextuality belong together.[9] Retrieving the catholic context affirms that the tribal church belongs together with the catholic church. In this project, the terms *catholic* or *catholic sensibility* are used in recognition of God's action across history, including the contemporary context; when the terms are used in connection with the local church or context, it means keeping track of the continuity of the confessing community of the Christian faith, i.e., from across space and time to the present tribal community. Moreover, affirming the tribal context—in this case, the local-tribal confessing community—recognizes the theological contribution that comes out of a particular historical context and period.

The current project proposes that TIS, particularly through the work of Vanhoozer, has something to offer to the divide between the academy

[9] Kevin J. Vanhoozer, email to the author, February 13, 2018.

and the church, in both the Western and Majority World settings. This project also proposes the view that TIS has something to learn from contextual theology. This is to argue that TIS adds catholic sensibility to contextual theology's sensitivity of context, and contextual theology adds sensitivity to local context to TIS's catholic sensibility. Primarily, this project contributes to the discussion of TIS as it attempts to provide *an entryway to the discussion between theological interpretation of Scripture and contextual theology* (i.e., tribal theology). This project thus finally asserts that biblical interpretation must be both local and catholic, like the church it serves. I argue for the importance of reading the Bible from multiple contexts as an attempt is made to address the tension between the church and the academy (i.e., the neglect of theology). This approach of reading the Bible will be referred to as a *multi-contextual biblical-theological interpretation of Scripture.* It pays attention to the original historical context, the canonical context, the context of catholic tradition, and the contemporary cultural context. The fundamental premise of this project is based on the understanding that God has revealed Godself through Jesus Christ in the Bible, which was written down by the human authors through the work of the Holy Spirit. It recognizes what God said and did in the past through Christ and anticipates what God might be saying and doing in different ethnic-cultural contexts—in this case, the local-tribal confessing community—through the Spirit.[10]

The purpose of this project is to appreciate the contribution of TIS in the contemporary discussion of biblical interpretation. In addition, it identifies the need for the TIS (i.e., Western in orientation) to engage with contextual theology (i.e., Majority World in orientation) to truly appreciate catholic context as a context to do theology. In such interpretative tasks, the church or the ecclesial context is seen as the location to do theology.

We begin to approach this task by focusing on Bible interpretation in the West. The first chapter traces and explains the shift of biblical interpretation in the eighteenth and nineteenth centuries in the West and argues that the privileging of the original context in biblical interpretation in the modern period resulted in a gap between what is discussed in the academy and what is preached in the church.

The second chapter provides a historical sketch of tribal theology in late twentieth-century NEI and captures tribal biblical interpretation, which suggests that it is moving toward a plurality of interests. While

[10] Kevin J. Vanhoozer, *The Drama of Doctrine: A Canonical Linguistic Approach to Christian Theology* (Louisville: Westminster John Knox Press, 2005), 17.

privileging the sociopolitical concern in their theological-interpretative task, the ecclesial context is being ignored or neglected.

The third chapter captures the emergence and development of theological interpretation in the late twentieth century, which addresses the division between theological disciples over biblical interpretation and the dichotomy between academy and church in biblical interpretation. It then highlights that TIS is yet to engage with contextual theology, while prioritizing its theological engagement with the discipline of biblical studies, systematic theology, or biblical theology.

And the fourth chapter contributes to the discussion of TIS as it attempts to provide *an entryway to the discussion between theological interpretation of Scripture and contextual theology*. It argues for the importance of reading the Bible from multiple contexts, i.e., the original historical context, the canonical context, the context of catholic tradition, and the contemporary cultural context.

1

MODERN BIBLICAL INTERPRETATION IN THE WEST: THE TENSION BETWEEN BIBLICAL STUDIES AND THEOLOGY AND THE PRIVILEGING OF THE ORIGINAL CONTEXT

Introduction

A distinct shift took place in modern biblical interpretation in the West. This shift is intrinsically linked with the rise of biblical criticism, which was conceptualized in the seventeenth century, (began to be) practiced in the eighteenth century, dominated the nineteenth century, and continues to influence (and gradually decline, if not a total decline)[1] in the twentieth century. This shift in biblical interpretation resulted in a certain demarcation between the church and the academy:[2] from using Scripture, the true story of the world, as the framework for understanding everything else, to using a critically reconstructed history (and what we know about the natural world) as the framework for reading (and criticizing) the biblical narrative. This is a shift from the enchanted worldview (presence of miracle, divine involvement, etc.) to the disenchanted worldview (absence

1 Yet there are scholars who still argue for the relevance of biblical criticism (or historical criticism) in the contemporary context. See John Barton, "Historical-Critical Approaches" in *The Cambridge Companion to Biblical Interpretation*. ed. Barton John (Cambridge: CUP, 1998), 9–20; John Barton, *The Nature of Biblical Criticism* (Louisville: Westminster John Knox, 2007); David R. Law, *The Historical Critical Method: A Guide for the Perplexed* (New York: T&T Clark, 2012); Roy A. Harrisville, *Pandora's Box Opened: An Examination and Defense of Historical-Critical Method and Its Master Practitioners* (Grand Rapids: Eerdmans, 2014).

2 This is different from what Legaspi said in *The Death of Scripture*. The rise of the academic Bible is a net result of the crisis in authority where ecclesial underpinning to the scriptural Bible was weakened after the Reformation. Michael C. Legaspi, *The Death of Scripture and the Rise of Biblical Studies* (Oxford: OUP, 2010), viii.

of the divine, miracle, etc.) in biblical interpretation. Hans Frei calls this shift "the great reversal," where biblical interpretation is now "a matter of fitting the biblical story into another world with another story rather than incorporating that world into the biblical story."[3]

This chapter tries to historically trace and explain the shift of biblical interpretation in the eighteenth and nineteenth centuries in the West. The task will be carried out with a thesis: The privileging of the original context in biblical interpretation in the modern period resulted in a gap between what is discussed in the academy and what is preached in the church.[4] This privileging is a direct outcome of the rise of biblical criticism. The precritical interpreters (e.g., the Reformers) privileged the original context, but with the affirmation of the divine inspiration of the Bible (i.e., they had an enchanted worldview). However, modern critics privileged the original context but without a sense of divine inspiration (i.e., the disenchanted worldview), leading to the rise of biblical criticism.[5]

With the emergence and advancement of biblical criticism, biblical scholarship began to serve the interest of the academy instead of the church. This is motivated and influenced by methodological naturalists where they refute, "quite vigorously, the notion that a Supernatural Being has interacted with nature in a manner deemed miraculous."[6] They were interested in acquiring knowledge through cognitive means, and without believing in divine revelation or miracles. This was evidently a reaction to the supernaturalists who were "defending the relation of the Bible to divine revelation by almost entirely removing it from the sphere of historical contingency, through the elaboration of an increasingly formalised and doctrinally isolated theory of inspiration."[7] The supernaturalists were only interested in the enchanted worldview, where they believe that the

---

3 Hans W. Frei, *The Eclipse of Biblical Narrative: A Study in Eighteenth and Nineteenth Century* (New Haven: YUP, 1974), 130; 6–9.

4 Much of my work interacts with Hans W. Frei. But it differs in our theses. He traces the eighteenth- and nineteenth-century biblical interpretation with the attempt to highlight the realistic or history-like feature of the Bible which was observed but ignored in the modern period. Frei, *The Eclipse of Biblical Narrative*, 10.

5 The terms *precritical* or *critical* are used as accepted categories to differentiate their approach to the Bible and its interpretation. But this is done with the recognition of the difficulties that come with these categories. See J.W. Rogerson, "Biblical Criticism" in *A Dictionary of Biblical Interpretation*, ed. R. J. Coggins and J. L. Houlden, (London: SCM, 1990), 84.

6 Joseph B. Onyango Okello, *A History and Critique of Methodological Naturalism: The Philosophical Case for God's Design of Nature* (Orlando: WIPF & Stock, 2015), 1.

7 John Webster, *Holy Scripture: A Dogmatic Sketch* (Cambridge: CUP, 2003), 20.

Bible is a reliable document of divine revelation, and miracles and prophecy of the biblical narrative are historical facts.[8] John Webster captures the tension between methodological naturalists and supernaturalists in the following manner:

> From one angle, the result is docetic—a text without any kind of home in natural history. From another angle, the result is ironically historicising, a de-eschatologizing of the text's relation to revelation by envisaging the text as an apparently creaturely object endowed with divine properties.[9]

The reality of this twofold direction is this: "Either the naturalness of the text is safeguarded by extracting it from any role in God's self-communication, or the relation of the text to revelation is affirmed by removing the text from the historical conditions of its production."[10] It can be said that this differing reading is a shift in the ontology (or nature) of the text, in what they think the Bible is from supernatural perception of the text to natural investigation of the text. It is also a shift in the teleology (or purpose) of the text, which is no longer to deliver divine instruction but to serve as a source for reconstructing "what actually happened."[11] The problem of modern critics is this: the Bible is read not as God-given but solely as human made. The result of such methodological naturalism is that ministers or scholars with critical influence read the Bible differently, and for different purposes, i.e., scholars cannot read the Bible as divine revelation. The crisis of such reading is that the community of faith cannot find the help they need in modern biblical interpretation/commentaries—which eventually resulted in a divide between the academy and the church in biblical interpretation.

Considering the immensity and the complexity of the subject, the discussion of the present chapter will be limited to eighteenth- and nineteenth-century Western (Protestant) biblical interpretation. This is further narrowed down to the discussion of how there was a shift from the church to the academy in the modern biblical interpretation—a shift that concerns the primary location where the Bible was interpreted. The nature of how this chapter is presented will be descriptive and not prescriptive—but with necessary efforts to make decisive suggestions as the case may require. The current project comes out of the concern of where biblical criticism is moving toward: while modern interpreters were prioritizing the original context (to find out what actually happened, behind the text), the ecclesial context (what can build up the community

---

8 Frei, *The Eclipse of Biblical Narrative*, 87.

9 Webster, *Holy Scripture*, 21.

10 Webster, *Holy Scripture*, 21.

11 Kevin J. Vanhoozer, email message to author, January 21, 2019.

of faith) was being ignored, leading to a crisis in biblical interpretation. The outcome of methodological naturalism or disenchanted worldview is that interpretation and commentaries of the modern biblical criticism were no longer accessible to the church, while the supernaturalists or the enchanted worldview reading of the text (i.e., that which edifies the community of faith) were being ignored or neglected in biblical interpretation.

Modern Biblical Interpretation

This section tries to capture the rise and thrall of biblical criticism in the eighteenth- and nineteenth-century West. A focus on this period is important because biblical interpretation became the primary focus of the academy, making it inaccessible to the church. One of the major disagreements between precritical and critical interpreters is their understanding of the one real world.[12] *This is a tension between the enchanted worldview and the disenchanted worldview.* The precritical interpreters, those who hold the enchanted worldview, tend to trust the story of the Bible and they are supernaturalists, while (most of) the modern interpreters or the disenchanted worldview adopt a different story of the real world and they are methodological naturalists. This is a bifurcation of worldviews: the precritical readers are soaked in the transcendent understanding of God, while the modern readers are consumed in the creaturely texts of the Bible.[13] The precritical interpreters assumed a supernatural view of the world where miracle is acceptable in their narrative. Hence, in practice, they tended to interpret the Bible literally, i.e., the literal sense was the true meaning of the text and what seemed obscure (figural sense) was read considering the clearer texts.[14] While the modern critics are naturalists, divine intervention or miracle is not natural, i.e., it is not compatible with the historical narrative. While emphasizing the original context of the text, they are interested in the single meaning of the text, which is the historical reference. This is done by historical investigation of the text referring to the extrabiblical sources and reconstructing the biblical narrative.

The shift from precritical to critical interpretation is influenced by a host of emergences in the areas of science and philosophy.[15] While the

[12] Frei, *The Eclipse of Biblical Narrative*, 2–3.

[13] Webster suggests an appeal to "a Christian doctrine of the trinitarian works of God" as solution to this predicament. Webster, *Holy Scripture*, 18.

[14] See Jean Grondin, *Introduction to Philosophical Hermeneutics,* trans. Joel Weinsheimer (New Haven: YUP, 1994), 39–41; D. C. Steinmetz, "John Calvin as Interpreter of the Bible," in *Calvin and the Bible*, ed. D. K. McKim (Cambridge: CUP, 2006), 285.

[15] Still others suggest that the study of the rise of criticism reflects a deep relation between biblical interpretation and politics.

full impact of science in the area of biblical interpretation was felt only in the nineteenth century, "the scientific spirit" began surging in the early eighteenth century.[16] Advancement in science brought a questioning of the traditional understanding of earth or the universe, Christendom, chronology, and geography. It brought the assumption that the evidence of observation is equally reliable, if not more reliable than the Bible.[17] In addition (and consequently), instead of using the Bible as the authority for writing history or geography, arguments were made using *reason* for historical/geographical study. For instance, using a combination of geography and chronological study, Isaac La Peyrère argued that the first human predated the first biblical man.[18] Along with such an impact, the rise of natural philosophy brought a drastic change in modern thinking. Natural philosophy is "that science which considers the powers of nature, the properties of natural bodies, and their actions upon one another."[19] Science then refers to deductive reasoning of humankind—not the senses, but the operation of the human mind.[20] With its rise came the question of the presence of divine purpose in the natural order, and the placing of humankind with a clearly defined place and position.[21] It planted the seed that though God may have constituted the created order, the laws of nature function without God's interference. This development is aimed at acquiring scientific-objective knowledge "in all areas of life," but with "the steady marginalization and then elimination of God from the picture" (i.e., elimination of the enchanted worldview).[22] The early impetus of such thinking is found in the works of René Descartes and Thomas Hobbes. Their teleological work (i.e., the purpose of nature) shifted gears from "the centrality of [humans] in the cosmos" to "an anthropocentrism" (in this case, human reasoning).[23] The result of such thinking, when imported to the task of biblical interpretation, is the reconstruction of the biblical

16 Neil, "The Criticism and Theological Use of the Bible 1700–1950," 238–239.

17 Krentz, *The Historical-Critical Method*, 11–12.

18 Jeffrey L. Morrow, *Three Skeptics and the Bible: La Peyrère, Hobbes, Spinoza, and the Reception of Modern Biblical Criticism* (Eugene: Pickwick, 2016), 54–84.

19 Charles Hutton, *A Philosophical and Mathematical Dictionary, Vol. II: Containing an Explanations of Terms, And an Account of Several Subjects, Comprised Under the Heads Mathematics, Astronomy, and Philosophy Both Natural and Experimental* (London: S. Hamilton, 1815), 86.

20 See Thomas Parkinson, *A System of Mechanics, Being the Substance of Lectures upon That Branch of Natural Philosophy* (Cambridge: J. Archdeacon, 1785), 8.

21 Peter Harrison, *The Bible, Protestantism, and The Rise of Natural Science* (Cambridge: CUP, 2001), 183–84.

22 C. G. Bartholomew and M. Goheen, *Christian Philosophy: A Systematic and Narrative Introduction* (Grand Rapids: Baker, 2013), 114–15.

23 Harrison, *The Bible, Protestantism, and The Rise of Natural Science*, 183–84.

narrative with a question mark of not just the inspiration of the text, but of the miracle narratives and the appearance of the text.

The implication of these developments is seen in terms of how the early modern interpreters entered the theological discourse with a sense of intensification of interest in the original languages of the biblical text, along with interest in other ancient languages.[24] This development led to two diversified pursuits: those who were interested in the question of origin and reliability of the biblical text and those who were interested in the proper ways of ascertaining the meaning and value of the biblical texts.[25] There were conflicts whenever the first query brushed with the second query.

In addition, development of metaphysical naturalism (also known as *ontological naturalism*)[26] and methodological naturalism made a huge impact in biblical interpretation. The former "holds that what is ultimately real is material reality," while the latter "refers to the methodology of science, which in looking for explanations brackets out appeal to the supernatural."[27] The metaphysical naturalist makes "substantive claims about what exists in nature and then adds a closure clause stating 'and that is all there is.' "[28] The focus is on nature, instead of the supernatural. The methodological naturalists refer to "a set of methods as a reliable way to find out about the world—typically the methods of the natural sciences, and perhaps extensions that are continuous with them and indirectly to what those methods discover."[29] Metaphysical naturalism gave the early impetus of biblical criticism (through philosophers like Hobbes and Baruch Spinoza), while methodological naturalism was influential in the thrall of biblical criticism. The result of employing methodological naturalism is that it is "defeasible on the basis of new evidence, so whatever tentative substantive claims the methodological naturalist makes are always open to revision or abandonment on the basis of new, countervailing evidence."[30] This became quite evident as biblical criticism dominated biblical studies in the nineteenth century—showing a diversified approach of biblical interpretation.

---

[24] Richard A. Muller, "Biblical Interpretation in the 16th and 17th Centuries," in *Historical Handbook of Major Biblical Interpreters*, ed. D. K. McKim (Downers Grove: InterVarsity, 1998), 139.

[25] Frei, *The Eclipse of Biblical Narrative*, 17.

[26] There appear to be two types of metaphysical naturalists: those who deny God's existence and those who believe in the presence of God's attributes in the natural ontology. Robert R. Pennock, *Tower of Babel: The Evidence Against the New Creationism* (London: MIT, 1999), 190.

[27] Kevin J. Vanhoozer, email message to author, January 21, 2019.

[28] Pennock, *Tower of Babel*, 190–191.

[29] Pennock, *Tower of Babel*, 190–191.

[30] Pennock, *Tower of Babel*, 191.

With the advancement and dominance of biblical criticism, biblical texts were put to the subjection of natural experience and explanation theory. The biblical text must be examined by the reconstruction of what appeared to be the natural, historical, cultural, and individual life of the time. The claimed authority of the Bible no longer determined the enchanted reality. The appeal to "divine causation either of the biblical history or the biblical writings" was ignored or dismissed.[31] This was the dawn of a new phase in the history of biblical interpretation driven by the conception of methodological naturalism—setting the "stage for which deistic convictions, empirical philosophy, and historical criticism form part of the technical intellectual background."[32] This was a period of cultural transition, i.e., from "a traditional conception of reality to a mode of understanding we recognize as distinctly modern."[33] This is the beginning of the great reversal of the modern period, whose influence and impact can be seen throughout the modern period.

Early Modern Period

Authority and Reason

The seventeenth-century West saw the rise of reason as the ultimate criterion. It saw the questioning of the authority of the Bible. Klaus Scholder states, "One can say with some justification that the beginnings of biblical criticism are initially far more a philosophical than a theological problem . . . The church historian finds himself or herself transported into a largely uncharted area which lies between philosophy and theology."[34] This has much to do with the rise of natural philosophy; and with it, the loss of supernaturalism (i.e., the possibility of divine intervention, miracles). It is the influence of metaphysical naturalism that took away the exceptional status, privilege, and authority of the Bible.[35] The seventeenth-century philosophers provided the early impetus of critical thinking. René Descartes (1596–1650) raised doubts about the authority of the Bible, Thomas Hobbes (1588–1679) disputed the Mosaic authorship of the Pentateuch, and Baruch Spinoza (1632–1677) inserted the idea

31 Frei, *The Eclipse of Biblical Narrative*, 18; 31.

32 Frei, *The Eclipse of Biblical Narrative*, 2.

33 Harrisville and Sundberg, *The Bible in Modern Culture*, 24.

34 Klaus Scholder, *The Birth of Modern Critical Theology: Origins and Problems of Biblical Criticism in the Seventeenth Century* (London: SCM, 1990), 5–6.

35 According to Preus, this is particularly true of Spinoza. He argues that the original hearers (the prophets and apostles) of the Bible were without "divine aid" and "spiritual infusion." Preus, *Spinoza and The Irrelevance of Biblical Authority*, 179–180.

of reading the Bible like any other book. While the church was holding onto the enchanted worldview, critical thinking started to influence how they read the Bible. This is evident in how Hugo Grotius (1588–1645) and Richard Simon (1638–1712) maintained the divine conception of the Bible, but began to engage in critical thinking, i.e., read the Bible using extrabiblical sources.

Descartes's *Discourse on the Method* (1637) is instrumental in the starting of rationalist thinking.[36] It raised doubt about the Christian faith and its truth claims. It raised doubt to "a universally valid principle and changed philosophic, scientific, and historical method down to the present day."[37] It placed the source of truth as rooted in the human subject: humans as the center of philosophical inquiry. Everything is to be questioned (e.g., tradition), and only that which is certain in the eyes of reasoning is accepted. What is handed down as truth in tradition was questionable if it stands contrary to reason. Reason (understood as doubt) is the sole criterion of truth. In other words, epistemology replaced metaphysics as "first philosophy." Instead of beginning with real things (like God!), philosophers began with the question, How can we *know* real things? This precipitated what has been called "the turn to the subject" (i.e., the knowing subject). The real question now becomes, "What are the limits of knowledge? How can we know things that we don't experience for ourselves?"[38] Gradually, reason became the norm not just of religion but also of how we read Scripture. It suggested a sense of suspicion of the final text. Consequently, Bible readers/interpreters began to question the appearance of the text in light of history.

This was a shift in how truth is ascertained—from ontology to epistemology.[39] This was the beginning of a change in perspective of the source of truth—from the Scripture to the human subject. If Descartes raised doubt about the criteria of truth, Hobbes raised doubt about the authority of the Bible. Hobbes's *Leviathan* (1651) suggests that humans are by nature unsocial if an effective government does not govern them.[40] Our focus is to show how Hobbes's view of the Bible helped in the growing influence of rationalism and questioned the authority of the Bible. Hobbes

---

36 See René Descartes, *Discourse on Method and Meditations*, trans. Elizabeth S. Haldane and G. R. T. Ross (Mineola: Dover Publications, 2003).

37 Krentz, *The Historical-Critical Method*, 13.

38 Kevin J. Vanhoozer, email message to author, January 21, 2019.

39 Craig G. Bartholomew, *Introducing Biblical Hermeneutics: A Comprehensive Framework for Hearing God in Scripture* (Grand Rapids: Baker, 2015), 345.

40 See Thomas Hobbes, *Leviathan: With Selected Variants from the Latin Edition of 1668*, edited, with Introduction and Notes by Edward Curley (Indianapolis: Hackett Publishing Company, 1994).

suggests that the Old Testament (hereafter, OT) was "written by many people, whose names are unknown to us, over a long period of time, long after the occurrence of the events they described."[41] He also suggested that Moses was not the author of the Pentateuch.[42] He states,

> And first, for the *Pentateuch*, it is not argument enough that they were written by Moses, because they are called the five Books of *Moses*, no more than these titles, the Book of Joshua, the Book of Judges, the Book of Ruth, and the Books of the Kings, are arguments sufficient to prove, that they were written by Joshua, by the Judges, by Ruth, and by the Kings.[43]

He found it strange that Moses would speak of his own death or grave in Deuteronomy 34:6. The phrase "no one knows his burial place to this day" suggests two things: this was written after Moses's death, and there is a time gap between the event and the account of the said book.[44] He holds on to the possibility that someone else wrote the last part of the book and Moses wrote the rest. According to him, this is evident in Genesis 12:6: "Abram passed through the land to the place at Shechem, to the oak of Moreh. At that time, the Canaanites were in the land." He holds that Moses could not have been the author as the Canaanites were killed by Israelites after his death. Similarly, in Numbers 21:14, the author cites another ancient book (*The Book of the Wars of the Lord*), where Moses's deeds are recorded.[45] Like the above accounts, Hobbes argues that the books of Judges, Samuel, Kings, and Chronicles were written long after the events happened.[46] To suggest that many people wrote the OT and question the authorship of Moses was to move away from the traditional understanding of the Bible. Such a suggestion and questioning inserted doubt or a sense of suspicion of the textual appearance created a sense of suspicion. In addition, there was also an appeal to critical reasons to find out what *really* happened. Such thinking brought distrust of the appearance of the text, encouraging readers to doubt what the Bible seems to be teaching to the church. Hobbes's suggestion raised the question of whether the information in the Bible is reliable or not. For example, Hobbes no longer saw the Bible as the revelation of God, but the record of that

41 A.P. Martinich, "The Bible and Protestantism in *Leviathan*" in *The Cambridge Companion in Hobbes' Leviathan*, Patricia Springborg, ed. (Cambridge: CUP, 2007), 375–91, 377.

42 Though Hobbes was not the first person to make such a suggestion, it is likely that he was the first European writer to argue the case in the print. Martinich, "The Bible and Protestantism in *Leviathan*," 377.

43 Hobbes, *Leviathan*, 252.

44 All Bible quotations are taken from the New Revised Standard Version (NRSV).

45 Hobbes, *Leviathan*, 252.

46 Martinich, "The Bible and Protestantism in *Leviathan*," 377–79.

revelation.[47] If it seems contradictory, it is to be the unskilled errors of the interpreters or the errors of reasoning.

If Hobbes raised doubt on the authority of the Bible, Spinoza made Scripture subject to reason. He leveled Scripture with any other books. Frei suggests that Spinoza's *Tractatus theologico-politicus* (1670) has the foundation of "the important principles of an interpretation at once rationalistic and historical-critical which were to be developed over the course of the eighteenth century."[48] Roy Harrisville and Walter Sundberg share this opinion, where they hold that Spinoza is "the first to practice the fledgling 'science' of historical criticism of the Bible."[49] In *Tractatus*, Spinoza argued that true interpretation could be achieved by examining the meaning of the biblical statements and the intention of the authors.[50] He suggests that the correct method to interpret nature requires "constructing a natural history, from which we derive the definitions of natural things, as from certain data."[51] Interpreting scripture needs the assembling of "a genuine history of it and to deduce the thinking of the Bible's authors by valid inferences from this history, as from certain data and principles."[52]

Such historical inquiry of Scripture will involve the following. First, it means being accustomed to the original language of the biblical books and authors, especially of its nature and properties. Spinoza found it essential to understand the history of the Hebrew language since both the testaments have a Hebrew background.[53] Second, it also means gathering the opinions of each individual book and organizing them subject-wise. Such a task would include taking note of what is ambiguous, obscure, or contradictory in the biblical narrative. The focus is on the intended meaning of the text—not its truth. It means investigating "a passage's sense only from its use of the language or from reasoning which accepts no other foundation than Scripture itself."[54] Third, such historical inquiry requires an explanation of the circumstances of all the books of the prophets. It means considering "the life, character and particular interests of the author of each individual book, who exactly he was, on what occasion he

47 Curley, "*Introduction to Hobbes' Leviathan*," xxxii.

48 Frei, *The Eclipse of Biblical Narrative*, 42.

49 Harrisville and Sundberg, *The Bible in Modern Culture*, 33.

50 Benedict de Spinoza, *Theological-Political Treatise*, edited and trans. Michael Silversthorne and Jonathan Israel (Cambridge: CUP, 2007).

51 Spinoza, *Theological-Political Treatise*, 98.

52 Spinoza, *Theological-Political Treatise*, 98.

53 Spinoza, *Theological-Political Treatise*, 100.

54 Spinoza, *Theological-Political Treatise*, 100.

wrote, for whom and in what language."[55] Such discourse points to a new direction of biblical interpretation. It means delving into the history of the text by trying to ascertain the intention of the author and the language of the biblical books. The focus is now what lies *behind* the text, namely, the process of its composition. This is done by way of referring to reliable sources, i.e., the extrabiblical sources. What Spinoza set out to achieve was to bring out the true meaning of Scripture and its message—guiding the readers to "a simple moral principle" of the biblical narrative.[56] This was done to help the readers move away from the dominant ecclesial authority that apparently hindered them from seeing the true meaning of Scripture. He saw the purpose of Scripture as not just about teaching the right kind of religion but moving the heart of the people to do it, in practice. However, in doing so and by attempting to set the proper method of interpreting the text, he gave foundation to modern biblical criticism. This was done by introducing the idea of surveying the historical background of the Bible and raising historical questions of the individual books. Those who use the tools of natural reason are viewed as able interpreters who did not need the help of divine illumination. Biblical criticism, at this point, means being suspicious of the biblical appearance—trusting in critical methods.

In the area of biblical interpretation, an early conception of critical method is evident in Grotius' *Notes on the New Testament* (1641).[57] He attempted to interpret the New Testament (here on, NT) in light of its ancient setting, i.e., the classical, Jewish, Hellenistic, and early Christian texts. He used non-biblical sources of ancient writings as resources for the interpretation of the biblical text. Earlier than Grotius, a similar work was found in the mid-sixteenth century. In a commentary on select NT, Joachim Camerarius (1500–1574) argued for the interpretation of NT texts from the perspective of the authors.[58] The assumption is that interpreters will be able to understand the biblical texts *if only* they can understand the text as the authors intended. This is also to assume that it is the context of the authors or the ancient setting that determines the meaning. The world *behind* the text was critical of the works of the church fathers, the text, and the dictate of the tradition, i.e., the kind of interpretation

55 Spinoza, *Theological-Political Treatise*, 100.

56 See Steven Nadler, "The Bible Hermeneutics of Baruch de Spinoza" in *Hebrew Bible/Old Testament: The History of Interpretation, Vol. II: From Renaissance to the Enlightenment* (Gottingen: Vandenhoeck & Ruprecht, 2008), 827–36.

57 See Hugo Grotius, *Annotationum in Novum Testamenturn II* (Paris: n.a. 1646).

58 Werner Georg Kümmel, *The New Testament: The History of the Investigation of its Problems*, trans. S. McLean and Howard C. Kee (London: SCM, 1978), 31–33.

that recognizes divine intervention, miracle, or prophesy. These conceptions are the early formulation of modern biblical criticism.

Though the Roman Catholic Church ruled out biblical criticism, there were some who applied critical thinking in their interpretative task.[59] For example, Richard Simon made use of certain aspects of biblical criticism (textual criticism) to analyze the Reformers and to affirm the role of the church in interpreting the Bible, and with the hope that his work would be useful for the Catholic Church. He published a series of books making use of biblical criticism.[60] Werner Kümmel suggests that Simon is "the first to employ critical methods in a historical study of the origin of the traditional form of the text of the New Testament and of the question of the proper understanding of it."[61] He tried to show the unattainability of the Reformers' assertion for *sola scriptura*, suggesting that they cannot arrive at the meaning of the text by solely relying on the Scripture. But it can only result in multiple meanings, considering the diversity of the text. In *Critical History of the Old Testament* (1678), Simon argued that Moses was not the author of the books that are ascribed to him.[62] The writings of the Bible, especially the first five books, suggest that someone collected the materials and put them together.[63] He was of the view that some biblical books have a long history of compilation, and there is uncertainty about the textual tradition.[64] With such argument, he moved away from the ancient practices of biblical interpretation (i.e., from church and its tradition) toward a critical observation of ancient interpretation or of its documents/manuscripts. Like Hobbes, his work brought doubt on the authorship of Pentateuch. Biblical criticism, at this point, refers to using extrabiblical evidence and rationalistic thinking as criteria for biblical interpretation.

Naturalists and Criticism

What was inaugurated in the seventeenth century came to fuller fruition in the eighteenth century. If the seventeenth-century philosophers raised

---

59 n.a. "The General Council of Trent, Fourth Session (8 April 1546)," in *The Christian Faith in the Doctrinal Documents of the Catholic Church*, Sixth Edition. J. Neuner S. J. and J. Dupuis S. J., eds., (New York: Alba House, 1996), 97–98.

60 Kümmel, *The New Testament*, 40–44.

61 Kümmel, *The New Testament*, 41.

62 Despite his good intentions, his work, especially on the authorship of Moses, was not well received by the Roman Catholic Church. Henning Graf Reventlow, *History of Biblical Interpretation, vol. 4: From the Enlightenment to the Twentieth Century*, trans. Leo G. Perdue (Atlanta: SBL, 2010), 84.

63 Simon, *A Critical History of the Old Testament*, 3.

64 Law, *The Historical Critical Method*, 89.

doubts on the authority of the Bible, if reason is projected as the supreme criterion, it is the eighteenth-century theologians (the English Deists and German liberals) who laid the foundation of rationalistic criticism.[65] Frei suggests that the modern theological discourse began in England—at the beginning of the seventeenth century to the eighteenth century—and later, moved to Germany.[66] Henning Reventlow also suggests that the Deists and German liberals changed the nature and the course of biblical interpretation.[67] The consolidation of critical approach began with the English Deists, while its dominance is found in the German liberal scholars.

The Deists' controversy was marked with debates and discussion on the interpretation of the biblical narratives. These debates are fueled with a sense of suspicion of the church's traditional dogma in favor of the historical study of the biblical text.[68] They were preoccupied with the question of the intelligibility/scrutiny of the historical revelation, the fact claims of the gospel, or the credibility of miracles, particularly of the NT. The focus of this discussion, while keeping note of the contribution of other English Deists, will be on the debate between Anthony Collins and William Whiston.[69] Frei saw this conversation as helpful to understand the kind of divide that began to emerge in the eighteenth century between history-like and real historical events, realism and real facts, words/narrative and subject matter.[70] However, for our purposes, we look at the kind of critical concepts that began to take shape—as an impetus of biblical criticism in the debate between Collins and Whiston.

In *An Essay Towards Restoring the True Text of the Old Testament, and for Vindicating the Citations thence Made in the New Testament* (1722), Whiston suggested that the OT references of Jesus and disciples apply to

65 While asserting reason and observation as a defining category of truth/meaning, the English Deists are the ones who reject revelation as a source of knowledge. Neil, "The Criticism and Theological Use of the Bible 1700–1950," 239.

66 Frei, *The Eclipse of Biblical Narrative*, 51. Cf. J. W. Rogerson, *Old Testament Criticism in the Nineteenth Century: England and Germany* (London: SPCK, 1984), ix.

67 Reventlow, *The Authority of the Bible*, 289–410.

68 This was motivated by a high view of humanity. It came with much reconstruction of what was perceived in the precritical period—their view of humanity (capacity and condition of humans) and salvation.

69 The works of Deists like John Locke (1632–1704), John Toland (1670–1722), and Matthew Tindal (1653–1733) played an important role in putting forward the understanding that Jesus taught natural religion, which was not dogmatic. They hold that the church corrupted, distorted, or diluted the Christian faith.

70 See Frei, *The Eclipse of Biblical Narrative*, 66–85.

Jesus as the Messiah, the one who was promised.[71] He proposed that "The Greek Version of the Old Testament, call'd the Septuagint Version, as it stood in the Days of Christ and his Apostles, was agreeable to the genuine Hebrew Text, as it was in that age."[72] He was of the view that those who were spreading the gospel alleged that "*Christ must* fulfil the Old Prophesies" (i.e., Christ must suffer and rise from the dead).[73] And in such accordance, Christ did suffer and rise from death as it had been prophesied. However, since the OT has been corrupted by the Jewish sources in early Christianity to destroy any possible claims of evidence in favor of Christianity, the OT prophecies are found incompatible with the fulfilment. Whiston was of the view that "The present Hebrew Copies of the Old Testament are different in many Places from those genuine Hebrew and Greek Copies thereof, which were extant in the Days of Christ and his Apostles."[74] These differences, or corruption of the text, are evident from early Christianity, particularly from the time of Origen and Jerome. The Jews have made a change in the characters of the Hebrew Bible at the beginning of the second century.[75] To bolster his claims, he investigates those who used "the Sacred Books of the Old Testament" in history—the Samaritans and the Twelve Tribes of Israel.[76]

The corruption, as Whiston suggests, came into being because of opposition to Christianity.[77] And he argued for the restoration of the original text, which was corrupted by the the Jewish interpretation and its sources. He holds that the texts, which were cited by Christ and his apostles and other NT writers, were truly cited by them, and these citations were in agreement with the genuine Hebrew and Greek Bibles of that age.[78] He tried to restore the original text with the following suggestions: (1) The NT citations of the OT still agree with the Septuagint version of the present day; (2) These citations could not have the kind of impact it had back then, unless they were convinced of the truth of the Christian religion; (3) If the credibility of the citations were to be measured, it appears similar to the copy of the Septuagint version of Philo the Jew, who was contemporary with the Christ and his apostles; (4) Josephus, who is considered the most accurate historian and contemporary of the apostles, confirms the

---

[71] William Whiston, *An Essay Towards Restoring the True Text of the Old Testament, and for Vindicating the Citations thence Made in the New Testament* (London: n.a., 1722).

[72] Whiston, *An Essay Towards Restoring the True Text of the Old Testament*, 3.

[73] Whiston, *An Essay Towards Restoring the True Text of the Old Testament*, 14.

[74] Whiston, *An Essay Towards Restoring the True Text of the Old Testament*, 17.

[75] Whiston, *An Essay Towards Restoring the True Text of the Old Testament*, 149.

[76] Whiston, *An Essay Towards Restoring the True Text of the Old Testament*, 149.

[77] Whiston, *An Essay Towards Restoring the True Text of the Old Testament*, 220.

[78] Whiston, *An Essay Towards Restoring the True Text of the Old Testament*, 281.

citations and content of the NT; (5) The citations were just and authentic because even the enemies of the faith did not find fault in the account; (6) The citations are accurate as the apostolic fathers bear witness to these citations; and (7) These citations were also found in close proximity with other ancient readings of the time.[79]

What Whiston did here was to hold to the enchanted worldview and engage with tools of the disenchanted worldview. What he did was to go back to the sources to make his point (i.e., extrabiblical sources were used to make the readers understand that prophecies are fulfilled in Christ). This is an early formulation of biblical criticism, where scholars began to use sources outside of the Bible to understand the storyline of the Bible. This was not exactly a reconstruction of the biblical narrative, but it is criticism that makes a historical examination of the biblical text using extrabiblical sources—while founded in the authority of the Bible. This is a "believing" criticism, which is contrasted with the "skeptical" criticism. The former may accept supernaturalism, but the latter does not.

Anthony Collins's *A Discourse of the Grounds and Reasons of the Christian Religion* (1724) and *The Scheme of Literal Prophecy Considered* (1727) came out as a response to Whiston's suggestion of the fulfilment of the OT prophecy in the NT.[80] He argued against Whiston's claim of Jesus as the Messiah as false or absurd based on the fulfilment of the OT prophesies in the NT. It seems to make more sense that the Christian faith is based on the OT text itself, instead of holding to the idea that the OT prophecies lead to Jesus and Jesus's events. For Collins, basing the claims of Jesus as the Messiah in the OT text would reliably attest "the identity and authenticity of Jesus as the Messiah."[81] He is of the view that the messianic reading (i.e., prophetic fulfilment in Jesus) does not make sense without the context of the OT. Further argument is made suggesting that harmonizing the OT and the NT text is not possible if the text is not read literally or if the text is not read in its context. What is seen as a fulfilment of the OT in the NT (cf. Matthew 1:22, 2:15, 2:23, 11:4, and 13:14) is, in fact, read in a typological sense (allegorical or mystical).[82] However, there is only one fulfilment (i.e., the literal sense of the text). Literal sense, in this case, is to locate the text in the ancient and historical lineage in the context of the OT. This was said to disprove the references of NT writers of the OT (e.g., Matthew 1:22–23 citing Isaiah 7:14) to make the claim of the prophetic fulfilment of the conception and birth of Jesus Christ.

79 Whiston, *An Essay Towards Restoring the True Text of the Old Testament*, 281–301.

80 Anthony Collins, *A Discourse of the Grounds and Reasons of the Christian Religion* (London: n.a., 1724).

81 Frei, *The Eclipse of Biblical Narrative*, 68.

82 Collins, *A Discourse of the Grounds and Reasons of the Christian Religion*, 44.

When the reference is read literally (i.e., in its context), what seems to be a prophetic message conveys an altogether different message.

In this response, Collins did two things: literal interpretation of the text is endorsed (i.e., reading in the context of the OT), while non-literal sense (be it typology, allegorical, or mystical) was either meaningless or nonsensical. Instead, an emphasis was made to understand the text in its historical context. Though scriptural authority is still recognized, its value has changed. His emphasis is to ascertain the sense of the human writer, the words and meaning, and not necessarily the divine author.[83] This is to be done by relooking at the literal interpretation with a sense of historical reference.[84] In the modern critical context, it is no more a typological referent, but a historical referent.[85]

If not exactly contrary to Whiston, what Collins did was to go back to the historical context of the text. He reverses the hermeneutical polarities, making a critically reconstructed history the context for reading biblical narrative. Collins reverses the hermeneutical polarity: (in Frei's words) "the realistic or history-like narrative is identified with the literal sense which in turn was automatically identical with reference to historical truth," while historical narrative is identified with "a reconstruction of the process by which [biblical text] originated and of their cultural setting."[86] What is happening is that the meaning of the literal sense becomes historicized (naturalized). Though Whiston and Collins disagreed in their propositions (i.e., claims of Jesus as the Messiah), in terms of approach they appear to adopt a similar method. Moving away from the "realistic" or "history-like" sense of the text, they started to adopt the kind of method that uses biblical criticism or does the historical investigation by drawing attention to the extrabiblical sources (i.e., the historical reference).

Rationalism and Criticism

Theological discussion in Germany came from a different tradition of biblical study. Drawing its root back to the discussions of the Catholic Reformation (also known as Catholic Counter-Reformation), the discussion was on the centrality of the Bible for theological discourse and

83 Such thinking is influenced by John Locke, who suggested that the biblical texts can be understood within their contexts—as the authors understood the text and looked at the text out of the context. John Locke, "An Essay on the Understanding of St. Paul's Epistles, By Consulting St. Paul Himself" in *The Works of John Locke in Ten Volumes*, Vol. 8 (London: Thomas Davison, 1823), 8, 16, 19.

84 Frei, *The Eclipse of Biblical Narrative*, 76.

85 However, note must be made that typology is understood by many as containing a literary, historical, and theological connection between type and antitype.

86 Frei, *The Eclipse of Biblical Narrative*, 9–11.

conduct. The Reformers' focus has been on the authority and unity of the Bible, while the post-Reformation took the discussion to the principles of biblical interpretation. Further down this path, it moved away from not just ecclesial tradition but also away from the confessional formulae (such as the Thirty-Nine Articles and the Formula of Concord).[87] It also dismissed the possibility of the influence of the Holy Spirit in the interpretation of the Bible. The eighteenth century became a period of trying to ascertain the plain meaning of the text (i.e., historical reconstruction of the biblical narratives), leading to the disappearance of possible multiple meanings (such as literal, typological, and spiritual or mystical). Eventually, it is observed that "the harmony of historical fact, literal sense, and religious truth will at best have to be demonstrated; at worst, some explanation of the religious truth of the fact-like description will have to be given in the face of a negative verdict on its factual accuracy or veracity."[88] The latter is a key move toward reading the Bible as myth. This is the way critics could simultaneously say the Bible was historically false but religiously true.

Now, like the Deists of England, a new shift in biblical interpretation began to take shape in Germany in the early eighteenth century—the home of biblical criticism of the modern period.[89] The argument was between the supernaturalist and rationalist interpretation (i.e., liberal commentators). Supernaturalism or the supernaturalist is to be distinguished from the Protestant orthodox literalism and pietist spiritual interpretation.[90] Frei suggests that its rise is marked by the influence of deistic controversies in England and Christian Wolff's rationalistic philosophy.[91] They argued for "the literal truth of scripture, demonstrating what they thought to be the specific nature of its inspiration and also setting forth reasons for the factual reliability of its reports."[92] However, unlike Protestant orthodox and pietism, "they no longer used scriptural inspiration as a kind of automatic warrant for claims on behalf of the texts."[93] Frei states that the supernaturalist argued for,

> The historical factuality of the biblical reports of miracles and the fulfilment of prophecy, basing these claims on such arguments in favor of the

---

[87] Frei, *The Eclipse of Biblical Narrative*, 55.

[88] Frei, *The Eclipse of Biblical Narrative*, 56.

[89] Rogerson, *Old Testament Criticism in the Nineteenth Century*, ix.

[90] See Peter C. Erb, ed., *Pietists: Selected Writings* (New York: Paulist, 1983), 31–34.

[91] While Wolff defended the revealed knowledge or religion, it endorsed "natural religion and the deliverances of reason." Frei, *The Eclipse of Biblical Narrative*, 86, 96.

[92] Frei, *The Eclipse of Biblical Narrative*, 86.

[93] Frei, *The Eclipse of Biblical Narrative*, 86.

> Bible's reliable documentation of divine revelation as the apostolic origin of the New Testament writings, the integrity of the evangelists, the congruence of miracle with rational religion, the simplicity and life-likeness of the reports, and the historical fulfillment of Old Testament anticipations in the shape of New Testament events.[94]

On the other hand, liberal commentators doubted not just the inspiration but also the factual reliability of the biblical narratives. At this point the cause of disagreement is "the identity of explicative meaning with the historical or ostensive reference of the texts."[95]

Though the Pietists (who share similar lineage with the Orthodox) hold to the enchanted worldview, they also contributed to the rise of biblical criticism of the eighteenth century. A significant contribution of Pietism came from Philipp Jacob Spener (1635–1705). In *Pia Desideria*, Spener emphasized on Bible reading in context (i.e., the entire context of the Scripture): delight in Bible reading in the family, individual reading in the public service, and Bible study like the ancient and apostolic church meetings.[96] He was concerned that there was "too much dogma and too little devotion."[97] Echoing Martin Luther, he emphasized on reading the Bible properly. The criteria of such reading are to avoid dogmatic reading and language-oriented academic reading. Devotional reading of the Bible, be it personal, corporate, or to read like the apostolic church, setting needs to be emphasized. Such reading would entail "heartfelt prayer," "true repentance," be for the purpose of "praxis and action" and not just knowledge, but would give careful attention to the biblical texts.[98] A careful reading of the text meant paying attention to "how the verses fit together and then pay attention to each individual word."[99] It would also mean recognizing that the text is written not just for a particular time, but for all people across time. That way, the universality of Scripture is acknowledged, especially when referring to God's commandments and laws. The emphasis here is on the role of the Bible to help strengthen the faith of the Christian community. Instead of only engaging in philological studies of the Bible, the emphasis is on personal renewal of Bible

---

[94] Frei, *The Eclipse of Biblical Narrative*, 87.

[95] Frei, *The Eclipse of Biblical Narrative*, 87.

[96] Philipp Jakob Spener, "From the Pia Desideria" in *Pietists: Selected Writings*, ed. Peter C. Erb (New York: Paulist, 1983), 31–34.

[97] K. Gangel and W. S. Benson, *Christian Education: Its History and Philosophy* (Chicago: Moody, 1983), 173.

[98] Philipp Jakob Spener, "From the Necessary and Useful Reading of the Holy Scriptures, 1694" in *Pietists*, 73–74.

[99] Spener, "From the Necessary and Useful Reading of the Holy Scriptures, 1694," 74–75.

reading.[100] Apart from Spener, August Hermann Francke (1663–1727) is influential in formulating a clear Pietistic reading of the Bible. He uses a combination of historical reading and personal renewal reading. For instance, the Lutheran church of this time was interested in reading the Bible for ascertaining the doctrine in the text, but he emphasized reading the text by highlighting "the particular characteristics of the individual biblical authors."[101] His reading of the Bible involves a thematic reading of both the OT and the NT, in the form of "introductions to the individual biblical writings and guides to biblical hermeneutical."[102] The emphasis is on reading the text in its original languages, with a strong emphasis on personal renewal. This is also the point of departure between the Pietists and rationalists. The rationalist stays behind the text (i.e., reconstruction of the narrative), but the Pietist tries to move beyond the text, especially for personal edification through the text.

In the eighteenth century, there was a decisive shift in the understanding of revelation in relation to history and Scripture. Interpreters began to see the Scripture not just as the revelation of God but also as the sourcebook of ancient history. Biblical interpretation gradually shifted from being a concern of conflicting confessions to coming under the domain of scientific (i.e., non-partisan) criticism. Johann Salomo Semler (1725–1791), Johann David Michaelis (1717–1791), Johann Gottfried Eichhorn (1752–1827), Johann Philipp Gabler (1753–1826), and William Wrede (1859–1906) are some of the key voices who brought about such change.

Kümmel argues, "It was Johann Salomo Semler . . . who gave the scientific study of the New Testament the more vigorous impetus to further development."[103] Semler's teacher Siegmund Jakob Baumgarten (1706–1757), a conservative in his own right, suggested a natural and supernatural understanding of the Bible; the natural reading uses philology and historical criticism, while supernatural reading looked at the Bible as divine communication.[104] His approach was an engagement of the enchanted and the disenchanted worldview. He saw "the biblical revelation, though disclosing mysteries above nature and reason, contains nothing contrary to them."[105] He did not see it as problematic to use rationalistic, analytical

---

[100] Spener influenced August Herman Francke (1663–1726) to do not just an academic study but do a personal reading of the Bible.

[101] Wallmann, "Scriptural Understanding and Interpretation in Pietism," 910. See August Hermann Francke, *Commentatio de scopo librorum Veteris et Novi Testamenti* (Halle, 1724).

[102] Wallmann, "Scriptural Understanding and Interpretation in Pietism," 910.

[103] Kümmel, *The New Testament*, 62.

[104] Law, *The Historical Critical Method*, 43.

[105] Frei, *The Eclipse of Biblical Narrative*, 89.

means to examine the Bible (i.e., use extrabiblical resources to confirm or interpret biblical history). Moving further from Baumgarten, Semler argues for the study of the Bible and its tradition in its original language with its cultural nuances.[106] Like Baumgarten, he saw divine revelation in the Bible as compatible with truths of nature and reason. Unlike the Deist (who denied *special* revelation), he endorsed "a concept of the divine disclosure of truth, perceived in the depth of human experience."[107] He argued for the need to obtain skill and knowledge of the language of the Bible and its historical circumstances.[108] Such a task meant inquiring not just what happened but also trying to understand how the ancient authors felt and thought in their cultural and historical context. This is to assume that biblical interpretation can take place "in accordance with universal moral and religious principles;" moral, in this case, means spiritual truth or reality.[109] This is to say that natural religion, a function of philosophy, became the framework for reading the Bible *properly*. It became the interpretive framework for reading Scripture, not Scripture itself. This goes against the Reformation idea that "Scripture interprets Scripture."[110]

What came out of such an approach is to look at the Bible like any other book, a book of antiquity, a product of human authors, understandable only through the author's intention, and comprehensible in terms of historical analogy.[111] On a broader scale, Semler's work was influenced by attempts of universal hermeneutical methodology. Here, to read the Bible *like any other book* means reading it with the principles of general hermeneutics, not special hermeneutics. It is in this sense that the Bible becomes like any other document of the secular university. This reading of the Bible was further reinforced by the growing globalization of biblical scholarship. It was developed in the wake of emphasizing reason and rationality, both in biblical interpretation and religion. Moreover, he lived in a time where there was an emphasis on the subjectivity of religious faith and experience.[112] These developments in the eighteenth century, as shown in the works of Semler, are the actual beginning of the great reversal (as Frei suggested), moving away from the traditional understanding of reading Scripture. The biblical text is now read not as the Word of God

[106] Frei, *The Eclipse of Biblical Narrative*, 109.

[107] Baird, *History of New Testament Research*, 118.

[108] Frei, *The Eclipse of Biblical Narrative*, 109.

[109] Frei, *The Eclipse of Biblical Narrative*, 111.

[110] Kevin J. Vanhoozer, email message to author, January 21, 2019.

[111] Hayes, "Historical Criticism of the Old Testament Canon," 998.

[112] Hayes, "Historical Criticism of the Old Testament Canon," 998–1000.

but as a human construct, which requires reconstruction to understand the text. This is biblical criticism as understood in the eighteenth century.

Michaelis put Semler's critical conception forward in the historical study of the NT.[113] His work *Introduction to the Divine Scriptures of the New Covenant* is the first example of the "New Testament Introduction."[114] It is in the fourth edition of this book that Michaelis carried forward in the historical investigation of the NT and the individual books, which Semler posed. It was "a comprehensive discussion of the historical problems of the NT and its individual books, and thereby inaugurated the science of NT introduction."[115] For the first time, he dealt with the issues of language, textual criticism, and the origin of individual books.[116] Such a task means posing the variant historical questions using text-criticism: a hypothesis of "a lost original gospel," how to relate the gospel of John with Gnostic writings, the question of the apostolic writing of some of the NT books, and so on.[117] Though he did not deal with the historical formation of the canon, he saw the NT books that came from the apostles as canonical and inspired. Such concern of whether a book of the Bible is seen as canonical or non-canonical is clarified by historical examination.[118] His work was not only instrumental but it also added volumes and richness in how historical investigation was carried out in the eighteenth century.

Further development of the above historical investigation is evident in the work of Eichhorn. Particularly, his *Introduction to the Old Testament*, which culminated with five volumes (1823–1824), uses a non-theological approach to interpreting the OT.[119] He applied Christian Gottlob Heyne's understanding of myth in the OT using a philological and historical approach.[120] For Heyne myths are "summaries of the beliefs of primitive people in the pre-literary period, which were incapable of abstract thought, lacked knowledge, and were naively reliant on what was evident to their senses."[121] These can be historical myths (genuine historical events) or philosophical myths (an ethical principle). Such reading with

---

113 For detailed study, see Legaspi, *The Death of Scripture and the Rise of Biblical Studies*, 79–154.

114 It was published in 1750, the fourth edition in 1788. See Henning Graf Reventlow, "Towards the End of the 'Century of Enlightenment': Established Shift from *Sacra Scriptura* to Literary Documents and Religion of the People of Israel," in *Hebrew Bible/Old Testament*, Vol. II: 1052.

115 Kümmel, *The New Testament*, 69.

116 Kümmel, *The New Testament*, 69.

117 Kümmel, *The New Testament*, 69.

118 Kümmel, *The New Testament*, 69–70.

119 Law, *The Historical Critical Method*, 51.

120 Law, *The Historical Critical Method*, 51.

121 Law, *The Historical Critical Method*, 49–50.

philological and historical investigations of the biblical text became a norm in the eighteenth-century biblical investigation. The focus is now the exact grammatical and philological interpretation of the text. Such reading of the text eventually contributed to the beginning of "higher criticism."[122]

These developments of biblical criticism gradually led to a distinction between biblical theology and dogmatic theology. Specifically, this distinction is in a lecture—"An Oration on the Proper Distinction Between Biblical Theology and Dogmatic Theology and the Specific Objectives of Each"—delivered in 1787 by J. P. Gabler. [123] He argued for the necessity of making the distinction and the method to follow between biblical theology and dogmatic theology. On the one hand, biblical theology describes the theology of the biblical authors in the author's own terms, concepts, and categories; on the other, dogmatic theology, which is of didactic origin, teaches what theologians philosophize about divine things.[124] He categorized biblical theology into two tasks: first ("true" biblical theology), to provide a historically accurate description of the ideas and religion of the NT authors, and second ("pure" biblical theology), to sort out the theological wheat—the universal ideas that "apply today"—from the contingent cultural chaff.[125] He is of the view that biblical theology is a purely historical, descriptive science that aims at discovering "what it meant" and it has nothing to do with faith or theology. He claimed, "A biblical theology conceived along these lines would provide the historical and rationalistic scientific framework enabling systematic theology to relate biblical truths to contemporary life and thought."[126] He seems unclear as to how one ought to pursue the second task. Gabler's legacy lay in "putting New Testament theology, as a distinct historical discipline, on the academic map by distinguishing the theology contained *in* the New Testament from the theology brought *to* it or in accordance *with* it."[127]

---

[122] E. Earle Ellis, *History and Interpretation in New Testament Perspective* (Atlanta: SBL, 2001), 1.

[123] J. P. Gabler, "An Oration on the Proper Distinction between Biblical and Dogmatic Theology and the Specific Objectives of Each" trans. J. Sandys-Wunsch and L. Eldredge, *STJ* 33 (1980): 134–144.

[124] See John Sandys-Wunsch and Laurence Eldredge, "J. P. Gabler and the Distinction between Biblical and Dogmatic Theology: Translation, Commentary, and Discussion of His Originality," *Scottish Journal of Theology* 33 (1980): 133–44.

[125] Kevin J. Vanhoozer, "The New Testament and Theology," in *The Cambridge Companion to the New Testament*. ed. Patrick Gray (Cambridge: CUP, 2021), 401–418.

[126] Andreas J. Köstenberger, "The Present and Future of Biblical Theology," *Themelios* 37.3 (2012): 445.

[127] Vanhoozer, "The New Testament and Theology," 405.

Soon, Gabler's first task (i.e., "true" biblical theology) was carried forward by Wrede. He employed the principles of biblical criticism to "understand the history of early Christian religion as objectively and autonomously as possible, solely on the basis of its own cultural terms and concepts, no longer bound by doctrines like inspiration or the canon."[128] In *The Origin of the New Testament*, Wrede tries to explain the origin of the NT using critical tools.[129] He dismisses the idea of the supernatural origin of the NT, i.e., it was not "literally dictated to the human authors by God Himself."[130] The biblical text reflects "a question of historical origins, memorials of a religious history, and the history of Christianity at the epoch of its commencement."[131] The pursuit of understanding the origin of the NT is not theological but "a purely historical question."[132] The task is to trace "the influence of ideas and perceptions and so explain the development of early Christianity, from its roots in Palestine (Jesus) to the second-century church via Paul and John."[133]

By the end of the eighteenth century, what biblical criticism loses is the notion of the canon as something more than an arbitrary, socially constructed list of authoritative books. Biblical criticism became more about the historical investigation, a non-theological reading of the Bible. Such advancements of historical analysis mean deeper conversation on specific issues of the text—the grammatical and philological meaning, but less conversation of what the text means to the church. The discussion became more about how these tools allowed them to reconstruct the meaning or the nature of the text. In most academic settings, the church confessions were no longer deemed necessary for right (i.e., historical) interpretation.

High Modern Period

By the nineteenth century, biblical criticism (now popularly used as historical criticism) came to dominate biblical interpretation. The tasks of biblical interpretation became much more associated with biblical criticism with a strong emphasis on historical inquiries.[134] Several changes took place as "the result of the romantic and idealist revolution that was sweeping philosophy and historical study as well as the literary arts and

128 Vanhoozer, "The New Testament and Theology," 405.

129 William Wrede, *The Origin of the New Testament*, trans. James S. Hill (London: Harber & Brothers, 1909), 2.

130 Wrede, *The Origin of the New Testament*, 3.

131 Wrede, *The Origin of the New Testament*, 3.

132 Wrede, *The Origin of the New Testament*, 3.

133 Vanhoozer, "The New Testament and Theology," 405.

134 Frei, *The Eclipse of Biblical Narrative*, 122, 137.

criticism."[135] Biblical interpretation took a new turn in this century: toward a new historical process of biblical interpretation engaging in rethinking the traditionally held theological presuppositions.[136] It moved mostly to historical inquiries focusing on the reliability or unreliability of the sources related to the life of Jesus.[137] Apart from this new turn of criticism, there was a new "believing criticism" in mid-nineteenth-century England that responded to the growing influence of critical approach. The proponents of "believing criticism" attempted to incorporate critical methods to establish traditional doctrinal theology.[138]

Historicism and Criticism

The nineteenth-century biblical interpretation saw the climax, dominance, or the coming-of-age of biblical criticism. Advancement in history and historical method or historicism in Germany helped shape biblical scholarship in the nineteenth century. This advancement in modern thinking comes with an understanding that all cultures are influenced by history.[139] It comes with the assumption that human thinking is conditioned by history (i.e., it is influenced, if not determined, by its time and place). Such thinking is evident in the publishing of a series of books that helped in the development of historical criticism. Barthold G. Niebuhr's *Romische Geschichte* (1811–12) is considered one of the key voices of historicist work.[140] While studying the ancient sources, Niebuhr distinguished the materials from poetry to truth by attempting to discover the web of events and reconstruct the narrative.[141] Niebuhr states that the "[historian] must discover at least with some probability the general connectedness of events, and by a more credible story replace that which he has sacrificed to his [or her] better judgement."[142] Similar to Niebuhr's task, Leopold von Ranke's *Geschichte*

---

[135] Frei, *The Eclipse of Biblical Narrative*, 282.

[136] Alan Richardson, "The Rise of Modern Biblical Scholarship and Recent Discussion of the Authority of the Bible" in *The Cambridge History of the Bible: The West from the Reformation to the Present Day*, S. L. Greenslade, ed. vol. 3 (Cambridge: CUP, 1963), 295–96.

[137] Frei, *The Eclipse of Biblical Narrative*, 283.

[138] See Nigel Cameron, "Inspiration and Criticism: The Nineteenth-Century Crisis," *Tyndale Bulletin* 35 (1984): 129–59.

[139] See F. C. Beiser, *The German Historicist Tradition* (New York: OUP, 2012).

[140] See B. G. Niebuhr, *Romische Geschichre*, vol. 1–2, (Berlin: 1811–12); B. G. Niebuhr, *Lectures on the History of Rome: From the Earliest Time to the Fall of Western Empire*, Second edition. Leonard Schmitz, ed. (London: Taylor, Walton, and Maberly, 1850).

[141] Krentz, *Historical-Critical Method*, 22–23.

[142] B. G. Niebuhr, "The Critical Method: Barthold Niebuhr" in *The Varieties of History: From Voltaire to the Present*, ed. Fritz Stern (Cleveland: Meridian, 1956), 48.

der romanischen und germanischen Völker von 1494 bis 1535 (1824) made an effort to bring out an objective representation of history.[143] His work tries "to show what actually happened (*wie es eigentlich gewesen*)."[144] This task came with the assumption that historians have to be critical (i.e., be suspicious of the surface appearances, including biblical eyewitness testimony). Its sources were the "memoirs, diaries, letters, diplomatic reports, and original narratives of eyewitnesses; other writings were used only if they were immediately derived from the above mentioned or seemed to be equal to them because of some original information."[145] These works helped shape the development of historicism: it suggests that human life is shown in history with multiple manifestations requiring observation with complete and open empathy.[146] Their task to arrive at an objective description of events, as they actually were, required critical reconstruction of events, and at times, an alteration of events as they were traditionally understood (because it was *naively* accepted by faith).

One such work of historicity or historicism in biblical studies is found in the works of W. M. L. de Wette (1780–1849), who is claimed to be the founder of modern biblical criticism.[147] John Rogerson suggests de Wette's work "inaugurated a new era in critical Old Testament scholarship, and that his two-volume *Contributions to Old Testament Introduction* (Halle 1806–7) was his most significant contribution to this end."[148] *Contributions* presented a view of the Israelite religion, which is fundamentally different from what is found in the OT. De Wette suggests that Moses did not give the Israelites the full legal system, sacrificial culture, and priesthood, as it is traditionally understood.[149] Instead, he argued that most of the religious system was written much later than Moses, though it is unclear to what extent Moses contributed. He found this ascription to Moses as anachronistic or mystical. This is biblical criticism in the nineteenth century. De Wette formulates the basic principles of historical criticism in the following manner. The first has to do with the source of the knowledge of history. It is the report. However, the report of what has been narrated needs

---

143 See Leopold von Ranke, "The Ideal of Universal History: Leopold von Ranke" in *The Varieties of History*, 54–62.

144 von Ranke, "The Ideal of Universal History," 57.

145 von Ranke, "The Ideal of Universal History," 57.

146 See George G. Iggers, *The German Conception of History: The National Tradition of Historical Thought from Herder to the Present*, Revised Edition (Middletown: WUP, 1983), 3.

147 See Rogerson, *Old Testament Criticism*, 28–29.

148 Rogerson, *Old Testament Criticism*, 28.

149 A similar view is also found in J. S. Vater's *Commentary on the Pentateuch* which appeared in three parts between 1802 and 1805. Reventlow, *History of Biblical Interpretation, vol. 4*, 236–37.

interpretation to understand the perspectives of the narrators. The second concern is the critical determination of whether the report is believable or not. To be critical of the report requires a broader perspective of the events by making assumptions. The third task, having understood the report, is to ask whether it is believable. Such a critical task takes a negative approach by pointing out the errors in the narrative. It suggests that one's worldview of metaphysics influences one's decision as to what is or is not believable. This would mean rejecting tradition as history since it maintains loyalty to the history of its ancestors. And it means doubting the narrative "when God himself or through an angel speaks to humans, or when the narratives report processes that either contradict common experiences and natural laws or contain contradictions in themselves."[150] It is with such a critical construct that de Wette asserted that the books of the Pentateuch are unreliable as history, since most of the narratives are mythical. Such a construct is the result of methodological naturalism (i.e., it rules out supernatural explanation of the text). However, that does not mean that these narratives are not useful. Their value is in their view of the narrative as poetry and myth that interpreters find: a "product of the national religious poetry of Israel, in which is reflected in its spirit, its patriotism, its philosophy, and its religion, and therefore becomes among the first sources of its history of culture and religion."[151] Much of what de Wette said in *Contributions* is expanded in his *Commentary on the Psalms* (1811). Here, he took up the question of the authenticity of Psalms. He argued that most of the named authors were not actual authors, especially the Davidic psalms. In de Wette's opinion, "it is only the scholar of aesthetics who can determine and decide on the inner worth of each psalm, that is, what is original and what is but an imitation."[152] Psalms were seen more like a lyrical anthology. What de Wette established is to bring about a kind of critical approach where the task of interpretation is equated with understanding the perspective, assumptions, and being suspicious of the narratives that appear to contain divine communications. Truth or the meaning of the text is not in the text. However, it is found in the perspectives, assumptions, and the suspicious reconstruction of the biblical narratives.

Hermeneutics and Criticism

Further, with the rise of German universities, there was a new sense of freedom in historical research and philosophical inquiry.[153] Historical

150 Reventlow, *History of Biblical Interpretation, vol. 4*, 237.

151 Ct. in Reventlow, *History of Biblical Interpretation, vol. 4*, 237.

152 Reventlow, *History of Biblical Interpretation, vol. 4*, 239–40.

153 See Thomas Albert Howard, *Protestant Theology and The Rise of Modern German University* (Oxford: OUP, 2006).

criticism came to properly dominate biblical interpretation (and to a certain extent, it still does). Criticism came to be equated with exegesis or interpretation; there was also a close link between criticism and theological constructions. One of the key contributions came through the works of Friedrich Daniel Ernst Schleiermacher (1768–1834).[154] His *Hermeneutics and Criticism* (1838) attempted to understand the process through which humans arrive at understanding the text.[155] This was a move away from the question of biblical interpretation to the philosophical theory of interpretation—from exegesis to hermeneutics. His effort was to contribute to the philosophical theory of interpretation—"the art of understanding."[156] For Schleiermacher "Hermeneutics deals only with the art of understanding, not with the presentation of what has been understood."[157] Kurt Mueller-Vollmer suggests that the hermeneutical work of Schleiermacher should be seen in line with the early Romantic Movement, which changed the intellectual life of Europe, from 1795–1810.[158] Location of hermeneutical concerns was made with "the idea of the author as creator and of the work of art as an expression of his creative self."[159] Hermeneutics, in that sense, is "concerned with illuminating the conditions for the possibility of understanding and its modes of interpretation."[160] If that is the case, then authors of the text are seen as creators and their work as art and to understand their work is to relive or rethink the author's thought or feeling.[161] This is a move away from the earlier understanding of hermeneutics, which was occupied with decoding meaning from a given text or narratives. Schleiermacher distinguishes between "a less rigorous practice" where "understanding occurs as a matter of course" and "a more rigorous practice" where "misunderstanding occurs as a matter of course," and as such, "understanding must be willed and sought at

154 Frei suggests that Schleiermacher's influence was felt only at the end of the century. One reason has to do with his distinction of hermeneutics and criticism, the other has to do with the possibility that his work was overshadowed by Strauss's *Life of Jesus*. Frei, *The Eclipse of Biblical Narrative*, 284.

155 This was posthumously published by one of his students, F. Lucke, offering a coherent work of Schleiermacher's hermeneutics. Schleiermacher, "Foundations," 72–97.

156 Schleiermacher, "Foundations," 73.

157 Schleiermacher, "Foundations," 73.

158 Kurt Mueller-Vollmer, "Introduction" in *The Hermeneutic Reader: Texts of the German Tradition from the Enlightenment to the Present*, ed. Kurt Mueller-Vollmer (New York: Continuum, 2006), 8.

159 Mueller-Vollmer, "Introduction," 8.

160 Mueller-Vollmer, "Introduction," 9.

161 B. M. G. Reardon, *Religion in the Age of Romanticism: Studies in Early Nineteenth Century Thought* (Cambridge: CUP, 1985), 8.

every point."[162] This means that understanding a text or a narrative would require a sense of reexperiencing the thought or emotional process of the author. Such a task would require "grasping the text precisely with the understanding and in viewing it from the standpoint of both grammatical and psychological interpretation."[163] It requires knowledge of the language of the text, especially of its usage and the thought formulation of the author. This, according to Schleiermacher, is the task of interpretation. An interpreter would be an expert in the language of the concerned subject. Interpretation is no longer concerned with the ecclesial concern or their interpretation. Instead, it has to do with understanding the world behind the text—in this case, the thoughts and feelings of the author. This is to claim that "We understand the author better than he [or she] understood himself [or herself]."[164]

Historical Theology and Criticism

With the change of meaning and understanding in hermeneutics ("from determination of the rules and principles of interpreting texts to inquiry into the nature of understanding discourse and what is manifested in it"),[165] hermeneutical discussion is now seen in interaction with other historical concerns. This methodological procedure gave a twofold direction in theological-historical discourse: a critical-historical understanding and a faith-based understanding. This is a tension between the enchanted and the disenchanted worldview, where theological-historical inquiries are made with or without the conception of divine involvement (or with or without believing in miracles). These two perspectives were brought together by focusing on the same object—in this case, the story of Jesus of Nazareth.[166] By the end of the nineteenth century, there was some sort of hermeneutical recession as a result of the publication of David Strauss's (1808–1874) *Life of Jesus* (1846).[167] This book forced "the discussion away from hermeneutical and into historical questions, particularly the reliability or unreliability of the written sources for providing access to Jesus as he actually was and taught."[168] This development was a change from hermeneutical questions to historical questions.[169]

162 Schleiermacher, "Foundations," 81–82.
163 Schleiermacher, "Foundations," 82.
164 Schleiermacher, "Foundations," 87.
165 Frei, *The Eclipse of Biblical Narrative*, 282.
166 See Peter C. Hodgson, *The Formation of Historical Theology: A Study of Ferdinand Christian Baur* (New York: Harper and Row, 1966).
167 See David Friedrich Strauss, *The Life of Jesus, Critically Examined*, trans. George Eliot (London: Swan Sonnenschein, 1902).
168 Frei, *The Eclipse of Biblical Narrative*, 283.
169 Frei, *The Eclipse of Biblical Narrative*, 283.

In *The Life of Jesus*, Strauss argued that (most of) the narratives of the NT are a myth, and not historical. Though it contains timeless truth, he suggests that the biblical narratives are covered with unhistorical truth. He uses the category of myth as the hermeneutical key to interpreting the NT text. Otto Pfleiderer suggests that the novelty in *The Life of Jesus* is not in applying the myth in biblical interpretation but in "the uncompromising thoroughness with which the principle was applied to every section of the gospel story."[170] He also suggests that,

> The originality lay in the merciless acumen and clearness with which the discrepancies between the Gospels and the difficulties presented to the critical understanding by their narratives were laid bare, and with which all the subterfuges of supernaturalist apologist, as well as all the forced and artificial interpretation of semi-critical Rationalists, were exposed thereby cutting off all ways of escape from the final consequences of criticism.[171]

Strauss suggests two criteria to show the unhistorical (what is mythical and legendary) in the gospel narrative: one is a negative criterion and the other a positive one—it is not history and it is a fiction.[172] Within the *negative* criterion: First, an account is said to be *not historical* if "the narration is irreconcilable with the known and universal which governs the course of events."[173] Here, methodological naturalism shades into metaphysical naturalism. What is seen as divine apparitions and miracles, or prophecies, are to be seen as not historical (e.g., the narrative of angels and devils). Second, an account is to be considered historical if the narrative is "inconsistent [neither] with itself, nor in contradiction with other accounts."[174] This can be affirmative when one account affirms what the other denies. Alternatively, it can be contrary when the second account contradicts the other—in terms of time, place, number, names, or the essential substance of history. Within the *positive* criterion: the positive characters of "legend and fiction" are to be seen as "sometimes in the form, sometimes in the substance of a narrative."[175] If the form is poetical, or if the character talks in hymns, or if it is supernatural, it is not regarded as historical. However, that does not take away the historical validity of the narrative since myth can take a simple and apparent form. There is

---

170 Otto Pfleiderer, "Introduction" in David Friedrich Strauss, *The Life of Jesus, Critically Examined*, trans. George Eliot (London: Swan Sonnenschein, 1902), xi–xii, v–xxvi.

171 Pfleiderer, "Introduction," xii.

172 Strauss, *The Life of Jesus*, 87.

173 Strauss, *The Life of Jesus*, 87.

174 Strauss, *The Life of Jesus*, 87–89.

175 Strauss, *The Life of Jesus*, 89.

still room to consider the substance of the narrative. If a narrative shows similarity with certain existing and prevailing ideas "within the circle from which the narrative proceeded, which ideas themselves seem to be the product of preconceived opinions rather than practical experience, it is more or less probable, according to circumstances, that such a narrative is of mythical origin."[176] For example, if there were detailed studies of a character (say, Jesus) that describes the prophecies and prototypes of the OT, it is seen as mythical and not historical.

What Strauss did was to distinguish between historical and mythical narrative. In doing so he moved away from those who treated the gospel as literal, the factual account of the life of Jesus—those who believe in miracles, the supernaturalist. He also moved away from those who give a natural explanation of the narrative—those who explain away the miracle events, the rationalist. In addition, he adds the mythical elements in the text—a religious expression representing an event or idea in "a form which is historical."[177]

Strauss's attempt to reconstruct the life of Jesus—an exposition of the gospel with mythological elements—was widely critiqued, especially by rationalists or naturalists. Reordering or furthering the discussion along the line of the rationalist of the conventional nineteenth-century biblical criticism can be seen in the works of Eduard Reuss (1804–1891), Karl Heinrich Graf (1815–1869), Abraham Kuenen (1828–1891), and Julius Wellhausen (1844–1918).[178] These scholars are responsible for determining the chronological sequence of the source of the Pentateuch, which has come to be known as the JEDP theory.[179] Similar historical investigations of the NT were also carried out by scholars like Karl Lachmann (1793–1851), Christian Gottlob Wilke (1886–1854), and Christian Hermann Weisse (1801–1866).[180] They made the case that the gospels of Matthew and Luke depended on Mark and a lost source, known as Q.[181] This investigation of sources was not seen as an end in itself, but it became the basis for the reconstruction of the biblical narrative or the history of Israel. This is biblical criticism in the nineteenth century. It questioned not just the authority of the Bible but it also put suspicion in the minds of the readers.

[176] Strauss, *The Life of Jesus*, 89.

[177] Strauss, *The Life of Jesus*, 53.

[178] See E. W. Nicholson, *The Pentateuch in the Twentieth Century: The Legacy of Julius Wellhausen* (Oxford: OUP, 1998).

[179] See Reventlow, *History of Biblical Interpretation, vol. 4*, 315–17.

[180] Ronald Allan Piper, ed., *The Gospel Behind the Gospel: Current Studies on Q* (Leiden: E. J. Brill, 1995).

[181] See Sheppard, "Biblical Interpretation in the 18th & 19th Centuries," 276.

"Believing Criticism" and Criticism

While significant developments were seen in the direction of critical approach, their pursuit did not go unchecked. There were biblical scholars who responded to their claims while attempting to maintain the enchanted worldview in their interpretative task—and, to a certain extent, address the concerns of the church. One such group of scholars were seen in mid-nineteenth-century England who were collectively known as "believing criticism."[182] Since Deists attacked the authority of Scripture, reaction against them came in the form of arguments on the infallibility of the canon of Scripture.[183] The reaction is recorded in the series of "Bampton Lectures" in the early nineteenth century; they placed the Bible as "something apart from the other writings" (i.e., each book came out of divine superintendence).[184] Such a view of Scripture, the orthodox conception of the Bible, was held within a cluster of ecclesial settings. This discussion took a new turn with the publication of *Essays and Reviews* in 1860.[185] The essayists-reviewers attempted to combine the understanding of the infallibility of Scripture and the principles of criticism. Nigel Cameron states,

> The Conservatives were forced to move from treating the matter, in the context of positive exposition of their concept of the nature of Scripture . . . as an objection requiring response, to coming to grips with Critical writings and debating before the eyes of the Church which was the more faithful and the more credible way of treating the Bible.[186]

This new development is the focus of this section. Effort will be made to understand the argument of the "believing criticism" through the minds of Joseph Barber Lightfoot (1826–1889), Brooke Foss Westcott (1825–1901), and Fenton John Anthony Hort (1828–1892). Lightfoot, Wescott, and Hort (also known as the "Cambridge School") attempted to incorporate a critical approach to establish traditional doctrinal theology, especially with a focus on the NT.[187] They planned to work on "a 'tripartite' commentary on the New Testament—where Lightfoot would work on Pauline writings, Wescott on Johannine writings, and Hort on

[182] I have taken the help of Nigel Cameron to give a sense of the historical development of believing criticism. See Nigel Cameron, "Inspiration and Criticism: The Nineteenth-Century Crisis," *Tyndale Bulletin* 35 (1984): 129–59.

[183] See J. H. Pratt, ed., *The Thought of the Evangelical Leaders: Notes of the Discussions of the Eclectic Society, London, During the years 1798–1814* (London: n.p., 1856).

[184] V. F. Storr, *The Development of English Theology in the Nineteenth Century, 1800–1860* (London: Longmans, 1913), 177.

[185] Cameron, "Inspiration and Criticism," 137.

[186] Cameron, "Inspiration and Criticism," 139.

[187] See also Stephen Neill and Tom Wright, *The Interpretation of the New Testament, 1861–1986*, Second Edition (Oxford: OUP, 1988), 35–64.

the historico-Judaic" (the Synoptic Gospels, *St. James, St. Peter* and *St. Jude*).[188] Though their plan did not immediately fall into place, successive commentaries were published. They responded to the claims of German rationalism, especially the Tübingen scholars. Christian Baur and his Tübingen associates and pupils had attempted to provide "a chronological reconstruction of early Christian literature, which placed the Gospels and Acts so late as to be practically valueless as historical sources."[189] The result of such reconstruction was that it became impossible to place most of the NT in the second century, deeming them unreliable. The Cambridge school attempted to bring corrective measures to the Tübingen reconstruction of the biblical narratives.

Lightfoot responded to Tübingen scholars through the publication of *Saint Paul's Epistle to the Galatians* (1865) and *The Apostolic Fathers* (1885, especially his edition on Ignatius).[190] His commentary on the *Galatians* was the first installment of the project of Lightfoot, Westcott, and Hort. He took a historical approach of going back to the source like the rationalists, but with different results (i.e., holding to the enchanted worldview). F. F. Bruce suggests, "His strength lay on the historical side, and the need of the hour was for the reinforcement of the historical foundation of the Christian faith."[191] Lightfoot attempted to bring historical correction to the tasks of the rationalists, thereby maintaining the faith element.

Lightfoot dealt with some of the issues raised by the Tübingen scholars in his dissertations included in *Galatians*: "Brethren of the Lord" and "St. Paul and the Three."[192] He addresses the question of the identity of the *brethren of the Lord*, asking, "Who are the brethren of the Lord?" He considers the three traditional views and legitimizes them using historical insights. The first view holds that there is no blood relationship between the brethren and Jesus—the *Epiphanian* view; the second suggests that they were the brethren of the Lord as Mary was the Lord's mother—the *Helvidian* view; and the third view asserts that the brethren are the Lord's cousins—the *Hieronymian* view. Lightfoot dismisses the *Hieronymian* view, suggesting that it has no traditional sanction or any secondary

[188] Arthur Wescott, "Prefatory Note" in *The Gospel According to St. John, vol. 1: The Greek Text with Introduction and Notes*, Brooke Foss Westcott, ed. (London: John Murray, 1908), v.

[189] F. F. Bruce, "*J. B. Lightfoot (died 1889): Commentator and Theologian*," *Evangel* 7.2 (1989): 10–12.

[190] See J. B. Lightfoot, *Saint Paul's Epistle to the Galatians* (London: Macmillan, 1884); J. B. Lightfoot, *The Apostolic Father, Part II: S. Ignatius, S. Polycarp*, Second Edition (London: Macmillan, 1889).

[191] Bruce, "*J. B. Lightfoot (died 1889)*," 10.

[192] Lightfoot, *Saint Paul's Epistle to the Galatians*, 252–91, 292–374.

evidence to support its view. Using Scriptural references and other early Christian writings, he saw the *Epiphanian* view as historically accurate. Scriptural evidence, especially from John 19: 26–27, tells that the Lord would not have consigned the care of his mother to a stranger if the brethren were his own brothers. Moreover, in implication, the *Helvidian* view is disproved. Further, while referring to the early church writings (such as The Gospel of the Hebrew, the Gospel According to Peter, Protevangelium Jacobi, Clementine Homilies, The Clementine Recognitions, Hegesippus, Clement of Alexandria, Origen, etc.), he confirmed the *Epiphanian*, view which suggests that there was no blood relationship between the brethren and Jesus.[193]

Further, in "St. Paul and the Three," Lightfoot attempts to answer the prevailing tension in the apostolic age "between Paul and the Judaizers who tried to dilute his law-free gospel with an infusion of legalism."[194] Baur had argued that second-century Christianity consisted of two opposing views/groups—Jewish Christians (Peter) and Gentile Christians (Paul).[195] Against the theological controversy of the time, Lightfoot suggests that there was no sharp conflict or opposition between Paul and the three apostles—James, Peter, and John (especially Peter). He builds his argument by showing "the progressive history of the relations between the Jewish and Gentile converts in the early age of the Church," drawing from the Apostolic writings.[196] This suggestion is further aided by investigating the position of Paul and the apostles on the issue of circumcision. He explores the said concern by dividing its history into three parts: the extension of the church to the Gentiles, the recognition of the Gentile liberty, and the emancipations of the Jewish Churches.[197] In the first parts of the history, the early church appears to conform to the ways of Jewish customs. It was confined to one nation and to its rites and practices. The second part of the history shows the admission of Gentiles into the Church. This was a new turn in Church history. Paul was called to take on the responsibility to take the name of Christ to the Gentiles. The reversal of this position is assisted by two crucial circumstances letting the Gentiles into the Church: the martyrdom of Stephen and the severe famine in Palestine. The third part of history shows the emancipation of the Jewish churches. With the fall of Jerusalem and the discontinuing of

[193] Lightfoot, *Saint Paul's Epistle to the Galatians*, 252–91.

[194] Bruce, "*J. B. Lightfoot (died 1889)*," 10.

[195] See Martin Bauspiess et al., eds., *Ferdinand Christian Baur and The History of Early Christianity*, trans., Robert F. Brown and Peter C. Hodgson (Oxford: OUP, 2017).

[196] Lightfoot, *Saint Paul's Epistle to the Galatians*, 294.

[197] Lightfoot, *Saint Paul's Epistle to the Galatians*, 294.

the temple worship, the Jewish Church was led to rethink the purposes of the law (i.e., the law that once constituted the national institution and religious obligation), and their relationship with the unconverted Jews.[198] With the above response, what Lightfoot did was this: like modern critics, go back to the historical sources and Scripture, but affirm the Christian faith. Unlike the rationalists, instead of reconstructing the biblical narrative, he affirmed the narrative of the Christian faith as recorded in the Scripture. He went back to the sources (i.e., the extrabiblical sources), but recognized the internal sources and affirmed orthodox beliefs.

Like Lightfoot, Westcott's reaction to the Tübingen scholars is evident in his *Introduction to the Study of the Gospels, With Historical and Explanatory Notes* (1866).[199] His methodology is expressed in *The Bible in the Church, A Popular Account of the Collection and Reception of the Holy Scriptures in the Christian Churches* (1866).[200] In *The Study of the Gospels,* Westcott points out his theological position by stating "the conviction that truth is felt to be more precious in proportion as it is opened to us by our own work."[201] Through the historical study of the gospel, he wanted to show that "there is a true mean[s] between the idea of a formal harmonization of the Gospels and the abandonment of their absolute truth."[202] He suggests that the more the reader reads the Bible, the more fully they will realize its importance—and not move away from it by way of reconstructing its narrative. Instead of looking for a plausible history, he argues that critics should pay attention to the "mutual relations and constructive force" of the gospel.[203] He states, "We cannot remind ourselves too often that arguments are strong only as they are true, and that truth is itself the fullest confutation of error."[204] This is to suggest that the results of historical investigation should be preceded by theological interpretation. He, along with Lightfoot and Hort, remained careful from overstating the results drawn from textual and historical examination.[205] This view is firmly stated in *The Bible in the Church,* where Westcott states that "the Bible may be treated historically or theologically. Neither treatment is complete

---

198 Lightfoot, *Saint Paul's Epistle to the Galatians*, 313–14.

199 Brooke Foss Westcott, *Introduction to the Study of the Gospels, With Historical and Explanatory Notes* (Boston: Gould and Lincoln, 1866).

200 Brooke Foss Westcott, *The Bible in the Church, A Popular Account of the Collection and Reception of the Holy Scriptures in the Christian Churches* (London: Macmillan, 1866).

201 Westcott, *Introduction to the Study of the Gospels*, xi.

202 Westcott, *Introduction to the Study of the Gospels*, xii.

203 Westcott, *Introduction to the Study of the Gospels*, xii.

204 Westcott, *Introduction to the Study of the Gospels*, xii–xiv.

205 Westcott, *The Bible in the Church*, viii.

in itself."[206] However, he recognizes that in the recent past (referring to the modern critics), the Bible has suffered the inversion of historical investigation. He argues for a kind of historical investigation that brings to light the truth of the biblical text. Westcott affirms that the Bible is not just ancient writing. Instead, it is the "source and measure" of the religious faith of the Christians.[207] He goes on to suggest that the record of the Bible is according to the natural laws. Nevertheless, he means that "slowly and with an ever-deepening conviction the Churches received, after trial, and in some cases after doubt and contradiction, the books which we now receive: that the religious consciousness which was quickened by the words of prophets and apostles in turn ratified their writings."[208] What we have as Scripture did not come in rigid or uniform laws, but by means of ecclesial usage. It went together with the Christian body, as "the vital law of its action."[209] Wescott states that it is "the Church [which] offered a living commentary on the Book, and the Book an unchanging test of the Church."[210] Hence, for someone to suggest that the Bible should bear the mark of unquestioned divine origin is to reflect the person's view of revelation. It would seem evident that God works through humans, both in the church and the Bible. Such progress is to be appreciated for being truly human, but also to be recognized that it is divine.

Hort's theological position is evident in *The Way, The Truth, and The Life* (1893), which addresses the coexistence of critical mind with a belief in the biblical truths.[211] His thinking came with three distinct marks of expression: "the expression of personal conviction," "the furtherance of individual belief," and "the appeal to the relations between the Christian revelation and the sum of experience."[212] First, the expression of personal conviction comes from the right source. He holds that to be impersonal takes away the scope to convince others, "with little or no reference to what has actually exerted power over their minds." Their influence or persuasiveness is limited toward "those peculiar minds whose own beliefs or disbeliefs are formed or retained exclusively within these same limits." Second, the furtherance of individual belief is an essential element of imparting wisdom. He is of the view that "what is written with a view to being simply assented to and adopted has advantages of definite form

206 Westcott, *The Bible in the Church*, viii.
207 Westcott, *The Bible in the Church*, x.
208 Westcott, *The Bible in the Church*, xi.
209 Westcott, *The Bible in the Church*, xi.
210 Westcott, *The Bible in the Church*, xi.
211 Fenton John Anthony Hort, *The Way, The Truth, The Life: The Hulsean Lectures for 1871* (London: Macmillan, 1893).
212 Hort, *The Way, The Truth, The Life*, xxx.

and result denied to what is written with the hope of encouraging and aiding independent energy of heart and mind." He sees it as important to confront truth with personal life and knowledge. Third, the choice of personal efforts of understanding in speech and of reception of speech is dependent on "the true nature of Christian evidence taken as a whole."[213] Most of this search for Christian evidence is done at the expense of the credentials or the contents of the Christian faith. Such a task has resulted in much controversy with a sense of discontent with its search. What Westcott and Hort did was to translate the truth of the text to the readers. They were absorbed in the methodology of criticism, but their goal was to ascertain the truth of the text. Such emphasis comes from the assumption that the biblical text is infallible and inspired. Yet, both were engaged in textual criticism. Their focus was to hold on to the truth of the text and not reconstruct the text.

Late Modern Period

Moving to the twentieth century, biblical scholars continued the pursuit of biblical criticism: the pursuit of the author's intent by way of reconstruction of the text using extrabiblical sources.[214] The twentieth century biblical scholars now freely read the Bible as an ancient source, sitting together with other ancient books. The consequence of such practice is the collapse of the canonical status of the biblical texts. It saw the diversification of biblical scholarship taking the form of several schools of reading. These diverse forms of critical reading can be seen in the following manner: comparative studies of the Bible with other ancient Near Eastern documents, developments of distinctive schools with particular interest (Targumic and Septuagintal studies, myth and ritual studies, cultic rituals, anthological Midrash, etc.), Bible as a resource of reference of a salvation history, comparative study of Jewish and Christian reading of the Bible, and sociological and anthropological reading of the text.[215] If it is not exactly dominant, biblical criticism is still in operation in the academy—in one form or another.[216]

---

[213] Hort, *The Way, The Truth, The Life*, xxx–xxxiii.

[214] But by the late nineteenth century, a new critique called "New Historicism" argued that interpreters cannot gain "a full and authentic past, a lived material existence, unmediated by the surviving textual traces of the society in question." Louis A. Montrose, "Professing the Renaissance: The Poetics and Politics of Culture," in *The New Historicism*, ed. H. Aram Veeser (New York: Routledge, 1989), 20.

[215] See G. T. Sheppard, "Biblical Interpretation in Europe in the 20th Century," in *Historical Handbook of Major Biblical Interpreters*, 412–22.

[216] Mary Hesse, "How to Be Postmodern without Being a Feminist," *The Monist* 77.4 (1994): 445–61.

What is distinctive is the rise of studies in the history of religion coming from the Near Eastern excavation, especially focused on the pan-Babylonian school.[217] Biblical scholars like Hermann Gunkel (1862–1932), Hugo Gressmann (1877–1927), and Sigmund Mowinckel (1884–1965) studied the ancient texts as well as "the religious phenomena behind the text."[218] As they ask questions about the beginnings, development, and relationships, their "concern, tool, and data" were driven by "phenomenological, historical, and comparative" approaches.[219] They examined the characteristics and components of the Israelites religion to extrapolate "what took place and what conceptions or 'ideology' underlay the religious practices."[220] They made efforts to understand "the original form of the practices and ideas and how and why they developed and changed"; this included an attempt to understand the outside influence to formulate their religious elements.[221] As they "relativized the sacred literature out of which theological systems were constructed, challenging claims to uniqueness, absoluteness, revelation, and finality," they ignored theology.[222] Here, form criticism emerged from literary criticism, which attempted to determine "the structure or composition of larger literary works (the sources)."[223] It started with "the isolation of the small original units, the determination of their presumed oral origin (the so-called setting in life), and the generic classification of these units and of their functions."[224] For example, Hermann Gunkel sees literary types as constituted by a complex of: "(1) thoughts and moods, (2) linguistic forms (sounds or written symbols) and (3) a normal connection with life."[225] Such interest was further developed (in the 1960s and early 1970s) with growing interest in the ancient Near East (or Western) studies—especially on "treaty and covenant, from the new stylistic and rhetorical criticism, from the study of oral literature, from structuralism [structural linguists], and from careful scrutiny of the form-critical

---

217 Patrick D. Miller "Israelite Religion" in *The Hebrew Bible and Its Modern Interpreters*, ed. Douglas A. Knight and Gene M. Tucker (Chico: Scholars, 1985), 201–38.

218 Miller, "Israelite Religion," 201.

219 Miller, "Israelite Religion," 201.

220 Miller, "Israelite Religion," 201.

221 Miller, "Israelite Religion," 201.

222 Miller, "Israelite Religion," 202.

223 Rolf Knierim, "Criticism of Literary Features, Form, Tradition, and Redaction" in *The Hebrew Bible and Its Modern Interpreters*, ed. Douglas A. Knight and Gene M. Tucker (Chico: Scholars, 1985), 136.

224 Knierim, "Criticism of Literary Features, Form, Tradition, and Redaction," 136.

225 Cited in Martin J. Buss, *Criticism in its Context*, Journal for the Study of the Old Testament Supplement Series 274 (Sheffield: SAP, 1999), 15.

assumptions by some form critics themselves."[226] This further affected the understanding of "form or structure, genre, setting, function and/or intention, their interdependence, the relationship of genre and text, and of literature and orality."[227] With such advancement in critical approach, it brought distrust of historical and literary appearances. Source, form, and redaction critics suspected that the truth is something else even though biblical texts *appear* to be unified—hence, the attempt to reconstruct the original historical situation *behind* the text. In this sense, criticism is now seen as "*an attempt to part the veil of appearances in order to see the reality*"—the reality *behind* the text.[228]

Along with these developments, there were two others important (broadly speaking) developments in the area of biblical interpretation. One has to do with postmodern interpretation of the Bible, which reacts against the biblical criticism and develops its own distinctive interpretative strands; the other also responds to critical approach and it concerns the churchly interpretation of the Bible, which emphasized on locating the Bible and its interpretation in the church and recognizes the role of the church in interpretation.

Postmodernism (Ideology) and Criticism (Exegesis)

The mid-twentieth century began to see the confrontation of modernism or critical thinking from different fronts. Such critique is evident not just in biblical interpretation, but across disciplines—art, literature, philosophy, architecture, theology, etc. Moving further into the late twentieth century, the critique against critical commentators-interpreters began to increase, especially from postmodern interpreters. They argue against the modernist reconstruction of the biblical text suggesting that they failed to achieve the task that they set out to achieve. They saw it as impossible to bring out a scientific-objective and rationalistic interpretation of the biblical narratives because all knowledge claims reflect the knower's situation (race, class, gender) and power interest. This eventually led to a tension between exegesis and ideology—between modern and postmodern interpreters.

If modern biblical interpretation prioritized the text, postmodern interpreters prioritized the readers—a privileging of the context (location and identity) of the readers. According to Steven Connor, the development of postmodernism can be seen in four stages: accumulation,

---

[226] Knierim, "Criticism of Literary Features, Form, Tradition, and Redaction," 136.

[227] Knierim, "Criticism of Literary Features, Form, Tradition, and Redaction," 136–37.

[228] Kevin J. Vanhoozer, email message to author, December 13, 2018.

synthesis, autonomy, and dissipation.[229] In the first stage, which extends through the 1970s to the early 1980s, there were developments of postmodernism from different fronts—in the works of Daniel Bell and Jean Baudrillard, Jean-Francois Lyotard, Charles Jencks, and Ihab Hassan. At this stage there were no criteria to define a fixed term for postmodern; there was a difficulty to identify what seems to be a distinct shift from modernity to post modernity. In the second stage, from the middle 1980s onwards, the above features of postmodernism were clustered together, i.e., "what came to seem important was not so much the aptness of the explanations of particular varieties of postmodernism as the increasingly powerful rhymes that different accounts of the postmodern formed with each other." This is also the stage where syncretism began to take shape in postmodern thinking. In the third stage, by the middle 1990s, the term is seen in terms of how "the 'post' idea had achieved a kind of autonomy from its objects." By this time, it had become "a kind of data-cloud, a fog of discourse that showed up on the radar even more conspicuously than what it was supposed to be about." In the fourth stage, by the end of the 1990s, "'postmodernism' slowly but inexorably ceased to be a condition of things in the world, whether the world of art, culture, economics, politics, religion, or war, and became a philosophical disposition, an all-too-easily recognizable (and increasingly dismissible) style of thought and talk."[230] By this time the term postmodernism had come to "signify a loose, sometimes dangerously loose, relativism."[231] At this point postmodern studies began to proliferate; it came to be conceived as "a condition" or as "a project."[232]

The critique against modernism, especially their preoccupation with the author or the intent of the author, came as early as the 1940s. In the article "The Intentional Fallacy (1946)," W. K. Wimsatt and M. C. Beardsley suggested the possibility that critics are able to provide a legitimate interpretation without referring to the author.[233] This was the working-out of an earlier article on the author's "Intention (1943)," where it argued that the intention of the author cannot be found or desirable as a standard for judging the credibility of a literary art work.[234] Though

---

[229] Steven Connor, "Introduction" in *The Cambridge Companion to Postmodernism* (Cambridge: CUP, 2004), 1.

[230] Connor, "Introduction," 1–6.

[231] Connor, "Introduction," 6.

[232] Connor, "Introduction," 6.

[233] W. K. Wimsatt and M. C. Beardsley, "The Intentional Fallacy," *The Sewanee Review*, Vol. 54.3 (1946): 468–488.

[234] W. K. Wimsatt and M. C. Beardsley, "Intention" in *Dictionary of World Literature*, ed. Joseph T. Shipley (New York, 1943), 326–39.

such thinking might not have gained the needed access at that point of time, it opened doors for further discussion on the subject. A few years later, Roland Barthes's "The Death of the Author" (1967) argues against the idea of incorporating the author's intent and the biographical context of an author in a literary interpretation.[235] These works put a case against the task of ascertaining the intention of the author to derive the meaning of the given literature. Nevertheless, Barthes would suggest that such work is not possible. He would even argue that the writing and the author are unrelated. If not the author, then it is the readers (he calls them "the spectator") who determine the meaning of the text. Barthes states, "The birth of the reader must be ransomed by the death of the Author."[236] This shift from the author to the reader has been in the making for decades—from author-oriented approach to text-oriented approach, and finally, to reader-oriented approach.[237]

This shift of reading gave birth to the reader-centered criticism or reader-response criticism. This is concerned with how readers come to terms with the meaning of the text out of their experience with the text.[238] The *Reader-Response Criticism* (1980) probably marked the formalization of reader-response criticism.[239] For Jane Tompkins, such criticism would take into account "the words of the *reader, the reading process,* and *response* to mark out an area for investigation."[240] By the early 1990s, such criticism had influenced biblical scholars to take the context of the readers seriously. Within reader-response criticism, there are wide ranges of interests. Books like *Reading with a Passion* (1995) bring to mind how a person's experience is related to their reading of the Bible.[241] It showed that questions related to "the effect of narrative on audiences, theories of how texts affect particular response, and illustration of how a narrative can be transformed by the psychology of the individual reader or

---

[235] See Roland Barthes, "The Death of the Author" in *Image Music Text,* trans., Stephen Heath (New York: Hill & Wang, 1977), 142–49.

[236] Barthes, "The Death of the Author" 149.

[237] See Terry Eagleton, *Literary Theory: An Introduction*, Second Edition (Malden: Blackwell, 1983, 1996).

[238] Stanley Fish, *Is There a Text in this Class? The Authority of Interpretative Communities* (Massachusetts: HUP, 1980).

[239] Jane P. Tompkins, ed., "An Introduction to Reader-Response Criticism" in *Reader-Response Criticism: From Formalism to Post-Structuralism* (Baltimore: JHUP, 1980), ix.

[240] Tompkins, "An Introduction to Reader-Response Criticism" in *Reader-Response Criticism,* ix.

[241] Jeffrey Staley, *Reading with a Passion: Rhetoric, Autobiography, and the American West in the Gospel of John* (New York: Continuum, 1995).

by particular interpretative communities."[242] In *Reading from this Place* (1995), Fernando Segovia and Mary Ann Tolbert attempted to measure the influence of social location in "theory and practice" in the reading/interpretation of the Bible.[243] It takes seriously the social location and thus contextualization of the readers. Similarly, but taking an autobiographical direction, *The Personal Voice in Biblical Interpretation* (1999) emphasizes how "a person's unique character and life-story" are influential in reading and interpreting the Bible.[244] This criticism is technically referred to as autobiographical biblical criticism. Such criticism considers the role of the personal voice of the interpreter in the process of arriving at the meaning of the text. Reader-response criticism pays attention to the reader's context (social, cultural, or ethnic), instead of the author. In other words, the readers play an active role in recreating the significance of the text in mind. Yet, its outcome tends to be pluralistic—there is no definite meaning or answer in their recreation. This is a given since readers come from different backgrounds and influences.

Reader-oriented criticism that has gained much interest in the literary discussion is Jacques Derrida's deconstruction—referred to as deconstructive criticism. The concept first appeared in *Of Grammatology* (1967), where Derrida tried to understand the interplay between language and construction of meaning;[245] a further attempt to explain what deconstruction means is found in "Letter to a Japanese Friend"[246] Derrida used the term deconstruction to translate Martin Heidegger's words *Destruktion* or *Abbau* as these words signify "an annihilation or a negative reduction much closer perhaps to Nietzschean 'demolition.'"[247] He is of the view that deconstruction is "neither analysis nor a critique;" it is neither a method; it is not an action or operation; instead, it is an event.[248] He states, "Deconstruction takes place, it is an event that does not await the deliberation, consciousness, or organization of a subject, or even of

[242] Staley, *Reading with a Passion*, 1–2.

[243] Fernando F. Segovia and Mary Ann Tolbert, eds., *Reading from this Place, vol. 1–2: Social Location and Biblical Interpretation in Global Perspective* (Minneapolis: Fortress, 1995).

[244] See Ingrid Rosa Kitzberger, ed., *The Personal Voice in Biblical Interpretation* (London: Routledge, 1999); Janice Capel Anderson and Jeffrey L. Staley, *Taking it Personally: Autobiographical Biblical Criticism* (Atlanta: SBL, 1995).

[245] Jacques Derrida, *Of Grammatology*, Corrected Edition, trans., Gayatri Chakravorty Spivak (Baltimore: JHUP, 1974).

[246] Jacques Derrida, "Letter to a Japanese Friend" in *Psyche: Inventions of the Other, Vol. II*, ed. Peggy Kamuf and Elizabeth Rottenberg, (Stanford: SU, 2008), 1–6.

[247] Derrida, "Letter to a Japanese Friend," 2.

[248] Derrida, "Letter to a Japanese Friend," 4.

modernity."[249] Instead, "*It deconstructs itself. It can be deconstructed . . . It is in deconstruction.*"[250] It takes place by questioning the supposed connection between the "signifier" and "signified"—for instance, the supposed meaning between the word and the meaning of the word—by suggesting that there is no necessary connection between the two.[251] People use a word or term, instead of the other, because of many different sets of conventions that regulate the use of the language. It reacts to the concept of *logocentrism*: "a commitment to the principle that there is finally some metaphysical thread connecting words and their referents, signifiers and signified, and that if we can only find the right approach (or method, or foundation, or origin, or first principle), we can discern the logos of the cosmos."[252] The development of such thinking is a direct response to the modern interpreter's preoccupation with method and objectivity.

When deconstruction is applied to the biblical texts, it not only provides a wide range of possible readings but also gives insights that traditional readings might have not considered. Stephen D. Moore's "Deconstructive Criticism" (1992) provides a good example of deconstructive reading. Following the works of Paul de Man and Derrida, Moore draws out some key features of deconstruction looking at the Gospel of Mark.[253] First, the text itself is self-deconstructing. The ending of Mark, assuming that it ends in 16:8, undercuts its beginning (i.e., "Outside the tomb, as the women flee and say nothing, Mark rips up its own birth record").[254] This is to say that "the paradigm for all texts consists of a figure (or a system of figures) and its deconstruction."[255] Second, the text may mean more than what is traditionally assumed. While explaining the parable of the sower in Mark: 3–9, the insiders are differentiated with the outsider. Yet, at the end of the gospel, the insiders are depicted as though they were, in fact, the outsider.[256] Third, it concerns the assumed inferior position of the written voice, compared to the spoken voice in Western

---

[249] Derrida, "Letter to a Japanese Friend," 4.

[250] Derrida, "Letter to a Japanese Friend," 4.

[251] A. K. M. Adam, *What Is Postmodern Biblical Criticism?* (Minneapolis: Fortress Press, 1995), 27–28.

[252] See Derrida, *Of Grammatology*, 3; Adam, *What Is Postmodern Biblical Criticism?* 28.

[253] Stephen D. Moore, "Deconstructive Criticism: The Gospel of the Mark," in *Mark and Method: New Approaches in Biblical Studies*, ed. Janice Capel Anderson and Stephen D. Moore (Minneapolis: Fortress, 1992), 86.

[254] Moore, "Deconstructive Criticism," 86.

[255] Paul de Man, *Allegories of Reading: Figural Language in Rousseau, Nietzsche, Rilke, and Proust* (New Haven: YUP, 1979), 205.

[256] See Frank Kermode, *The Genesis of Secrecy: On the Interpretation of Narrative* (Cambridge: HUP, 1979), 27, 46–47.

thinking. It takes the reader to the question of, "What if speech were already the host of writing?"[257] Fourth, the relationship between speech and writing or what transpired in the transition between the two is shown in Jesus's three predictions (8:31; 9:31; 10:33–34). While his immediate listeners failed to understand the significance of Jesus's predictions, the contemporary readers can hear what was said then. It is as though "Jesus were *writing* instead of *speaking*, as if his disciples were *reading* instead of *listening*."[258] In other words, it is the text that "tells the story, the allegory of its misunderstanding."[259] Fifth, it has to do with the peculiarities of words that Mark used. For example, the term *parabole* (meaning "parable") is used to keep the insider and the outsider on one side each—the insider can understand, while the outsider fails to comprehend. However, the problem was, on some occasions, that even the insider struggled to understand—they were threatened to become the outsider. The contradiction of who seems to be inside or outside is kept unresolved. Sixth, the "literary text unravels itself." This is to say that, while the interpreters or critics attempt to interpret the text, they are "being comprehended, being grasped, by the text."[260] The critics are being enveloped by the content of the text. Seventh, the focus of reading and interpreting is not about what appears to be the most important or central, but it is to deconcentrate "the secondary, eccentric, lateral, marginal, parasitic, borderline cases."[261] Its reading takes the interpreters to the margin.

What postmodern scholars/interpreters have managed is to debunk the flaws and weaknesses in the works of modern biblical scholars. More specifically, they can redirect the flaws of preoccupying their interpretative task to only one context (i.e., the historical original context). Having done that, they have turned their attention to the readers, with whom their identity and location are not only acknowledged but emphasized. This development also encouraged the Majority World scholars to develop their interpretative task. Interpretative tasks that were previously controlled and dominated by scholars from a particular region are now confronted by scholars from different parts of the globe with their own distinctive historical and cultural particularities (see chapter 2). At this point, suggestions can be made that there is much interest and productivity of the reader-oriented interpretation in the contemporary context.

---

[257] See Stephen D. Moore, *Literary Criticism and the Gospels: The Theoretical Challenge* (New Haven: YUP, 1989), 157–59, 132–33.

[258] Moore, "Deconstructive Criticism," 90.

[259] de Man, *Allegories of Reading*, 205.

[260] Moore, "Deconstructive Criticism," 93.

[261] Jacques Derrida, *Limited Inc*, ed. Gerald Graff, trans. Samuel Weber and Jeffrey Mehlman (Evanston: NUP, 1988), 44.

However, what has happened with these developments and engagements is the multiplication of interpretative approaches. With the emergence of postmodern interpretation, it further contributed to the division between what is discussed in the academy and what is preached in the church. The church does not have access to these discussions nor do the academicians gather/speak to the needs of the church. Either the scholars have moved to the academy, away from the ecclesial setting, or the church has withdrawn itself away from academic discussions. The postmodern interpreters did not only sunder the text from the sociohistorical contexts, the context of the canon of Scripture, or from the traditions of interpretation but also deprived it "from whatever interpretive constraints might have been suggested by the texts themselves."[262] The result of such developments has been "equally debilitating to constructive or prescriptive theology and ethics, since the interpretive enterprise is alleged to offer no canons against which to measure a 'right' reading from a 'wrong' one, or a 'good' reading from a 'bad' one."[263] This situation of biblical interpretation in the late modern and postmodern period is seen as "a 'muddy ditch'—the quagmire of history, language, tradition, and culture—out of which it is impossible ever to extricate oneself."[264] While critical interpreters were trying to dismiss the faith-driven agendas of a confessional tradition, they seem to have invited ideological agendas in biblical interpretation.[265] Such pluralistic interests of the postmodern have led to a crisis where there is no decisive method to determine the "right" or "true" interpretation of the text; whether it is modern interpreters or postmodern interpreters, where the focus on what is "behind" or "in front of" the text misses the message of the text.[266] It misses the theological content of the text. Hence, the way forward would be to consider a constructive engagement with the Scripture by way of reading it as the Word of God—and in an ecclesial setting.

Church (Theology) and Criticism (Biblical Studies)

While modern biblical scholars were engaging in critical interpretation of the Bible, its products became an academic concern. Its exegesis or commentaries became less and less relevant for the community of faith. Such misdirection of Bible reading received responses from the church with the

[262] Joel B. Green, "Afterward: Rethinking History (and Theology)" in *Between Two Horizons: Spanning New Testament Studies and Systematic Theology*, ed. Joel B. Green and Max Turner (Grand Rapids: Eerdmans, 2000), 238.

[263] Green, "Afterward: Rethinking History (and Theology)," 239.

[264] Vanhoozer, "Introduction," 20.

[265] Vanhoozer, "Introduction," 21.

[266] Vanhoozer, "Introduction," 20–21.

understanding that biblical interpretation should address the concerns of the church and consider its theology as well. Karl Barth (and other dialectic scholars) confronted and analyzed the critical approach of making God the object of humanity's "theological apprehension and reasoning."[267] Barth's publication of *The Epistle to the Romans* (1919) was a dropping of a bomb in the playground of modern theological thinking.[268] He challenged the flawed conceptualization of natural theology, which placed the knowledge of God from sources other than the revelation of God in Christ. He also criticizes theological liberals for thinking that they could know more about God from their own religious experience, instead of biblical testimony.

By the mid-twentieth century, the negligence of the church and its theology had triggered initiatives to cultivate and develop the church's theology. It has encouraged the church and its custodians to take up the task of biblical interpretation, both responding to the dominance of modern biblical criticism and contributing to the growing needs of the church. One of the reasons for ecclesial reading is the acknowledgment that we understand Scripture better when we approach it on the presupposition of faith (i.e., its testimony is true). In addition, it holds that everyone comes to the text with some presuppositions—whether theological or historical or both.

In 1969, the book *The Bible Speaks Again* pointed out a gap between biblical scholars and congregation in the church.[269] The contributors try to "bridge the gap that has developed continuously during the last hundred years between the biblical scholars and the man [and woman] in the pew."[270] Rather than making the discourse entirely academic, it is directed to address the concerns of the church, which "lives from and for the proclamation of the prophetic and apostolic word, by the grace of the Spirit."[271]

Similarly, James Smart argued that there is an emerging gap between modern concepts and language and those of the Bible.[272] He argues that the essentials of the Bible are not being heard in the church. This made

---

267 Richardson, "The Rise of Modern Biblical Scholarship," 319.

268 Karl Barth, *The Epistle to the Romans*, Sixth edition, trans. Edwyn C. Hoskyns (Oxford: OUP, 1968).

269 William Barclay, "Forward" in *The Bible Speaks Again: A Guide from Holland, Commissioned by the Netherlands Reformed Church*, trans. Annebeth Mackie (Minneapolis: APU, 1969), 10.

270 Barclay, "Forward," 10.

271 Barclay, "Forward," 10.

272 James Smart, *The Strange Silence of the Bible in the Church* (Philadelphia: Westminster, 1970).

the church vulnerable to the dominant religious philosophy of the time.[273] This is perceived as that which "constitutes the crisis beneath all the other crises that endanger the church's future."[274] This situation, what he calls "the strange silence of the church," is not limited to preachers alone but it is shared by the community of faith at large.[275] He further made claims that this peculiar situation has emerged out of "a blindness to the complexity of the essential hermeneutical problem, which, in simple terms, is the problem of how to translate the full content of an ancient text into the language and life-context of late twentieth-century persons."[276] In other words, the critical interpreters are stuck in the past or in the world behind the text, and they are unable to speak to the contemporary context.

This perceived crisis also invited a denominational look in *The Lutheran Hermeneutics* (1979).[277] It addresses the nature and concerns of the Scriptures as the inspired-inerrant Word of God; its contributors are interested in coming to terms with the issues of the critical approach (and the divisions that rose among the Lutherans). Though such concern addresses the Lutheran church, what it conveys very much applies to the church at large. Similar concern was raised in *Biblical Interpretation in Crisis* (1989) by the Roman Catholics.[278] It points to the tendency of modern biblical scholarship toward a historical-critical method, which undermines the faith of the church. Critical interpreters had hoped to bring open what had long been forgotten, such as the original message of Jesus. However, the narrative that they hoped to reconstruct became confusing—and not only that, but their approach was also diversified with multiple possible outcomes. Interest in the Scripture itself was diminished. Even if they were to focus on the text, it required dissecting the text into little parts. Faith or what is considered divine is no longer a component of their task. The result of such tasks only leads to "a jungle of contradictions" fueled by a number of hypotheses.[279] Joseph Cardinal Ratzinger states, "In the end, one no longer learns what the text *says*, but

---

[273] Smart, *The Strange Silence of the Bible in the Church*, 10.

[274] Smart, *The Strange Silence of the Bible in the Church*, 10.

[275] Smart, *The Strange Silence of the Bible in the Church*, 10.

[276] Smart, *The Strange Silence of the Bible in the Church*, 10.

[277] John Reumann, Samuel H. Nafzger, and Harold H. Ditmanson, eds., *Studies in Lutheran Hermeneutics* (Philadelphia: Fortress, 1979).

[278] See Richard John Neuhaus, ed., *Biblical Interpretation in Crisis: The Ratzinger Conference on Bible and Church* (Grand Rapids: Eerdmans, 1989).

[279] Joseph Cardinal Ratzinger, "Biblical Interpretation in Crisis: On the Question of the Foundations and Approaches to Exegesis Today" in *Biblical Interpretation in Crisis: The Ratzinger Conference on Bible and Church*, ed. Richard John Neuhaus, (Grand Rapids: Eerdmans, 1989), 2.

what it *should* have said, and by which component parts this can be traced back through the text."[280]

As a result, according to Carl E. Braaten and Robert W. Jenson, the church lost its grip on the Bible as "the authoritative Scripture."[281] They are of the view that,

> The methods of critical reason have tended to take over the entire operation.of biblical interpretation, marginalizing the faith of the church and dissolving the unity of the Bible as a while into a multiplicity of unrelated fragments. The academy has replaced the church as the home of biblical interpretation.[282]

There is now a "gap between the historical-critical method of biblical studies and the church's dogmatic interpretation of the biblical faith."[283] Acknowledging such a gap, John Sandys-Wunsch asks why many modern scholars have lost the idea of inspiration that distinguishes the Bible from any other book.[284] He makes an attempt to fulfill this task by way of doing a historical survey of biblical interpretation from 1450 to 1889.[285] This concern is further discussed in *Reading Scripture with the Church* (2006).[286] Its contributors argued that "the church soundly attend both to the theological weights of diverse ancient texts and to the critical investigations of those text's grammar, milieu, and historical verisimilitude."[287] They argue that the theological dimensions of the text should not be an afterthought of biblical interpretation. Instead, theology ought to pervade "the operations by which [interpreters] endeavour to arrive at meaning, as it also pervades [their] efforts to articulate the meaning [they] discern."[288] This is a direct reaction against the task of critical approach, where theology is ignored in pursuit of their textual, historical, or analytical interest—basically, in the reconstruction of the text.

Clearly it is not just the gap, but there is a clear distinction in how biblical interpretation is endorsed and exercised in the church. Michael

---

[280] Ratzinger, "Biblical Interpretation in Crisis," 2.

[281] Carl E. Braaten and Robert W. Jenson, "Introduction: Gospel, Church, and Scripture" in *Reclaiming the Bible for the Church*, ed. Carl E. Braaten and Robert W. Jenson (Edinburgh: T&T Clark, 1995), ix–x.

[282] Braaten and Jenson, "Introduction," x.

[283] Braaten and Jenson, "Introduction," ix.

[284] John Sandys-Wunsch, *What have they Done to the Bible? A History of Modern Biblical Interpretation* (Minnesota: Liturgical, 2005).

[285] Sandys-Wunsch, *What have they Done to the Bible?*, ix.

[286] A. K. M. Adam et al., eds., *Reading Scripture with the Church: Toward a Hermeneutics for Theological Interpretation* (Grand Rapids: Baker, 2006).

[287] Adam, Fowl, Vanhoozer, and Watson, *Reading Scripture with the Church*, 7.

[288] Adam, Fowl, Vanhoozer, and Watson, *Reading Scripture with the Church*, 9.

Legaspi sees the unfortunate distinction between academy and church in terms of how people/community approach the Bible: as either "a *scriptural* Bible or an *academic* Bible."[289] A reality such as this invites the contemporary readers to come to terms with the issue of how one ought to read the Bible—either as the Word of God or as a source of history, or both. He argues that the story of the academic Bible began when "the scriptural Bible evoked by the liturgical scene . . . had already receded to the margins of modern Western cultural and public life."[290] Such an exegetical task (of the academic Bible) is no longer accessible to the church, or it is no longer beneficial for their faith journey. Biblical interpretation (since the eighteenth century) had the tendency of not just separating professional biblical studies and everyday biblical interpretation, but disconnecting the Bible itself from the theological enterprise.[291] Joel Green also suggests that contemporary interpreters ought to locate Scripture in relation to church to remold the works of critical biblical studies.[292] The emphasis is on biblical interpretation that concerns "the role of Scripture in the faith and formation of persons and ecclesial communities."[293] While modern biblical studies focused elsewhere (i.e., the original context), theological interpretation is "concerned with encountering the God who stands behind and is mediated in Scripture."[294] Though postmodern interpreters focus on hearing the voices (the implied author or narrator, voices of other texts, voice of the voiceless, or one's own voice), there is an urgent need to hear the divine voice. The concern, then, is to learn to hear "the voice of God" in the words of Scripture in "the present tense."[295] Green argues, "This *is* (and not simply *was* and/or might somehow *become*) the Word of the Lord."[296] Such a task, to endorse theological interpretation, would require a "show and tell" of how it ought to be endorsed.[297]

The above concerns of the church are an attempt to recapture the enchanted worldview, which was dismissed with the emergence of critical approach. It is an attempt to retrieve that which was missed out for centuries in biblical interpretation. This direction of churchly or theological interpretation requires certain philological constraints to bring about a constructive interpretation of Scripture in the church. It means that the

---

289 Legaspi, *The Death of Scripture and the Rise of Biblical Studies*, viii.

290 Legaspi, *The Death of Scripture and the Rise of Biblical Studies*, viii.

291 Joel B. Green, *Practicing Theological Interpretation: Engaging Biblical Texts for Faith and Formation* (Grand Rapids: Baker, 2011), 4.

292 Green, *Practicing Theological Interpretation*, 4.

293 Green, *Practicing Theological Interpretation*, 4.

294 Green, *Practicing Theological Interpretation*, 5.

295 Green, *Practicing Theological Interpretation*, 5.

296 *Emphasis* in original. Green, *Practicing Theological Interpretation*, 5.

297 Green, *Practicing Theological Interpretation*, 5.

Bible cannot be what anyone decides what it means. It does not mean taking the path of critical interpreters, where an attempt is made to reconstruct the biblical narrative. Instead, it would mean being sensitive to the final biblical narrative that considers the core, canonical, catholic, and contextual principles (see chapter 3). Such understanding entails the understanding that the Bible is divinely inspired as much as it is a historical text. This is to recognize that the Bible is both "a divine and human work."[298] This is to argue that "God has chosen to reveal himself in history, to Abraham, to Israel, and ultimately through Jesus."[299]

Conclusion

The dominance of biblical criticism has resulted in a conflict between a critical and (allegedly) objective reading and a theological reading of the Bible—a sense of preoccupation with two different constructs of the original context—and between modern interpreters and postmodern interpreters—a sense of preoccupation with the readers or appropriate methods of interpretation.

The dominance of critical interpretation in the modern period and pluralistic interpretation in the postmodern period has further pushed the church away to the periphery in biblical interpretation. The dominance of critical approach or the ignorance of the voice of the church means neglecting the contemporary and catholic context at the expense of privileging the original context or the location and identity of the readers—the world *behind* and *before* the text. Because of these conflicts and tensions, there is now a wide disconnect between what is discussed in the academy and what is practiced in the church. The above reality has encouraged some contemporary interpreters to take up the task of remolding biblical interpretation. Such a task to remold would require considering the ecclesial context (i.e., theology and the concerns of the church) in biblical interpretation. Considering such a task may mean valuing the core of Christian gospel, the canon, the concept of catholicity, and the context of the interpreter or contemporary concerns (see chapters 3 and 4).

---

[298] Gordon J. Wenham, "The Place of Biblical Criticism in Theological Study," *Themelios* 14.3: 85, 84–89.

[299] Christopher M. Hays, "Towards a Faithful Criticism" in *Evangelical Faith and The Challenge of Historical Criticism*, ed. Christopher M. Hays and Christopher B. Ansberry (Grand Rapids: Baker, 2013), 6.

2

TRIBAL THEOLOGY AND TRIBAL BIBLICAL INTERPRETATION IN NORTH EAST INDIA: THE TENSION BETWEEN DOMINANT VOICE AND VOICES FROM THE MARGIN AND THE PRIVILEGING OF THE TRIBAL CONTEXT

Introduction

While modern biblical interpretation in the West privileges the original context, it will be observed that tribal theology (and tribal biblical interpretation) in late-twentieth-century NEI privileges tribal culture/heritage and experience. Tribal theology emerged as a reaction to the dominant voice (i.e., the proponents of Indian Christian theology and Western mission and its legacy).[1] Tribal theologians/scholars are of the view that tribal culture/heritage and the concerns of the poor, downtrodden, and oppressed are ignored by the adherents of Indian Christian theology; they are also of the view that tribal churches in NEI are living in the legacy of the twentieth-century Western missionaries. In response, they reacted against the proponents of Indian Christian theology, which they believe ignored their issues and concerns, and to the tribal church in NEI, which they are convinced is still captivated by the Western missionaries. Whether it is Indian Christian theology or Western mission, they are unable to relate with the tribal culture/context. To make theology relevant, they are engaging with tribal culture/heritage and sociopolitical situations, primarily considering the experience of the tribals in contemporary India. Considering this, their theological task can also be a recovery of the enchanted worldview of tribal culture/heritage before the arrival of Western missionaries.

[1] In this case, the term *dominant* is used in reference to dominant interpreters over other cultures, worldviews, or schools of thought.

With the emergence and development of tribal theology in the late twentieth century, tribal biblical interpretation also began to take shape, especially in the academy. Their concern was to develop a reading of the Bible from the tribal perspective where their issues and concerns are considered.[2] While recognizing the significance of these developments, this chapter argues that tribal theology and tribal biblical interpretation are moving toward a diverse interpretative interest with no governing interest or value—which is detached from the concerns of the church or church setting. The multiple tribal contexts or readers' contexts determine the legitimacy of the tribal theological discussion or that of the meaning of the text.

Tribal Theology in North East India

This section historically traces the development of tribal theology in the late twentieth century in NEI. As indicated, the focus is to show that tribal theology emerged as a reaction to the dominant voice (i.e., against Indian Christian theology and Western mission and its legacy). An attempt is made showing that tribal theology is moving toward a diverse interpretative interest with no governing interest or value—and away from the concerns of the church or the church as the location to do theology.

Tribal is an indigenous ethnic minority, constituted as scheduled caste/scheduled tribe in India.[3] As per the 2011 Indian census, they cover 25.2 percent of India's population—201,378,372, or 16.6 percent scheduled caste; and 104,545,716, or 8.6 percent scheduled tribe.[4] They have always been part of Indian history, with its distinct social identity (i.e., with their own "customs and regulations"); yet, they have been living in isolation (i.e., living in the hills) from the dominant caste/class (i.e., living

[2] Before the emergence of *tribal theology* in NEI, there was no vibrant community of biblical interpretation. But Zhodi Angami suggests that there is a group of people in the church who practice literal interpretation of the Bible, and a group of individuals who are trained in Seminaries/Bible Colleges acquainted with historical criticism and literary methods. However, it is my contention that there is no distinctive presence of a vibrant community of Bible interpreters in the form of writing exegetical papers or Bible commentaries. Apart from active engagement in Bible translation, there is hardly any community of biblical interpretation in the NE region. One can suggest that apart from a *Mizo Study Bible*, there is scarcely any project of such nature. Zhodi Angami, *Empire and God: A Tribal Reading of the Birth of Jesus in Matthew's Gospel* (London: Bloomsbury, 2017), 1.

[3] K. Thanzauva, *Theology of Community: Tribal Theology in the Making* (Aizawl: MTC, 1997), 1–6.

[4] See https://www.census2011.co.in/ (October 29, 2019).

in the valleys).[5] References to their existence are evident as far back as the Ramayana, Mahabharata, Vedic literature, and Puranas.[6] Integral to the Indian civilization, they are able to maintain a distinct social/cultural identity (i.e., distinct from the dominant caste/class). This distinctiveness is extended to their religious and customary practices with its basic features.[7] However, despite their distinctive identity, they are mistreated or referred to with derogatory terms by the dominant caste/class.[8] Their history is tainted with suffering, oppression, exploitation, and discrimination in the hands of the dominant caste/class in India. This history of violation was not only in the past; it continues to this day.[9] They suffer from all sorts of injustice, which are evident in the form of social-economic exploitation, violation of human rights, alienation from their land, suppression of ethnic identity, and derogation of their culture and tradition.[10] Even within the Indian Christian community, they are a neglected group of people; their religious and cultural practices are treated as inferior to the dominant caste/class. Their history, religious beliefs, issues, and concerns are seen as less significant, even in the Indian Christian theological discussion (i.e., it was not included in the discussion).[11] Considering this reality, tribal scholars felt the need to provide a theological response to the Indian tribal reality-issues. Over the years, there have been several theological responses addressing tribal concerns in India—which is widely governed by the term *tribal theology*. The following section is an attempt to provide a historical sketch of tribal theology with special reference to NEI.

Early Tribal Discussions

Tribal theology has been in the making for (about) forty years. Since its inception, there have been several publications of monographs and

---

5 L. P. Vidyarthi and B. K. Rai, *The Tribal Culture in India* (Delhi: Concept Publishing Company, 1977), 25.

6 Vidyarthi and Rai, *The Tribal Culture in India*, 25–26.

7 Jonathan H. Thumra, "The Primal Religious Tradition" in *Religious Traditions of India*, ed. P. S. Daniel, David C. Scott, and G. R. Singh (Delhi: ISPCK, 1988), 45–74.

8 Nirmal Minz, *Rise Up, My People, and Claim the Promise: The Gospel Among the Tribes of India* (Delhi: ISPCK, 1997), 7–8.

9 See Longchar, *An Emerging Asian Theology*, 10–13; Nirmal Minz, "Tribal Issues in India Today" *Religion and Society* 50.3 (2005): 3–10.

10 R. J. Kr. Kootoom, "Tribal Voice Is Your Voice," *Tribal Voice of the Persecuted Tribals* 15 (1995): 1.

11 Nirmal Minz, "A Theological Interpretation of the Tribal Reality in India" in *Readings in Indian Christian Theology*, ed. R. S. Sugirtharajah and Cecil Hargreaves, vol. 1 (London: SPCK, 1993), 46–58.

articles on the subject. In the recent past, some efforts have been made to review or trace tribal theology in NEI. The tendency of these efforts is to locate the discussion of tribal theology in the works of the trio—Renthy Keitzar, K. Thanzauva, and A. Wati Longchar. While their contribution is foundational in the making of tribal theology, such tendency limits the discussion of tribal theology (i.e., it takes away the historical significance). To understand this reality, there is a need to trace its historical development.

Although tribal studies in India began as early as the eighteenth century, Christian response to "tribal concerns" in India began in the 1960s.[12] It emerged with the notion that tribal reality requires a proper Christian response. Corporate effort is seen in 1961 (Rajpur) and 1962 (Shillong) consultations, where individuals, who belonged to the tribal community and those who have worked with the tribals, addressed the social concerns confronting the tribals in India.[13] Their aim was,

> (1) *to understand the changes that are coming into being in the structures and values of tribal community life in India today,* (2) *to evaluate the policies and programmes of the Indian State and the Indian Church in relation to these changes in the light of the Christian understanding of community,* (3) *to help develop a proper approach to the political, economic and cultural requirements of tribal life in present-day India.*[14]

These consultations recognized that the tribal communities are living in "a context of change" in the areas of family, language, moral ideals/values, politics, and religion.[15] It recognized that these changes demand both a change in thinking and a need for Christian response. Moreover, it recognized that the church should relate with social change, contribute to the development programs of the government, and integrate the tribals to the Indian nation/state.[16] The emphasis for indigenous Christian thinking became significant for the development of tribal theology: they

---

[12] See n.a. "Consultation Findings: A Christian Approach to Tribal Communities in India Today," *Religion and Society* 8.3 (1961): 60–83; n.a. "Consultation Findings: The Mission of the Church and The Development of the Tribal Communities," *Religion and Society* 9.4 (1962): 80–85.

[13] John Thomas, *Evangelising the Nation: Religion and the Formation of Naga Political Identity* (New Delhi: Routledge, 2016), 188.

[14] *Emphasis* in original. n.a. "Consultation Findings: A Christian Approach to Tribal Communities in India Today," 60; n.a. "Consultation Findings: The Mission of the Church and The Development of the Tribal Communities," 80.

[15] n.a. "Consultation Findings: A Christian Approach to Tribal Communities in India Today," 60.

[16] n.a. "Consultation Findings: A Christian Approach to Tribal Communities in India Today," 60–82.

emphasized "a new form of Church life and order."[17] This helped Indian tribals to conscientize both the needs of the tribal community and the need to indigenize tribal Christian thinking. These consultations primarily came out of concerns/impacts of social change, which triggered the question of tribal identity. They were driven by the *felt* need to integrate tribal identity with the national identity (i.e., dominant identity) by those who were working with/for the tribals and by some educated tribals. But such theological engagement was carried forward, uncritical of the government programs and without the anticipation of possible negative impact of attempting to assimilate tribal identity with the dominant identity. In doing so, they failed to recognize the distinctiveness of tribal identity, which was already highly developed in terms of "the principle of sustainability."[18]

Out of these consultations, a study group was formed to "give expression to some sort of a common mind on the issues facing the tribals in India," resulting in the publication of *Tribal Awakening* in 1965.[19] The book carried forward in further detail the concerns that were raised in the previous consultations (i.e., 1961 and 1962 consultation). It brought forth *the role of Christians in tribal awakening.* From "a national and human point of view," it attempted to "critically assess" the role of Christianity on issues faced by tribals with the advancement of technology and developments.[20] Though it did not explicitly deal with "tribal theology," it gave a framework for an indigenous tribal Christian thinking.[21] This became more and more evident with an increasing search for "self-identity" amongst the tribals as "one of the most significant forces of social transformation in the country."[22] As the contributors hoped for, the book ignited several researches related to the tribals in India.[23] As the book operated with the parameter of assimilating minority with the dominant identity, the future tribal theological discussion would move away from it i.e., from a search for common tribal identity to multiple tribal/subtribal identities. This would become more evident with the gradual development of *tribal theology* in NEI.

---

17 See n.a. "Consultation Findings: A Christian Approach to Tribal Communities in India Today," 65–68; n.a. "Consultation Findings: The Mission of the Church and The Development of the Tribal Communities," 84.

18 Padel, "In the Name of Sustainable Development," 159.

19 M.M. Thomas and Richard W. Taylor, "Preface" in *Tribal Awakening: A Group Study*, ed. M. M. Thomas and Richard W. Taylor (Bangalore: CISRS, 1965), viii.

20 Thomas and Taylor, "Preface" in *Tribal Awakening*, viii.

21 Thomas, *Evangelising the Nation*, 194.

22 Saral K. Chatterji, "Foreword to Silver Jubilee Reprint," in *Tribal Awakening*, 5–6.

23 Chatterji, "Foreword to Silver Jubilee Reprint," in *Tribal Awakening*, 5–6.

Early Tribal Discussions in North East India

With the emergence of liberation theologies in Latin America and Majority World and the growing awareness of tribal issues, discussions on the need for contextual theologies in NEI began in the 1970s.[24] The early motivation for a relevant theology came from individuals like Gordon Jones and Jonathan H. Thumra.[25] Jones invited the tribals to "understand the Gospel in its essentials and to interpret it, to translate it, into terms that meet the needs of the people of [NE] India."[26] To develop a relevant theology for NEI, he suggests that the tribals look at Christ as the conqueror, the "Christus Victor".[27] This was said with the understanding that Jesus is the victor and liberator of all evils—be it social, political or both. The figure of Jesus is portrayed as the Victor of tribal issues present in the form of oppression, suppression, subjugation, etc. Similarly, Jonathan Thumra spoke of the need for contextual theologies that are relevant in NEI.[28] This is to hold that what is perceived as Christian theology in NEI is not relevant to the context of the people. About this time, Christians in NEI became suspicious of the dominant or prevalent theology, especially those that were associated with the Western mission or colonials.[29] With it, they also began to comment/critique the theology and practice of the tribal church (i.e., it is unable to relate with their beliefs and practices). Such talks marked a point of departure between tribal theology (academy) and tribal churches in NEI. Jones and Thumra did not exactly provide a framework for tribal theology, but they gave the early impetus of doing contextual-tribal theology in NEI.

A more distinct discussion of tribal theology came with the "Theological Consultation on Primal Vision and Hermeneutics in North-East India" at Shillong in 1981.[30] This consultation explored "whether there was a specific approach which Christians in North-East India with

24 Akala Imchen, "Development of Indigenous Theology in North East India: An Appraisal," in *Doing Indigenous Theology in Asia: Towards New Frontiers*, ed. Hrangthan Chhungi, M. M. Ekka, and Wati Longchar (Nagpur, India: NCCI/GTC/SCEPTRE, 2012), 1–24.

25 Renthy Keitzar, ed. *Good News for North East India: A Theological Reader* (Assam: CLC, 1995), i–ii.

26 Gordon Jones, "Good News for North-East India," in *Good News for North East India*, 1–7.

27 Jones, "Good News for North-East India," 5.

28 Jonathan H. Thumra, "Communicating Good News through Theological Education," *The Baptist Leader* 21.4 (1973): 5–7.

29 M. Horam, *Social and Cultural Life of Nagas* (Delhi: B.R. Publishing Corporation, 1977), 14.

30 H. S. Wilson, "Findings of the Theological Consultation on Primal Vision and Hermeneutics in North-East India," *IJT* 31.3–4 (1982): 323–32.

a tribal heritage could make to their task of interpreting Scripture and in understanding and communicating the Word of God in history."[31] It emphasized on integrating the heritage of "the people of Israel and the Christian community in the world," revaluing and reappropriating "Primal Vision,"[32] and the "socio-economic and cultural context" of the tribals to relevantly translate the gospel in NEI.[33] This integration took a twofold direction. First, J. L. Joy saw tribal hermeneutical as "transposing the biblical message from one situation to another—an attempt to understand how the Word of God, which was written and lived out some 2,000 or more years ago, can command obedience in today's contexts."[34] This meant investigating the relationship between tribal primal vision and hermeneutics, i.e., "the pre-Christian society, the Christian movement and its impact on society before independence and after."[35] It also came with the notion that there are gospel values in the tribal heritage.[36] Second, Renthy Keitzar suggests that a relevant translation of the Word of God requires an interpretation of the text according to "the life and thought patterns of tribal peoples so that the message of salvation can be more meaningful for them."[37] The purpose of hermeneutics was seen as communicating "the Gospel of Jesus Christ, the interpretation and ministration of the Word of God—in the world and to the world—in the context of contemporary culture."[38] It means there is a need to contextualize the Bible using indigenous terms and concepts.

The participants of the consultation were of the view that what is discussed in the church is not relevant to the tribal people. Keitzar would go on to argue that the Western missionaries failed to adapt the gospel to the NEI culture (e.g., Naga culture, Mizo culture, etc.).[39] He states that,

> The message of the Gospel has not gone deep into the cultural life of tribal Christianity; it is not rooted firmly in the tribal soil; it is still a *xerox-copy* of American Baptist Christianity, or a *duplicate* of western Presbyterianism or a *carbon-copy* of the charismatic movement of Pentecostalism, or even a *replica* of Roman Catholics of pre-Vatican II.[40]

31 Wilson, "Findings of the Theological Consultation . . . ," 323.
32 Wilson, "Findings of the Theological Consultation . . . ," 324.
33 Wilson, "Findings of the Theological Consultation . . . ," 325.
34 J. L. Roy, "Primal Vision and Hermeneutics in North-East India—A Protestant Tribal View," *IJT* 31.3–4 (1982): 314–22.
35 Roy, "Primal Vision and Hermeneutics in North-East India," 314.
36 Thanzauva, *Theology of Community*, 109.
37 Keitzar, "Tribal Perspective in Biblical Hermeneutics Today," 293–313.
38 Keitzar, "Tribal Perspective in Biblical Hermeneutics Today," 294.
39 Renthy Keitzar, *In Search of a Relevant Gospel Message* (Guwahati: CLC, 1995), 19.
40 Keitzar, "Tribal Perspective in Biblical Hermeneutics Today," 310.

He highlighted the reality that NEI Christians still live in the legacy of the Western missionaries. Considering this reality, Keitzar argues for "tribal Christianity that is founded on the historic faith of the Christian Church on the one hand, and an indigenous Christianity that is planted deep in the cultural life of the tribal people on the other."[41] Such emphasis may mean more than one thing. First, it is a critique of tribal churches, which have failed to address the sociopolitical concerns of the people.[42] Second, it means taking into account "the world-view of the tribal people, their concept of God, their forms of worship, their arts and culture, and their way of life must be taken into account in all seriousness in interpreting the Bible."[43] It is a recapturing of an enchanted worldview of the tribals before the arrival of Western mission. Third, the emphasis to recognize the tribal culture/heritage also comes with urgency to distinguish themselves from Hindu or Islamic culture. Their culture/heritage is perceived as distinct from other traditions (including other tribals in India). This distinction is a form of reaction to Indian Christian theology as its adherents ignored the tribal religion in the interfaith dialogue.[44] Traditional religion was not seen as significant to be included in the interfaith dialogue of the dominant religions.

The 1981 consultation reaffirmed the need to make the gospel relevant to the tribal people. While reinforcing the understanding that there are gospel values in the tribal heritage, it made an intentional attempt to do contextual theology in NEI. But it also uncritically carried forward some of the agendas of 1960 and 1961 theological consultation. First, it brought the idea of assimilating the NEI tribal identity with the dominant identity. This was a period where tribals in NEI were fighting for the recognition of their identity. By the 1980s, several NEI ethnic groups identified themselves with their own ethnic-national identities (i.e., Nagas in 1940s, Mizos in 1960s, Bodos and Khasis in1970s, etc.).[45] Hence, attempting to assimilate tribal identity with the dominant identity suggests insensitivity to the sociopolitical situation. Such insensitivity invited later tribal scholars to distance themselves from other tribals in India (i.e., NEI tribals are distinct from other tribals in India).[46] They were against the idea of

---

41 Keitzar, "Tribal Perspective in Biblical Hermeneutics Today," 310.

42 Larry E. David, "Can Tribal Theology Succeed? One "Outsider's" View," in *In Search of Identity and Tribal Theology: A Tribute to Dr. Renthy Keitzar*, ed. A. Wati Longchar (Jorhat: ETC, 2001), 115–34.

43 Keitzar, "Tribal Perspective in Biblical Hermeneutics Today," 310.

44 A. Wati Longchar, "Indian Christian Theology and Tribals in India," in *Tribal Theology*, 57–58.

45 Thomas, *Evangelising the Nation*, 194.

46 Thanzauva, *Theology of Community*, 5.

incorporating tribal identity of NEI with the national identity or "Indian Union".[47] This is also to assume that tribals in other parts of India are "more or less Hinduised" and assimilated with them.[48] But this was not the case with the tribes in NEI. Moreover, tribals in NEI are "still rooted in their own cultures, with their own laws of inheritance and marriage, and their own customs which were very different from those of their neighbours."[49]

Second, the Shillong consultation failed to address the derogatory connotations that come with the terms tribe/tribal. The constitution of India defines the term tribe or tribal using economic and religious categories: a homogenous community, which neither belongs to the Hindu or Muslim community, and those who are economically poor and socially marginalized.[50] But the ethnic groups in NEI prefer to be called by their respective ethnic names (e.g. Nanga, Mizo, Kuki, Khasi, etc.).[51] The terms tribe/tribal are now used with the acknowledgment of the derogatory connotations, but synonymous with "Indigenous people," "ethnic minorities," "aborigines," or "first people" in search of "a common identity."[52] It is used to bring about a common platform to address the concerns of the tribals.[53] However, apart from the search for liberative motifs of the tribals, tribal theological discussion would eventually move away from the search for a common identity to diversified theological or interpretative interests of particular tribes and sub-tribes. The concerns of the consultation were further carried forward by subsequent consultations organized by the Board of Theological Education of the Senate of Serampore and North India Students Conference (BTESSC).[54]

Emergence of Contextual Concerns

With the influence of the above consultations, the 1980s saw significant contextual attempts, addressing the urgency to make the gospel relevant to NEI. While some of these attempts were aimed toward tribal theology, others emerged to encourage the church to engage in sociopolitical affairs. For instance, the Mizo Theological Conference organized a forum on

---

47 Longchar, *An Emerging Asian Theology*, 16, 14–24.

48 Thanzauva, *Theology of Community*, 5.

49 Thanzauva, *Theology of Community*, 5.

50 Thanzauva, *Theology of Community*, 3; Longchar, *An Emerging Asian Theology*, 2–3.

51 Longchar, *An Emerging Asian Theology*, 2.

52 A. Wati Longchar, "Jesus Christ in Tribal Theology: A Critique, A Response," *JTS* 7.2 (2003), 248–89.

53 Thanzauva, *Theology of Community*, 1–9.

54 Thomas, *Evangelising the Nation*, 187.

March 3, 1984, addressing the need for contextual theology in the Mizo context.[55] This forum explored how a relevant theology can be developed in the Mizo context, resulting in the publication of *Towards a Tribal Theology* in 1989.[56] It attempts to construct "a tribal Christian theology" that considers the homogeneity and affinities of various tribal traditions.[57] Their interest was to help envision "a theological self-understanding" of the Mizos in particular and other tribals in general.[58]

Similarly, Nagas made an attempt at theological appropriation in 1984.[59] The Naga theological consultation was aimed toward the need to "develop relevant theology for the Nagas."[60] It urged "the churches to study seriously the social, economic, political, religious and cultural dimensions of the gospel."[61] While encouraging the church to engage in contextual concerns, the focus was on a relevant theological engagement. The consultation reaffirmed that "all Naga Baptist Churches must come together and work for a wider, effective and meaningful ministry of the Lord."[62] Similar to this consultation, there was a 1995 consultation that tried to "discern and understand the theological significance of issues facing the truth about the Nagas," considering the sociopolitical situation.[63] In their pursuit of self-determination from the Indian government, it affirmed that the Naga society-community is in political, social, and economic turmoil. It also affirmed the authority of the Bible as "a divine revelation" by God to humankind, and suggests the need for a holistic understanding of salvation.[64] These consultations invited the Naga churches to "formulate a theology, which can save and liberate the people from political oppression, economic exploitation, and religious apostasy."[65] Such discussion was initiated by the church and its leaders to help the church move toward a relevant theological engagement. Till this point there was *no clear*

---

55 Rosiamliana Tochhawng, "Tribal Theology: Which Way Forward?" in *Search for a New Society: Tribal Theology for North East India*, ed. Yangkahao Vashum, Peter Haokip, and Melvil Pareira (Guwahati: NESRC, 2012), 41–61.

56 K. Thanzauva, ed. *Towards a Tribal Theology: The Mizo Perspective* (Aizawl: MTC, 1989).

57 K. Thanzauva, "Introduction" in *Towards a Tribal Theology*, 3–8.

58 Thanzauva, "Introduction" in *Towards a Tribal Theology*, 3.

59 V. K. Nuh, "Preface" in *In Search of Praxis Theology for the Nagas*, ed. V. K. Nuh (New Delhi: Regency, 2003), v–vi.

60 Nuh, "Preface" in *In Search of Praxis Theology for the Nagas*, vi.

61 Nuh, "Preface" in *In Search of Praxis Theology for the Nagas*, vi.

62 n.a. "Appendix I: Resolution of the First all Naga Theological Seminar," 165.

63 n.a. "Appendix II: In Search of a Theological Statement" in *In Search of Praxis Theology for the Nagas*, 168–77.

64 n.a. "Appendix II: In Search of a Theological Statement," 170–75.

65 See Nuh, *In Search of Praxis Theology for the Nagas*, v–vi.

dichotomy between the church and the academy in theological engagement. It only became apparent after the distinctive development of *tribal theology* in the 1990s.

Distinctive Developments of Tribal Theology

What was discussed in the 1980s was extensively carried forward in the 1990s. This decade saw several creative efforts of tribal theology. As indicated, this period saw a clear demarcation between what is discussed in the academy and practiced in the church (or between liberals and conservatives). Specific to the Naga context, John Thomas suggests that this theological distinction is evident between those who studied in the United States and those who studied in India.[66] He states,

> On one hand, there were those who graduated out of Bible colleges, which were generally established and sponsored by the myriad independent and charismatic evangelical groups and churches especially from the United States . . . In contrast, there were those who graduated out of theological colleges, especially in India, which were far more liberal, inter-denominational, accommodative of divergent trends within Christianity, and therein open to interaction with other 'secular' disciplines and ideas.[67]

In addition, the continuing influence of Western mission should not be ignored. Most, if not all, of the nineteenth-century missionaries in the NE region were conservatives or evangelicals.[68] It is only from the mid-twentieth century that the NEI churches began to see the influence of liberal scholars. While the scattered theological position of the conservatives is apparent in NEI churches, an organized pursuit of contextual interests is evident in the academy, particularly within the Senate of Serampore. For example, the *Good News for North East India* addressed the need to make the gospel relevant to the lives of people.[69] It argued for a new understanding of Christian theology that can bring the tribals as "one people of God, accepting one another as fellow tribals and affirming one Lord, one faith, one baptism, one God and one Spirit, and as joint heirs with Christ (cf. Ephesians 4:4ff; and Romans 8:17)."[70] This initiative took the form of engaging with the tribal culture/heritage to develop "a creative Christian theology that is meaningful for our people as well as contextual to our contemporary realities."[71] This is *an attempt to recapture*

---

66 Thomas, *Evangelising the Nation*, 185–86.

67 Thomas, *Evangelising the Nation*, 185–86.

68 Boyd, *An Introduction to Indian Christian Theology*, 88.

69 Keitzar, "Introduction" in *Good News for North East India*, i–v.

70 Keitzar, "Introduction" in *Good News for North East India*, i–ii.

71 Keitzar, "A Study of the North-East India Tribal Christian Theology," in *Good News for North East India*, 32.

the enchanted worldview. There were also those who argued for theological reorientation to address the sociopolitical concerns of the tribals in NEI.[72] It argued for Christian theology to be relevant to the tribal context and address the issues and challenges faced by the tribals in NEI.

The developing stage of tribal theology came with cautionary remarks to avoid romanticizing "the tribal worldview."[73] It cautions tribal theologians from the nature of the gospel shaped and influenced by tribal culture/heritage. Some also reminded them of the need to be "a globally-informed contextual theology, a theology that emerges from a hermeneutic which takes the issues of identity, otherness, and equality seriously."[74] Such remark is against an exclusively theological direction—toward *only* NEI tribal theology.

By the mid-1990s, the tribal theological discussion moved toward a distinctive thinking with the institution of the "Tribal Study Centre" at Eastern Theological College in 1995.[75] This center would become the heart of tribal theological discussion in NEI (and in India). The first book from the center, *An Exploration of Tribal Theology*, explored possible methodologies to do tribal theology.[76] It aimed to provide "a methodological perspective in the search for a relevant theology in tribal context, especially for the Christians in North East India."[77] With the institution of the center, the subject of "tribal theology" became part of the curriculum of the Bachelor of Divinity from 1996–1997; it was then recognized by the Senate of Serampore as "a course of study for theological students" in India.[78] Along with this development, further advancement on tribal theology came with the beginning of a biannual journal on tribal theology, *Journal of Tribal Studies*.[79] This journal gave "a venture of faith with a mission to contribute [their] tribal sources to scholarship hitherto not known to the outside world."[80] The aim was to theologically ponder the "tribal experience of struggle," "rediscover traditional values," and understand

---

72 Thanzauva, *Theology of Community*, 50–51.

73 Roger Gaikwad, "Doing Theology with Tribal Resources: Cautionary Remarks" in *Doing Theology with Tribal Resources*, 127–42.

74 Lalsangkima Pachuau, "In Search of a Context for A Contextual Theology: The Socio-Political Realities of Tribal Christians in Northeast India," *JTS* vol. 1.1 (1997): 29, 13–29.

75 Angami, *Empire and God*, 67.

76 Longchar, "Preface" in *An Exploration of Tribal Theology* (Jorhat: The Tribal Study Centre, 1997), i.

77 Longchar, "Preface" in *An Exploration of Tribal Theology*, i.

78 Angami, *Empire and God*, 67.

79 Renthy Keitzar, "Introducing Journal of Tribal Studies," *JTS* vol. 1.1 (1997): i–iv.

80 Keitzar, "Introducing Journal of Tribal Studies," i.

tribal heritage.[81] With these developments, a new way of doing theology in NEI is proposed and constructed responding to the dominant-conventional theology.

With the dawn of the twenty-first century, tribal theological discussions have identifiable features and approaches.[82] Seminal to the discussion of tribal theology is the publication of *Tribal Theology: A Reader.*[83] This book is a "sourcebook" for doing tribal theology; it attempts to "frame out a better shape towards doing tribal theology."[84] It provides both the definition and methodology of tribal theology; it also discusses the socioeconomic and political concerns of the tribals. By this time distinctive approaches to tribal theology were identifiable in the works of Keitzar, Thanzauva, and Longchar. Shimreingam Shimray saw the conceptualization, method, and critique of tribal culture as "the stepping stone" to formulate a more concrete tribal theology.[85] With their contribution, the tribal theological discussion moved to more or less three approaches of tribal theology.[86] The *first* approach attempts to contextualize the Christian faith with the tribal heritage/culture prevalent in the works of Keitzar. His theological method can be located in the Bible and context. He saw his theological task in a twofold manner: "exegetical and contextualization, an attempt to interpret the Bible in the context of socio-cultural change."[87] In the discussion of tribal theology, he saw the need to be relevant to the tribal context. It means arguing for "a new theology along the line of sound biblical teaching" and "a message that can penetrate into the core of tribal mentality."[88] It means engaging with tribal heritages of the past and present to make the Christian gospel relevant to the life and thought patterns of tribals and contemporary context.[89] He argues that "The Word of God must be interpreted in its relevance to the life and thought patterns of tribal peoples so that: thought patterns of tribal peoples so that the message of salvation can be more meaningful

81 Longchar, "Jesus Christ in Tribal Theology," 251–252.

82 K. P. Aleaz, "A Tribal Theology from a Tribal World-View," *IJT* 44.1–2 (2002): 20–30.

83 Shimreingam Shimray, ed., *Tribal Theology: A Reader* (Jorhat: TSC, 2003).

84 Shimray, "Preface" in *Tribal Theology*, i.

85 Shimray, "Preface" in *Tribal Theology*, i.

86 See Aleaz, "A Tribal Theology from a Tribal World-View," 20–30.

87 Keitzar, "Theology Today," in *In Search of Praxis Theology for the Nagas*, 21, 32.

88 Renthy Keitzar, "The Editorial Column: A Relevant Theology," *The Baptist Leader*, vol. 21 (1973).

89 See Keitzar, "Tribal Perspective in Biblical Hermeneutics Today," 294; Keitzar, *In Search of a Relevant Gospel Message*, 1; Keitzar, "Tribal Theology in the Making," 212.

for them."[90] Specific to the Naga context, it means interpreting the Word of God in light of the contemporary realities of the Nagas.[91] The *second* approach holds that gospel values are present in the tribal heritage/culture seen in the works of Thanzauva. He argues for the tribal understanding of communitarianism as a foundation for doing tribal theology. He attempts to "rediscover the essence of tribal communitarian life for an alternative doctrine of humanity for [the] transformation of tribal society" with the hope of contributing to the Christian understanding of community.[92] He argues for the synthesis-praxis methodology: by synthesis, he means "a synthesis of gospel and culture" and "a synthesis of our inherited theology from the West and tribal culture in the context of North East India"; and by praxis, he means reinforcing the concept of "action-reflection" with "appropriate action for the transformation of society towards the realization of the Kingdom of God" with an emphasis on "liberation, social justice, and wholeness."[93] The synthesis model will help preserve tribal culture and enable them to confess Christ as they understand him; the praxis model will challenge the culture, social system, and social structure, which is not compatible with gospel values. The *third* approach argues that tribal theology should emerge from the tribal worldview evident in the works of Longchar. He is of the view that tribal theology should be rooted in the tribal worldview. He argues for "space" or "creation/land" as "the foundation for understanding the tribal people's culture, identity, personhood, religion, and ethos."[94] He argues for the liberation of the tribals by means of the perspective of space—"a sacred space" that gives identity and sustenance to the tribals.[95] This is to assume that tribal culture, identity, religion, or spirituality cannot be conceived without the understanding of space or creation/land. In other words, relooking at Christian theology from the perspective of space will make the gospel relevant to the tribal context.

Contemporary Concerns and Issues

What is laid out by Keitzar, Thazauva, and Longchar is carried forward with a plurality of interests. Such research interests have invited diversity and critique of the tribal theological discussion. The twenty-first

---

90 Keitzar, "Tribal Perspective in Biblical Hermeneutics Today," 294.

91 Keitzar, "Theology Today," in *In Search of Praxis Theology for the Nagas*, 32.

92 Thanzauva, *Theology of Community*, 109.

93 See Thanzauva, "Issues in Tribal Theology" in *Tribal Theology*, 19; Thanzauva, *Theology of Community*, 71–114.

94 See Longchar, "The Need for Doing Tribal Theology," 8; Longchar, "Dancing with the Land: Significance of Land for Doing Tribal Theology," 16–28.

95 Longchar, *An Emerging Asian Theology*, 25.

century saw multiple directions in the discourse of tribal theology. In addition to publications from the Tribal Study Centre, several publications, such as BTESSC, Senate Centre for Extension and Pastoral Theological Research, and Aizawl Theological College contributed, reinforced, and reaffirmed the discussions of tribal theology. Such increasing interests have an impact on tribal theology, both at the local and global level. Along with it, some issues began to surface concerning multiplicity of interests, source, methodology—and the relationship between church and academy.

In the contemporary context, there is a shift from the early discussions of a search for common tribal theology to diverse tribal theologies (e.g., Ao, Khasi, Mizo, etc.) leading to a legitimation crisis of theologizing/interpretation with no governing interests or shared values. Most, if not all, current research interest is to develop a particular ethnic theology (e.g., Mizo Christology), instead of a common tribal theology. Such diversity of research interests is resulting in a multiplicity of interests with no "governing interest"[96] or "shared values" [97] and shared traditions[98]—with concerns of a legitimation crisis. This reality has confronted them with the question of whose tribal interpretation/theologizing counts, and which one does not—this is keeping in mind the (about) four hundred tribes and subtribes.[99]

Their effort is using tribal "traditions, ethos and experience" as "the prime source and the starting point" to develop tribal theology.[100] Tribal scholars recognize God's revelation in the tribal heritage. They also recognize the continuity and influence of tribal heritage/culture in their Christian faith. In addition, such research is seen as the way forward to create/provide new frontiers for the discussion of tribal theology. While labelling Christian orthodoxy as Western theology, some aspects of tribal theology confront the belief system that came through the Western missionaries. Such tasks appear to place tribal heritage *before* Christian heritage (inclusive of the Bible and Christian tradition) as a key source of theologizing.

---

96 Vanhoozer, "Introduction" in *Dictionary for Theological Interpretation of the Bible*, 19–25.

97 R. S. Sugirtharajah, "Introduction: Still at the Margins" in *Voices from the Margin: Interpreting the Bible in the Third World*, ed. R. S. Sugirtharajah, Revised and Expanded Third Edition (Maryknoll, NY: Orbis, 2006), 1–10.

98 Peter Haokip, "Tribal Theology: Sources, Methodology and Hermeneutics," in *Search for a New Society*, 31.

99 Zhodi Angami, "Looking at Jesus from a Tribal Optic" in *Bible Readings from the Northeast India Context*, ed. Takatemjen (Mokokchung: CTC, 2014), 17–42.

100 n.a. "Communique of the International Theological Symposium," 226.

The direction of contemporary tribal research is a way of adapting (if not a corrective) to relevant theologizing. In its earlier attempt, tribal theology came out as a reaction to the dominant voice and tribal situations—bringing a distinctive tribal theology. They now must deal with the question of whose tribal theologizing-interpretation counts, and which one does not. They must deal with the question of whether the dominant tribe should dictate the smaller tribe or not; they must deal with domination or assimilation of the smaller tribes with the larger tribes. If they do, tribal theological discussion is likely to go through the same cycle of the voice of the margins reacting against the dominant. If that were the case, their search for the recognition of tribal identity, primal religion, or justice would then be self-defeating. Hence, to avoid such repetitive reactions, contemporary tribal scholars are compelled to search for tribal values in every tribe and subtribe. However, such discourse would eventually lead to a legitimation crisis of tribal theology. Their only commonality is the location of tribal land and the liberative motif of tribal theological discourse.

Also, some concerns are raised regarding the division between academy and church and the credibility/viability of tribal methodology (or methodologies).[101] These concerns come out of the question of effectiveness of tribal theology in the ecclesial context and the question of the viability of tribal methodology in the academic context. It takes the readers to the lacuna between what is discussed in the academy and what is practiced in the church in NEI: tribal scholars argue that tribal churches are living in the legacy of Western mission, and tribal churches argue that tribal theology is a syncretism of tribal tradition and Christianity.

Tribal theologians argue that the church needs to update their theology to stay relevant, while the church holds that tribal theology is not viable for church ministry.[102] Tribal theology is mostly discussed in the academy within a particular school of thought (i.e., the Senate of Serampore). However, those who come from other theological persuasions, such as fundamentalists, conservatives, or evangelicals, see tribal theology as a "compromise and syncretism" or even "unbiblical."[103] The church would avoid or ignore engaging with tribal theology; if they do, the tendency is to be dismissive of tribal theology.[104] In light of this reality, this lacuna

101 See Lalnghakthuami, "Theologizing Tribal Heritage," *MTJ* vol. 1.3 (2010): 83–94.

102 Tikhir, "Tribal Theology Now and Then," 9–11.

103 Renthy Keitzar, "Theology Today," in *In Search of Praxis Theology for the Nagas*, 21.

104 Visakuolie Vakha, "Jesus Christ in Tribal Theology: A Critique" in *Perspectives: Current Issues in Theological Thinking*, ed. Akheto Sumi (Mokokchung: Jongshinokdang Trust, 2002), 64–81.

is being recognized by the contemporary tribal scholars.[105] They seem to acknowledge that tribal theology is unable to connect with the lives and experience of the tribal church i.e., "the spiritual needs of the church and community."[106] This observed disconnect between the academy and the church has invited contemporary tribal scholars to seriously reconsider and revisit the sources and methodology of tribal theology.

In the recent past, some of them have raised questions about the continuing validity of the methodology of the earlier tribal theologians. B. J. Syiemlieh questions the viability of Thanzauva's "synthesis/praxis" method with the notion that a genuine tribal theological method ought to be original and creative.[107] He seems to imply that borrowed methods (i.e., borrowed from Stephen B. Bevans)[108] cannot be genuinely tribal. Similarly. Yangkahao Vashum argues that synthesis/praxis does not consider the post-colonial context of the NE region.[109] If tribal theological methods should be viable, it should consider the liberating struggle of the people, consider the memoirs and history of the people, and move beyond the simplistic post-colonial binaries between same/other, spirit/matter, and civilized/primitive. However, Rosiamliana Tochhawng argues for the necessity of the synthetic-praxis method and warns the proponents of tribal theology of being eclectic (i.e., selective of the gospel/culture) and "romanticizing" the tribal worldview.[110] A suggestion is made to incorporate the synthesis-praxis method (i.e., communitarianism) and a space-creation method (i.e., land/space cantered).

While the above discussion highlights some concerns of tribal methodology, it is still in the academy. *The church or ecclesial context is absent from the conversation.* Considering this reality, this project suggests that the lacuna between the church and academy can be addressed by way of speaking from the *gap* (i.e., between the church and the academy); by *ushering* the Church to join the conversation with the tribal theologians/scholars and by *acknowledging* that the academicians need to converse with the church. It can take the shape of addressing the neglected areas

---

[105] See Yangkahao Vashum, "Tribal/Indigenous Theology and Its Methodology: A Review and Proposal," *JTS* vol. 13.1 (2008): 35.

[106] Lalnghakthuami, "Theologizing Tribal Heritage," 83.

[107] Brightstar Jones Syiemlieh, "The Future of Tribal Christian Theology in Northeast India: Possible Directions" in *Tribal Theology on the Move*, ed. Shimreingam Shimray and Limatula Longkumer (Jorhat: Tribal/WSC, 2006), 41.

[108] See Stephen B. Bevans, *Model of Contextual Theology*, Revised and Expanded Edition (Maryknoll: Orbis Books, 2002).

[109] Yangkahao Vashum, "Revisiting Tribal Theology Methodology" in *Search for a New Society*, 1–20.

[110] Rosiamlian Tochhawng, "Methodological Reflection on Theologizing Tribal Heritage in North East India" in *Theologizing Tribal Heritage*, 19–28.

of tribal theology (i.e., Scripture and Christian tradition); it can also take the form of recognizing the need to consider the contextual concerns of the tribals in NEI. The next section of this chapter provides the scope for such discussion. It opens the door to the discussion—an entryway to the discussion of tribal theology in NEI with an ecclesial concern.

Biblical Interpretation in North East India

Influenced by tribal theology, tribal biblical interpretation began to emerge by the end of the twentieth century. The earliest suggestion to read the Bible with tribal concerns came through Keitzar in the 1980s.[111] Since then, there have been some exploratory attempts at reading the Bible using tribal lenses. In the recent past, tribal scholars have been taking the initiative to develop a distinctive tribal biblical interpretation (i.e., read the Bible from the tribal perspective). Most, if not all, of these interpretative efforts come out as reaction to historical criticism or as an alternative to modern biblical interpretation.

Keitzar's attempt of tribal Bible reading emerged as a response to the question of "whether there was a specific approach which Christians in North-East India with a tribal heritage could make to their task of interpreting Scripture and in understanding and communicating the Word of God in history."[112] This concerns gathering to the immediate cultural context and the experience of the tribals. While reacting against modern Bible reading, Keitzar argues for biblical interpretation that stays true to the life and thought patterns of the tribal people.[113] He calls for "a fresh approach to the theology of Bible translation in the tribal languages of North-East India."[114] Such an argument is made with the assumption that the earlier translation works are not rooted in the tribal culture/tradition. It is also said with the assumption that the canonical Bible holds authority within the tribal community. In his opinion, a fresh theology of translation may mean considering two concerns: first, it means considering the literary convention and the style and thought pattern of the local language where the Bible will be translated, and second, it means seeing Bible translation as the source of relevant theological terminology communicating the biblical text meaningfully.[115] He saw the Bible as "the central authority" with tribal heritage as a key to understanding what the Scripture says.[116]

---

[111] Keitzar, "Tribal Perspective in Biblical Hermeneutics Today," 293–313.

[112] Wilson, "Findings of the Theological Consultation . . . ," 323.

[113] Keitzar, "Tribal Perspective in Biblical Hermeneutics Today," 308.

[114] Keitzar, "Tribal Perspective in Biblical Hermeneutics Today," 308.

[115] Keitzar, "Tribal Perspective in Biblical Hermeneutics Today," 308–9.

[116] Keitzar, "Tribal Perspective in Biblical Hermeneutics Today," 313.

Taking a step further from Keitzar, Thanzauva and Hnuni argued that Bible translation should be much more than making "a written book available in the tribal language."[117] They suggest that tribals transferred their understanding of supernatural power to the book of Bible. When the tribals embraced Christianity in NEI, the Bible was accepted as "a propositional truth about God and human life supernaturally communicated to human beings by the Holy Spirit."[118] In doing so, Bible translation from a foreign language to tribal language brought about a new tribal identity. It transformed the tribal society. However, it also alienated the tribals from their culture.[119] Seeing the Bible as some sort of a magical book had its negative impact. With this concern, they argue for a new hermeneutical approach that is socially dynamic and liberating.[120] It means recognizing the autonomy of the biblical text, instead of looking at it as a magical book or distancing from the original context. It means considering "the tribal, social, and cultural conditions" in the reading of the Bible.[121] This is reading the Bible in "the context of identity crisis" i.e., their "alienation from their land and culture, exploitation and economic dependency."[122] This is to assume the importance of the contemporary concerns of the tribals in biblical interpretation.

Specifically, tribal Bible reading can take the form of being attentive to "the story of the authors" of the Bible and sensitive to "the reader's context".[123] Such reading would result in a new meaning of the text. The interfacing of the narrative approach and reader's approach will not only maintain "the unity of the text," but also help discover a new meaning of the text.[124] Thanzauva and Hnuni call this approach "a multi-task hermeneutics" as it will help the readers to "understand themselves in the process of understanding the text that they may be inspired to respond to the issues that confront them."[125] Employing such a tribal hermeneutical approach means rereading the text that addresses tribal reality and providing a new light to it.

[117] K. Thanzauva and R. L. Hnuni, "Ethnicity, Identity and Hermeneutics: An Indian Tribal Perspective," in *Ethnicity and The Bible*, ed. Mark G. Brett (Boston: Brill, 2002), 343–58.

[118] Thanzauva and Hnuni, "Ethnicity, Identity and Hermeneutics," 346.

[119] Thanzauva and Hnuni, "Ethnicity, Identity and Hermeneutics," 347.

[120] Thanzauva and Hnuni, "Ethnicity, Identity and Hermeneutics," 348.

[121] Thanzauva and Hnuni, "Ethnicity, Identity and Hermeneutics," 348.

[122] Thanzauva and Hnuni, "Ethnicity, Identity and Hermeneutics," 351.

[123] Thanzauva and Hnuni, "Ethnicity, Identity and Hermeneutics," 351.

[124] Thanzauva and Hnuni, "Ethnicity, Identity and Hermeneutics," 352.

[125] Thanzauva and Hnuni, "Ethnicity, Identity and Hermeneutics," 352.

After the above individual works, a substantial corporate contribution came in the recent past. The *Tribal Theology and The Bible* was published with the following objectives:

> To deliberate on the various approaches to contextual reading of the Bible and search for appropriate approach to tribal-contextual reading of the Bible; to enable the participants to read and study the Bible from one's perspectives; and to enable the participants to critically examine the significance of the Bible for tribal Christian faith, ministry and life.[126]

Similarly, *Bible Readings from the Northeast Indian Context* came out with an attempt to develop contextual reading of the Bible in NEI.[127] These books are an intentional effort to bring contextually sensitive and relevant interpretation of the Bible. Though it is exploratory in nature, it shows a clear mark of interest (i.e., *toward a multiplicity of interests*). At this point, there is no clear structure or streams of thought that can be identified as a distinctive tribal biblical interpretation. However, the priority of tribal biblical interpretation is recognizable (i.e., prioritization of the sociopolitical contexts).

While developing tribal biblical interpretation, the contributors of *Tribal Theology and The Bible* are critical of historical criticism. Thanzauva argues for the liberation of the aliens as the hermeneutical key for the tribals in NEI.[128] It aims to explore two horizons: the tribal and the textual horizon. Similarly, after raising concerns of the relevance of historical criticism, Razouselie Laseto argues that biblical interpretation in NEI should consider the contemporary tribal situation and condition.[129] This is to suggest that contextual reading of the Bible has become imperative. B. J. Syielieh also questions the methodological priority of historical criticism in the interpretation of the NT.[130] He proposes "principles and methods of interpreting the NT in Northeast India by taking special note of the identity of the readers in the context."[131] He holds that there is a scope to interpret the NT in light of the NEI context through the eyes of the implied readers and with the use of social sciences. While recognizing the importance of the text, these scholars pay attention to the context of

---

[126] Vashum, "Preface" in *Tribal Theology and The Bible*, i–ii.

[127] Angami, "Forward (a)" in *Bible Readings from the Northeast India Context*, vii–x.

[128] Thanzauva, "Tribal/Indigenous Interpretation of the Bible," in *Tribal Theology and The Bible*, 13–25.

[129] Razouselie Lasetso, "Methods of Biblical Interpretation," in *Tribal Theology and The Bible*, 26–38.

[130] B. J. Syiemlieh, "Contextual Interpretation of the New Testament in Northeast India," in *Tribal Theology and The Bible*, 39–56.

[131] Syiemlieh, "Contextual Interpretation of the New Testament in Northeast India," 39.

the readers attempting to add the significance of identity and location in biblical interpretation.

Bible Readings from the Northeast India Context takes the shape of re-reading the Bible with the intent of making Bible reading relevant and meaningful to the tribals in NEI.[132] It is an attempt to reclaim the place of the Bible in theologizing and understanding tribal culture and tradition. K. Lallawmzuala identifies the challenges and implications of liberation theology, postcolonial, and postmodern theories, and its bearing on the OT hermeneutics in the context of tribals of NEI.[133] This attempt to develop tribal biblical interpretation is built on the assumption that each *context* needs an indigenous contextual reading of the Bible. It can be developed by associating it with a liberation approach of reading the Bible (i.e., it should result in the "liberation of the poor and oppressed").[134] It would also mean associating with the social location and cultural background of the tribals to locate the meaning of the text. Along with the reader's context, Lallawmzuala recognizes the importance of historical context of the text/author.[135] The goal of such interpretation, then, is to bring together the ancient and contemporary meaning. Similarly, Zhodi Angami suggests three underlying principles of tribal biblical interpretation.[136] The first is an attempt to decolonize the Bible (i.e., interpret the text from "the perspective of tribal worldviews, tribal cultures, and tribal experiences"). The second considers the marginal position/state of the tribals in NEI (i.e., read from a marginal perspective). The third invites the tribals to read the text with new eyes (i.e., read with the ordinary people).[137] This is to hold that the tribal interpretation of the Bible is unique and tribal perspective can appropriate the text for the tribals.

He further expanded the notion of reading the Bible from tribal perspective in his book, *Tribals, Empire and God.* It employs "contextual reader-response criticism to read Matthew's infancy narrative from the perspective of tribal communities of [NEI]."[138] He brings out a tribal interpretation of the Bible from a marginal perspective while integrating the method of historical criticism, postcolonial hermeneutics, and contextual reading. Angami aims to "provide an interpretation of the narrative that makes sense to the tribals by reading it with tribal concerns, sensitive

[132] Takatemjen, "Preface" in *Bible Readings from the Northeast India Context*, xiv–xv.

[133] K. Lallawmzuala, "Issues in Biblical Interpretation: Towards a Tribal Biblical Hermeneutics" in *Bible Readings from the Northeast India Context*, 1–16.

[134] Lallawmzuala, "Issues in Biblical Interpretation," 13.

[135] Lallawmzuala, "Issues in Biblical Interpretation," 15.

[136] Angami, "Looking at Jesus from Tribal Optic," 17–42.

[137] Angami, "Looking at Jesus from Tribal Optic," 23–29.

[138] Angami, *Tribals, Empire and God*, x.

to the spirituality, the culture and the social and political experiences of the tribal people."[139] He gives attention to two areas as interpretative clues: "the tribal political context of military occupation" and "the tribal experience of being at the margins—socially, politically and academically."[140] While offering an alternative to Matthew's infancy narrative for the tribal communities, the biblical narratives are depicted as "coherent and relevant" to the tribal people, and not necessarily foreign or alien.[141] It is hoped that such reading of the Bible will "challenge and transform tribal social and political circumstances."[142]

With these developments, some efforts are made to interpret/theologize from the perspective of tribal women. This has much to do with the formation of "the Department of Women Studies" in the Eastern Theological College in 1996—which helped recognize the role of women in the church, ministry or in doing theology.[143] The first and second consultation on tribal women was held on December 10–13, 2002; and April 22–25, 2004, respectively, culminating in the publication of *Weaving New Patterns of Ministry for Women in North East India*.[144] Along with other concerns, it argued for theology or biblical interpretation from the perspective of tribal women. Specific to biblical interpretation from the tribal women's perspective, Angami suggested the need to reread the biblical text from the tribal women's perspectives in NEI.[145] The Bible identified as a product of the patriarchal system and suggested for a reading of the Bible from a justice perspective, recognized the experience of tribal women, and implemented tribal feminism.[146]

The need to do theology from tribal women's perspective was further developed with the publication of *No More Sorrow in God's Garden of Justice*.[147] It invites tribal women to do theology from the perspective of justice and women. This is a search to do theology by tribal women in "a search and call for justice, solidarity and partnership [with men] in

[139] Angami, *Tribals, Empire and God*, xi.

[140] Angami, *Tribals, Empire and God*, xi.

[141] Angami, *Tribals, Empire and God*, 268.

[142] Angami, *Tribals, Empire and God*, 268.

[143] Narola Imchen, "Preface" in *Weaving New Patterns of Ministry for Women in North East India*, ed. Narola Imchen (Jorhat: WSD, 2004), viii–xi.

[144] Narola Imchen, ed. *Weaving New Patterns of Ministry for Women in North East India* (Jorhat: WSD, 2004).

[145] Angami, "Constructing Tribal Feminist Hermeneutics" in *Weaving New Patterns of Ministry for Women in North East India*, 7–16.

[146] Angami, "Constructing Tribal Feminist Hermeneutics," 9–14.

[147] Limatula Longkumer, ed. *No More Sorrow in God's Garden of Justice: Tribal Women Doing Theology* (Jorhat: WSD, 2007).

theological journey."[148] Such theologizing is "a product of deep cries, screams, tears and extreme sufferings in their daily lives. It is a cry from pain, starvation, rape, poverty; it says no to discrimination. Theology from 'sorrow' calls for a paradigm shift in doing theology. It calls for a new interpretation of the Bible."[149] Here, Limatula Longkumar argues that the Bible has been used to suppress women in the tribal society (and church).[150] As a reaction to the masculine tendency and the tendency to suppress women, she argues for a Bible reading that will help empower both women and men to "build communities of justice and peace for all."[151] This idea is further developed by emphasizing the role and influence the Bible has in the tribal community in "Tribal Feminist Reading of the Bible."[152] She argues for Bible reading from a holistic perspective (the whole humanity and creation perspective), using the language of inclusiveness, mutuality, and partnership, without hierarchy, creatively, and from a liberation perspective.[153] What it tries to achieve is to arrive at a just or inclusive interpretation of the Bible—where the voice of women is part of the interpretative process. With the recognition of the neglected and marginalized, it encourages women to develop their voice by responding to what is oppressing in the tribal community and church.

In summary, tribal biblical interpretation in NEI emerges from the discussion of tribal theology and with an awareness of the sociopolitical reality of the tribals. As indicated, it operates within the framework of tribal theology—and reacts to the dominant-masculine social/ecclesial structure. However, what can be differentiated between tribal theology and tribal biblical interpretation is its source. While tribal theology prioritizes the tribal culture and its tradition, tribal biblical interpretation recognizes both the context of the text (i.e., the ancient meaning) and the context of the tribals (i.e., tribal culture/heritage and experience). In the tribal theological discourse, the location of Scripture tends to be marginalized while prioritizing tribal culture and tradition;[154] in the tribal biblical interpretation, the location of Scripture is prioritized with attempts to reinterpret biblical texts from the tribal perspective. In their theological

148 Limatula Longkumer, "Editorial" in *No More Sorrow in God's Garden of Justice*, v–vi.

149 Longkumer, "Editorial" in *No More Sorrow in God's Garden of Justice*, vi.

150 Limatula Longkumer, "Contextual Reading of the Bible" in *No More Sorrow in God's Garden of Justice*, 129–45.

151 Longkumer, "Contextual Reading of the Bible," 129.

152 Limatula Longkumer, "Tribal Feminist Reading of the Bible" in *Tribal Theology and The Bible*, 139–51.

153 Longkumer, "Tribal Feminist Reading of the Bible," 149.

154 Eyingbeni Humtsoe, "Tribal Theology and the Bible: A Review," in *Tribal Theology and The Bible*, 59–72.

discussion, the context of the readers takes center stage in the theological/biblical interpretation.[155]

What is significant in these developments is the multiple directions or pursuits. Their theological key is location- and identity-driven (i.e., it takes a diverse or varied direction). However, the question of which interpretation counts or does not count is still a relevant question. While the current tribal biblical interpretation provides some consolidated strategy to address the neglected aspect of tribal theology (i.e., engaging with Scripture), it is not quite there yet. Though their intent is to provide a relevant interpretation of the Bible, the larger context of the tribal community is being neglected (i.e., the local-tribal ecclesial community). It only deals with the sociopolitical situation of the tribals in NEI. Apart from devotional reading of the Bible,[156] evangelical or ecclesial contribution to biblical interpretation is scarce. Contribution to tribal biblical interpretation that stays true to Christian orthodoxy and engages with the tribal church appears to be the need of the hour.

Conclusion

This chapter attempted to historically trace the emergence of tribal theology in late-twentieth-century NEI. Further attempts were made to show that tribal biblical interpretation emerged from the discussion of tribal theology. It was shown that both these developments are moving toward a multiplicity of theological/interpretative interests. The current state of tribal theology/biblical interpretation indicates that its discussion is limited within the indigenous/tribal community—and it primarily sits in the academy. It neglects the ecclesial context (i.e., the concerns of church). It neglects the church as a potential location of doing theology. Considering this reality, the current project hopes to contribute to the discussion of tribal theology/biblical interpretation by way of engaging with TIS. In doing so, it hopes to contribute to the discussion of both contemporary tribal theology/biblical interpretation and TIS.

---

155. Iralu warns that the tribal context should not be equated with the Bible as it can lead to "a syncretistic trap." Iralu, "Tribal Hermeneutics," 360.

156. See, for example, M. Sashi Jamir, "Inductive Bible Study: Contextual Appropriation in Northeast India," *Asbury Journal* 68.1 (2013): 42–55.

3

THEOLOGICAL INTERPRETATION OF SCRIPTURE: THE TENSION BETWEEN THEOLOGICAL DISCIPLINES OVER BIBLICAL INTERPRETATION AND THE PRIVILEGING OF THEOLOGY

Introduction

The rise and dominance of biblical criticism resulted in crises in biblical interpretation (see chapter 1). It resulted in a tension between biblical studies and theological studies, and between modern interpreters who focused on objectivity and history and postmodern interpreters who allowed for ideology and context. More significantly, it resulted in a divide between academy and church. This was a gradual result of how the text was seen (i.e., ontology of the text): "Is it merely human or human and divinely authored?"[1]

This tension in the contemporary biblical interpretation gravely contributed to the division between academy and church. In response, a quest to recover distinctly TIS emerged in the early twentieth century and developed in the late twentieth century.[2] The attempt to rectify *the marginalization of theology* is being done by addressing the division between theological disciples over biblical interpretation and the dichotomy between the academy and the church in biblical interpretation. Recovery of TIS is being made by engaging the discipline of biblical studies, systematic theology, and biblical theology. TIS that is being recovered in the contemporary context broadly concerns the interpretation of the Bible in the ecclesial context.

---

1 Kevin J. Vanhoozer, email message to author, February 26, 2020.

2 Daniel J. Treier, *Introducing Theological Interpretation of Scripture: Recovering an Ancient Christian Practice* (Grand Rapids: Baker, 2008), 11.

As TIS makes its strides, theology is being recovered in biblical interpretation. According to Joel B. Green, it is once again "moving into the limelight after hundreds of years of shadowy exile from academic biblical and theological studies."[3] As TIS attempts to retrieve theology, it interacts with theological disciplines that are traditionally associated with biblical interpretation (i.e., systematic/dogmatic theology, biblical studies, and biblical theology). However, to date, it has failed to engage with the discipline of contextual theology. This neglect is evident in how introductory works (i.e., companion, manifesto, introduction, or dictionary) to TIS are ignored to interact with the discipline of contextual theology.[4] Until this point, there is no monograph that has explored a possible relationship between TIS and contextual theology. This oversight of TIS will be the entryway of this project: *an entryway to the discussion between theological interpretation of Scripture and contextual theology* (i.e., tribal theology). This chapter partly sets the stage by drawing the chronological development of TIS in the late twentieth century and its approaches; and partly by providing Kevin J. Vanhoozer's answer to the tension between biblical studies and theology and between exegesis and ideology.

The Reemergence of Theological Interpretation of Scripture

This section captures the reemergence of TIS in the late twentieth century identifying the key advocates and concerns of TIS. While capturing the reemergence of TIS, we will be able to identify why the retrieval of *theology* was required and favorably initiated. The *Manifesto to Theological Interpretation* broadly defines TIS as an "*interpretation of the Bible for the church*," which is the kind of interpretation that has "never been fully lost in the church."[5] It recognizes that throughout Christian history, "it has been the norm for Christians to read their scripture theologically."[6]

---

3 Green, *Practicing Theological Interpretation*, 3.

4 See, for example, Stephen E. Fowl, *Theological Interpretation of Scripture*, Cascade Companions (Eugene: Cascade Books, 2009); Daniel J. Treier, *Introducing Theological Interpretation of Scripture: Recovering an Ancient Christian Practice* (Grand Rapids: Baker, 2008); Craig G. Bartholomew and Heath A. Thomas, eds., *A Manifesto for Theological Interpretation* (Grand Rapids: Baker Academic, 2016); ed. Kevin J. Vanhoozer *Dictionary for Theological Interpretation of the Bible* (Grand Rapids: Baker, 2005).

5 *Emphasis* in original. Craig G. Bartholomew and Heath A. Thomas, "Preface" in *A Manifesto for Theological Interpretation* (Grand Rapids: Baker Academic, 2016), ix, 1.

6 Stephen E. Fowl, "Introduction" in *The Theological Interpretation of Scripture: Classic and Contemporary Readings*, ed. Stephen Fowl (Cambridge: Blackwell, 1997), xiii.

As opposed to reading like any other book, history, or literature, the Bible is read "to guide, correct, and edify their faith, worship, and practice as part of their ongoing struggle to live faithfully before the triune God."[7] This practice of Bible reading comes with a long tradition of accepting it as authoritative to the church (i.e., the very means to hear God's voice). It is not a mere academic exercise, instead to read the Bible is to "encounter God."[8] This type of theological reading is present in many forms, both across Christian history and church. Regardless of some differences, they all showed a common interest to "reconnect biblical reading to the faith and practices of the catholic church and to establish, in a variety of ways, how faithful interpretation should engage with secular ways of reading the text."[9] In that sense, TIS is a response to the dominance of biblical criticism leading to the marginalization of theology in biblical interpretation.

Early attempts to do TIS emerged in the early twentieth century. Daniel Treier suggested that Karl Barth was the "forerunner" of the twentieth-century TIS movement;[10] this opinion is shared with other TIS scholars.[11] Barth is identified as "the opening salvo in the twentieth-century's renewed theological engagement with Scripture."[12] As indicated in chapter 1, the publication of *The Epistles to the Romans* in 1919 confronted the dominance of modernist thinking—more specifically, the dominance of biblical criticism.[13] Though Barth recognized the contribution of critical interpretation, he favored the doctrine of inspiration.[14] While it took some time to realize the value of Barth's work, he set course to what is now known as TIS. Barth reacted against what was seen as the proper methodological tools of reading the Bible: "A proper reading of the text was to read 'what' the author said but then to also look to see what was 'behind' the text."[15]

7 Fowl, "Introduction," xiii.

8 Treier, *Introducing Theological Interpretation of Scripture*, 13.

9 Bartholomew and Thomas, "A Manifesto for Theological Interpretation," 2.

10 See Treier, *Introducing Theological Interpretation of Scripture*, 11; Richard E. Burnett, *Karl Barth's Theological Exegesis: The Hermeneutical Principles of the Römerbrief Period* (Grand Rapids: Eerdmans, 2004).

11 See Bartholomew and Thomas, "A Manifesto for Theological Interpretation," 1; Angus Paddison, "The History and Reemergence of Theological Interpretation," 27.

12 Bartholomew and Thomas, "A Manifesto for Theological Interpretation," 1.

13 See Karl Barth, *The Epistle to the Romans*, Sixth edition, trans. Edwyn C. Hoskyns (Oxford: OUP, 1968). Cf. Amy Marga, "Karl Barth's Romans Commentary 1919: A Document to the Living God, One Hundred Years Later," *Word & World* 39.3 (2019): 236–45.

14 Barth, *The Epistle of Romans*, 1.

15 Marga, "Karl Barth's Romans Commentary 1919," 237.

Barth's contemporaries did not immediately pick up his arguments. This probably has to do with their inability to come to terms with the significance of his work.[16] Until the 1960s people were still trying to make sense of his work, as it did not follow any conventional approach to biblical criticism.[17] Decades later in 1975, Peter Stuhlmacher raised the issue of the relationship between theological understanding and the historical investigation of the Scripture.[18] This book "put the term front and center, and it considered many of the same issues now at hand."[19] It confronted the claims of biblical criticism that had come to dominate modern biblical interpretation and argued for listening to the claims of the texts. He argued for theological concerns of the text and the church as its reading location; his concerns were not to be carried forward blindfoldedly nor take "a reformational-spiritual or even biblicistic and uncritical exposition of scripture" nor from "a socio-critical political hermeneutics."[20] Instead, Stuhlmacher addressed the concerns of biblical interpretation from in-between the above positions (i.e., "a considered, self-critical adaptation of historical criticism to the scientific and theological needs and possibilities of the present, however viewed and judged").[21]

Along with the Protestant scholars, changes were happening amongst the Roman Catholic Church. There were cautions about Protestant biblical studies. So, open engagement with the critical approach came only after the mid-twentieth century. The Second Vatican Council was the turning point, engaging with critical approach. As Roman scholars engaged with biblical criticism, there were concerns about the sources of the ecclesial faith. It opened "Catholics to learning from, and cooperating with, biblical scholars outside the [Roman] Catholic Church."[22] Gradually, some concerns were raised about the interpretation of critical approach—with the notion that "the church's tradition of theological interpretation was being lost."[23] Tension between exegesis and systematic theology became apparent. This reality triggered the Catholic Church to examine the

16 Burnett, *Karl Barth's Theological Exegesis*, 16.

17 Marga, "Karl Barth's Romans Commentary 1919," 238–39.

18 Peter Stuhlmacher, *Historical Criticism and Theological Interpretation of Scripture: Toward a Hermeneutics of Consent*, trans. Roy A. Harrisville (Philadelphia: Fortress, 1977).

19 D. Christopher Spinks, "Catching up on a Conversation: Recent Voices on Theological Interpretation of Scripture," *ATR* 99.4 (2017): 769–86.

20 Stuhlmacher, *Historical Criticism and Theological Interpretation of Scripture*, 20.

21 Stuhlmacher, *Historical Criticism and Theological Interpretation of Scripture*, 20.

22 Peter S. Williamson, "Catholic Biblical Interpretation" in *Dictionary for Theological Interpretation of the Bible*, 103.

23 Williamson, "Catholic Biblical Interpretation," 104.

presuppositions of the critical approach.[24] Consequently, what can be seen as a contribution to the current TIS movement is Joseph Ratzinger's interest and concern in biblical interpretation.[25] While recognizing the situation of biblical interpretation as *in* crisis, Ratzinger questions whether the interpretation of critical approach can speak in the present; he also questions the validity of the conceptual approach to reading the Bible.[26] While he was critical (and skeptical) of the critical approach in his earlier discussion with no clear answer (yet, hopeful), in his later writings, he puts the church as the "primary setting" of biblical interpretation.[27] Its primary task is to hear the revealed Word of God (i.e., Jesus). Putting the Church in context "ensures that faith serves as the fundamental hermeneutic."[28] This is to recognize that "Everything begins by acknowledging Scripture for what it really is, the word of God in human words (1 Thess 2:13), but one can only acknowledge the Spirit who inspired Scripture if one reads it in the faith that the same Spirit bestows."[29]

On the Protestant front, the conversation of *theological* interpretation was distinctly shaped with the birth of the journal of *Ex Auditu* in the 1980s.[30] It privileged theological interpretation of Scripture, instead of prioritizing the hermeneutical theories.[31] According to Thomas W. Gillespie, the *theological interpretation* in question is that which comes "out of a patient, open, and faithful 'hearing' of the Word of God."[32] It is not so much about the hermeneutical rules or experience, but a careful examination of "how and where we have to live in accordance with [the Bible]."[33] Meaning then arrives in light of the text, and not the world behind the text. It will not be wrong to suggest that *Ex Auditu* became one

24 Richard John Neuhaus, ed., *Biblical Interpretation in Crisis: The Ratzinger Conference on Bible and Church* (Grand Rapids: Eerdmans, 1989).

25 Kevin J. Vanhoozer, "Expounding the Word of the Lord: Joseph Ratzinger on Revelation, Tradition, and Biblical Interpretation," in *The Theology of Benedict XVI: An Evangelical Appreciation of the Theology of Joseph Ratzinger*, ed. Tim Perry (Washington: Lexham, 2019).

26 Joseph Cardinal Ratzinger, "Biblical Interpretation in Crisis: On the Question of the Foundations and Approaches to Exegesis Today" in *Biblical Interpretation in Crisis*, 4–5.

27 Benedict XVI, *Verbum Domini: The Word of the Lord* (Boston: Pauline Books & Media, 2010), 46.

28 Vanhoozer, "Expounding the Word of the Lord," (forthcoming).

29 Vanhoozer, "Expounding the Word of the Lord," (forthcoming).

30 See *Ex Auditu: An International Journal for the Theological Interpretation of Scripture* (Eugene: Pickwick, 1985).

31 Thomas W. Gillespie, "Introduction" *Ex Auditu*, vol. 1 (1985): xv–xvi.

32 Gillespie, "Introduction," xvi.

33 Peter Stuhlmacher, "Ex Auditu and the Theological Interpretation of Holy Scripture," *Ex Auditu* 2 (1986): 1.

of the key platforms that enriched the discussion of TIS.[34] They cultivated an understanding of TIS as "the focal point" of scholarly interpretation and enforced TIS as the "priority in the use of the Bible by the church."[35]

Significant contributions also came from individual scholars shaping the reemergence of TIS in the 1990s. The foundational contribution came from the likes of Francis Watson, Stephen E. Fowl, and Kevin J. Vanhoozer. They established the baseline by suggesting that TIS can help address the tension in contemporary biblical interpretation (i.e., the tension over *which context* to privilege).

According to Watson, the rise of modernity resulted in the division of "three autonomous interpretative communities" (i.e., OT scholars, NT scholars, and systematic theologians), which are ideologically motivated and systematically distorted their subject matters.[36] One demarcation comes out of how biblical scholars treat their work as non-theological, and the other comes from how theologians tend to operate outside the sphere of biblical studies.[37] Biblical studies are criticized for their lack of theological awareness in their interpretation and theologians are criticized for the misuse of biblical texts while supporting their theological position. Though there is an overlapping of these fields, it is not seen as the primary focus. Watson observes that this "demarcation" appears to come out of professional necessity and division of labor for specialization.[38] However, that may not necessarily be the case. In biblical studies the presence of theological concerns is assumed but found to be either half-concealed or rarely identified. This results in an indirect relation with the practice of theology; theological concerns are seen in a second-hand relationship with the Bible distorting the process of biblical exegesis.[39] The other demarcation has to do with the division of the Bible as OT and NT and those who engage in it. These interpretative communities acknowledge each other's existence, but with mutual indifference. One tendency is to regard OT as the background upon which NT scholars can draw; the other tendency is the disinterest in the NT by OT scholars.[40] For instance, some OT scholars have gone to the extent of renaming the OT as

---

34 See, for example, Kevin J. Vanhoozer, "Body-Piercing, the Natural Sense, and the Task of Theological Interpretation: A Hermeneutical Homily on John 19:34," *Ex Auditu* 16 (200): 1–29.

35 Rolf P. Knierim, "On the Interpretation of the Old Testament by the Church," *Ex Auditu* 16 (2000): 55–76.

36 Watson, *Text and Truth*, 6–7.

37 Watson, *Text and Truth*, 2–3.

38 Watson, *Text and Truth*, 3.

39 Watson, *Text and Truth*, 3–4.

40 Watson, *Text and Truth*, 5.

the "Hebrew Bible," assuming its completeness and self-containability.[41] The result of this fragmentation of disciplines is this: "The separation and self-efficiency of biblical scholarship's two interpretative communities ensure that serious and informed reflection on the relation between the Testaments is kept to a minimum."[42] It brought not only indifferences between Christian disciplines but also hindered any form of constructive theological engagement with the Bible.

Similarly, Fowl argued that the rise of professional biblical scholarship resulted in dwindling of TIS, especially in the academy.[43] The marginalization of theology in the universities, divinity schools, and seminary colleges was influenced by three factors. The first came from the dominance of biblical criticism. Critical reading meant a historical reconstruction of the text, instead of the theological concerns. It is the reconstructed framework that shapes biblical interpretation. The second factor concerns the discrete activities of theology where "the work of professional biblical scholars is often seen by professional theologians as both too technical and irrelevant for their own interests." Similarly, the work of professional theologians is seen as "abstract and ill-suited" for biblical interpretation. In addition, the third factor has to do with the professionalization of biblical studies and theology in the modern universities—which further demarcated these disciplines.[44] To be a professional requires a certain efficiency or mastery in one's discipline, whose interests and agendas may not intersect.

As Vanhoozer responded to modern and postmodern interpretation (like Watson and Fowl), he is also of the view that the rise and dominance of biblical criticism resulted in an "ugly ditch" between exegesis and theology.[45] He also suggests that it resulted in a "muddy ditch" between exegesis and ideology, which came because of the multiplying of interpretative approaches in the late modern period.[46]

While attempting to address these tensions, Watson initially argued for "a theological hermeneutics for biblical interpretation—that is, a theoretical framework within which an exegesis oriented primarily towards theological issues can come into being."[47] His aim was to outline biblical interpretation from a theological perspective by keeping track of contemporary approaches of biblical interpretation. In his subsequent

[41] Watson, *Text and Truth*, 5.

[42] Watson, *Text and Truth*, 5.

[43] Fowl, "Theological Interpretation of Scripture and Its Future," 673.

[44] Fowl, "Introduction," xiii–xiv.

[45] Vanhoozer, "Introduction," 20.

[46] Vanhoozer, "Introduction," 20.

[47] Watson, *Text, Church and World*, 1.

publication, he argued for biblical theology as "an interdisciplinary approach to biblical interpretation which seeks to dismantle the barriers that at present separate biblical scholarship from Christian theology."[48] With a coherent approach of the Testaments, he argues for *biblical theology* that entails relativizing the demarcation between biblical scholars and theologians, and between OT and NT scholars.[49] This is "a renewed practice of biblical theology" where there is theologically-oriented biblical interpretation "unconstrained by conventional disciplinary boundaries and critical of the distortions that these boundaries engender."[50]

While acknowledging the contribution of Watson, Fowl argues that biblical theology cannot result in theological interpretation. He sees biblical theology (i.e., associated biblical criticism) in line with the structure of the modern university, instead of TIS of the late twentieth century.[51] Instead, Fowl argues for a "practice whereby theological concerns and interests inform and are informed by a reading of Scripture."[52] Such an argument comes with the supposition that "Christian interpretation of scripture needs to involve a complex interaction in which Christian convictions, practices, and concerns are brought to bear on scriptural interpretation in ways that both shape that interpretation and are shaped by it."[53] It also comes with the understanding that faithful Christian life and Christian biblical interpretation are "both ongoing and a matter of discussion, debate, and disagreement."[54] Fowl associated with those who are dissatisfied with modern critical reading and its results; this growing dissatisfaction mirrors "a more general dissatisfaction with the various intellectual projects which came to characterise modernity."[55] It seeks to "correct the mistaken idea that the right concept of meaning, together with the right method of establishing meaning, will repair the interpretative disputes that plague both the Church and the academy."[56] While dismissing determined meaning, he argues for an *underdetermined* meaning of the text, which may be located between biblical text and Christian doctrine. Underdetermined interpretation values "a plurality of interpretative

---

48 He continues to develop this argument by way of integrating history, hermeneutics, and theology—within a canonical perspective. Francis Watson, *Gospel Writing: A Canonical Perspective* (Grand Rapids: Eerdmans, 2013).

49 Watson, *Text and Truth*, 8.

50 Watson, *Text and Truth*, 13, 17.

51 Fowl, "Introduction," xvi.

52 Fowl, "Introduction," xiii.

53 Fowl, *Engaging Scripture*, 8.

54 Fowl, *Engaging Scripture*, 9.

55 Fowl, "Introduction," xv.

56 Spinks, *The Bible and Crisis of Meaning*, 42.

practices and results without necessarily granting epistemological priority to [a general theory of meaning to determine interpretation.]"[57]

Differing and working on determined meaning (that Fowl dismissed), Vanhoozer attempts to reinvigorate "author-oriented interpretation through a creative retrieval of Reformed theology and speech-act philosophy."[58] He sees meaning as existing before the reading of the text. Holding a realist view, Vanhoozer argues, "There is something prior to interpretation, something 'there' in the text, which can be known and to which the interpreter is accountable."[59] In another context, such conception is referred to as *First Theology*, emphasizing on "God-centered biblical interpretation."[60] It argues for TIS where the "doctrine of God affects the way we interpret the Scriptures, while simultaneously acknowledging that our interpretation of Scripture affects our doctrine of God."[61] Similar to Watson and Fowl, his proposal of TIS is a reaction against modern and postmodern biblical interpretation. Much has been said on this matter, both by Watson and Fowl. However, mention must be made why Vanhoozer finds this divide problematic: the concern is not so much about "reconstructing historical context and the history of the text's composition," but it has to do with the modern interpreter's tendency to treat "the biblical texts as sources for reconstructing human history and religion rather than as texts that testify to God's presence and action in history."[62] In other words, the Bible is no longer read as the Word of God, but like any ancient book. This was a shift in teleological understanding of the Bible: its purpose is no longer to deliver divine instructions, but to serve as a source for reconstructing "what actually happened."[63] In addition, there is also the divide between exegesis and ideology.[64] Dissatisfied with the modern interpretation, several interpretative approaches emerged in the late modern period—resulting in a plurality of interpretative approaches. The postmodern interpreters located their interpretative task to the "history, culture, class, and gender" of the readers.[65] Bible reading, in this case, is the meaning shaped by the "location and identity" of the readers.[66] Interpreters come to the text with "a plurality of interpretative interests," giving rise to "a plurality of interpretative approaches," but with

57 Fowl, *Engaging Scripture*, 33.
58 Vanhoozer, *Is There a Meaning in This Text?*, 10.
59 Vanhoozer, *Is There a Meaning in This Text?*, 26.
60 Vanhoozer, *First Theology*, 9–10.
61 Vanhoozer, *First Theology*, 10.
62 Vanhoozer, "Introduction," 20.
63 Kevin J. Vanhoozer, email message to author, January 21, 2019.
64 Vanhoozer, "Introduction," 20.
65 Vanhoozer, "Introduction," 20.
66 Vanhoozer, "Introduction," 20.

"no independent standards or universal criteria for determining which of many rival interpretations is the 'right' or 'true' one."[67] This situation has resulted in a legitimation crisis. The interpreters must deal with the question of: "Whose interpretation of the Bible counts, and why?"[68] Hence, in response to the crisis of biblical interpretation, Vanhoozer calls for "a more constructive engagement with Scripture."[69]

In response to the crisis of biblical interpretation, contributions also came from the schools of Yale and Duke.[70] *Theological Exegesis* tried to bring out a "comprehensive vision of biblical and theological studies that Childs has never ceased to outline, illustrate, and defend throughout the corpus of his scholarship."[71] For example, in the section on "Canonical Method," George Lindbeck focuses on hermeneutics by situating Childs with two other retrieval methods; Paul C. McGlasson argues for the significance of canon (i.e., a kind of canonical context) in the history of theology, and Roy A. Harrisville directly dealt with Childs's canonical method.[72] While acknowledging the works of Childs, they added a significant voice in the contemporary attempts of theological appropriation.

For Childs, the canonical context is more than a literary phenomenon. Emphasis on canon is to recognize the role and function Scripture has on the community of faith. Childs was disturbed by the division "between the descriptive and constructive elements of biblical interpretation, that is, the distance between 'Biblical Theology' as a primarily historical task *and* subsequent theological reflection."[73] He saw this division as the cause of or lack of theology in biblical interpretation.[74] While recognizing the need for critical engagement with the text, Childs prioritized the need for theological reflection. He recognized *canon* as "the locus at which the descriptive and constructive aspects of interpretation combine" (i.e., as the process by which "the church's sacred writings were formed and by which

---

67 Vanhoozer, "Introduction," 20–21.

68 Vanhoozer, "Introduction," 20.

69 Vanhoozer, "Introduction," 21.

70 See Christopher R. Seitz and Kathryn Greene-McCreight, eds., *Theological Exegesis: Essays in Honor of Brevard S. Childs* (Grand Rapids: Eerdmans, 1999); Ellen F. Davis and Richard B. Hays, eds., *The Art of Reading Scripture* (Grand Rapids: Eerdmans, 2003).

71 Kathryn Greene-McCreight and Christopher Seitz, "The Work and Witness of Brevard S. Childs," in *Theological Exegesis*, 3.

72 See Roy A. Harrisville, "What I Believe My Old Schoolmate Is Up To" in *Theological Exegesis*, 7–25; George Lindbeck, "Postcritical Canonical Interpretation," 26–51; Paul C. McGlasson, "The Significance of Context in Theology," 52–74.

73 Harrisville, "What I Believe My Old Schoolmate Is Up To," 7.

74 Brevard S. Childs, *The Book of Exodus* (Philadelphia: Westminster, 1974), xiii.

they exercised their roles in the life of each generation of believers").[75] Similarly, *The Art of Reading Scripture* attempted to "overcome the fragmentation of our theological disciplines by reading scripture together."[76] They proposed the idea of giving priority to the church as a context for reading the Bible. This means trying to bring out "a seamlessly integrated theological activity that spoke directly to the needs of the church," instead of letting biblical criticism dictate interpretation.[77] They tried "to recover the church's rich heritage of biblical interpretation in a dramatically changed cultural environment."[78] Such an initiative was carried out with the hope that it would help bring "a quiet revolution in the way Bible is taught in the theological seminaries . . . it also calls pastors and teachers in the churches to rethink their principles of using the Bible."[79] With these initial contributions, the twenty-first century saw exponential growth in the study of theological interpretation.

Further response to the contemporary reality of biblical interpretation also came through book series. The *Renewing Biblical Interpretation* series aims to "facilitate a renewal of biblical interpretation in the academy that will help reopen the Book for our cultures."[80] It is an academic initiative aimed at "biblical interpretation in the academy;" it recognizes the intersection of interdisciplinary insights for biblical interpretation to be "saved from some of its isolation and fragmentation, and for new ways forward to be forged;" the Christian faith forms "the heart of the Seminar," and this project recognizes "a renewal of biblical interpretation [which] will require communal work."[81] Recognizing that critical interpretation stifled Bible reading in the church, they emphasized the need to reconnect. This is done by considering the situation of contemporary biblical interpretation—of history, literature, and theology or the integration of it.

This series was followed by *Studies in Theological Interpretation*, which seeks to "appreciate the constructive theological contribution made by Scripture when it is read is its canonical richness."[82] Its contributors are in "the pursuit of constructive theological interpretation of the church's inheritance of prophets and apostles in a manner that is open to

75 Harrisville, "What I Believe My Old Schoolmate Is Up To," 11.

76 Ellen F. Davis and Richard B. Hays, "Introduction" in *The Art of Reading Scripture*, xv.

77 Davis and Hays, "Introduction," xv.

78 Davis and Hays, "Introduction," xv.

79 Davis and Hays, *The Art of Reading Scripture*, xx, 1–5.

80 See Craig Bartholomew, Colin Greene and Karl Moller, eds., *Renewing Biblical Interpretation* (Cumbria: Paternoster, 2000), xxvi.

81 Bartholomew, "Introduction," xxvi.

82 Markus Bockmuehl, *Seeing the World: Refocusing New Testament Study* (Grand Rapids: Baker, 2006), 7.

reconnection with the long history of theological reading in the church."[83] Similar to the earlier works, they try to bring back the discussion of biblical interpretation to the lives and practices of the church by way of constructive theological engagement with the Scripture in its canonical context. For example, Christopher Seitz argues for the place of the OT as Christian and theological as providing "the signal point of reference by which to understand the second witness [i.e., NT] to the work of God in Christ," considering the recent discussion of NT scholars' use of the OT.[84]

A consolidated effort of TIS is seen in the publication of *Dictionary for Theological Interpretation of the Bible* in the early twenty-first century. TIS is defined as undergirded by three premises: (1) it is "the joint responsibility of all theological disciplines and of the whole people of God," (2) "a governing interest in God, the word and works of God, and by a governing intention to engage in what we might call 'theological criticism,'" and (3) "a broad ecclesial concern that embraces a number of academic approaches."[85] Instead of focusing on the historical background of the text, the task is to focus on *the message* or the content of the biblical text. It is being done with the presupposition that the purpose of biblical interpretation is "to hear God's word and know God better."[86]

What the advocates of TIS are propagating grew with much enthusiasm with the establishment of more theological journals. The launching of the *Journal of Theological Interpretation* prioritized "a theological hermeneutics of Christian Scripture [concerning] the role of Scripture in the faith and formation of persons and ecclesial communities."[87] According to Green, it appeals to a kind of theological interpretation that considers "the potentially mutual influence of Scripture and doctrine in theological discourse and, then, the role of Scripture in the self-understanding of the church and in critical reflection on the church's practices."[88] Though it is not without challenges, the need for "exegetical study from within and in the service of the community of disciples who turn to the Bible as Christian Scripture" is seen as urgent.[89] It put into context the Christian Scripture in the faith developments of individuals and ecclesial communities. Individual areas of research are also carried forward in the *Journal of*

---

83 Bockmuehl, *Seeing the World*, 7.

84 Seitz, *The Character of Christian Scripture*, 11, 17.

85 Vanhoozer, "Introduction," 21–22.

86 Vanhoozer, "Introduction," 20.

87 Joel B. Green "The (Re-)Turn to Theology," *JTI* vol. 1.1 (2007): 1–3.

88 Green "The (Re-)Turn to Theology," 2.

89 Green "The (Re-)Turn to Theology," 2.

Theological Interpretation Supplements.[90] For instance, Thomas Holsinger-Friesen argues that the biblical interpretation of Irenaeus and his use of the Genesis creation text is understood as "pivotal backgrounds in the early struggle to identify ecclesial boundaries."[91] Significantly, such studies give the readers insights and the means of biblical interpretation that contemporary interpreters can carry forward. What can be learned from Irenaeus is not just his hermeneutical method but how he brings out "biblical truth claims about God and humanity."[92]

With the above publications, TIS has been able to construct the key principles of theological interpretation. And with the publications of theological commentaries, they were able to put together the theories into practice. They responded to the critique that TIS needs more examples of how to do theological interpretation.[93] In *The Two Horizons Old/New Testament Commentary*, the commentators address "the gaps which exist between the exegetical work typical of modern commentaries and disciplined theological reflection."[94] With similar concerns, *Belief* theological commentary can "provide new theological resources for the church, but also to encourage all theologians to pay more attention to Scripture and the life of the church in their writings."[95] *Brazos Theological Commentary on the Bible* also tries to draw out insights from the premodern biblical interpretation. The contributors assume that "the Nicene tradition, in all its diversity and controversy, provides the proper basis for the interpretation of the Bible as Christian Scripture."[96] According to R. R. Reno, reading the Bible through the lens of the Nicene tradition means:

> God the Father Almighty, who sends his only begotten Son to die for us and for our salvation and who raises the crucified Son in the power of the Holy Spirit so that the baptized may be joined in one body-faith in *this* God with *this* vocation of love for the world is the lens through to view the heterogeneity and particularity of the biblical texts.[97]

Doctrine is seen as foundational to understand the meaning of the text. More specifically, the *Ancient Christian Commentary on Scripture*

---

[90] See *Journal of Theological Interpretation Supplements* (Winona Lakes: Eisenbrauns, 2009).

[91] Thomas Holsinger-Friesen, *Irenaeus and Genesis: A Study of Competition in Early Christian Hermeneutics* (Winona Lakes: Eisenbrauns, 2009), ix.

[92] Holsinger-Friesen, *Irenaeus and Genesis*, x.

[93] John Webster, "Editorial," *IJST* 12-2 (2010): 116–17.

[94] Stephen E. Fowl, *Philippians* (Grand Rapids: Eerdmans, 2005), 1.

[95] D. Stephen Long, *Hebrews* (Louisville: WJK, 2011), xii–xiv.

[96] R. R. Reno, "Series Preface" in *Acts*, Jaroslav Pelikan, ed. (Grand Rapids: Brazos, 2005), 13–14.

[97] Reno, "Series Preface," 14.

takes the reader back to the patristic interpretation of the Bible.[98] It seeks to fulfill three goals:

> The renewal of Christian *preaching* based on classical Christian exegesis, the intensified study of Scripture by *lay* person who wish to think with the early church about the canonical text, and the stimulation of Christian historical, biblical, theological and pastoral *scholarship* toward future inquiry into the scriptural interpretations of the ancient Christian writers.[99]

Instead of focusing on critical approach, they focused on the theological interpretation of the ancient writings. Also, *The Church's Bible* paid attention to the interpretation of the Bible in the first millennium, drawing extensively from "the ancient commentaries, not only on random comments drawn from theological treatises, sermons, or devotional works."[100] They hold that when contemporary readers immerse themselves in "the ancient sources," they will be able to access the "spiritual and theological world of the early Church and hence of the Bible."[101] They also hoped that reading ancient commentaries would help them in their private and communal life.

As the TIS movement continues to make progress, their concerns can be narrowed down to three distinct emphases of precritical interpretation, church community, and canon: *divine authorship*, *reader*, and *text*. The *first* emphasis can be further categorized as divine address, divine action, and divine discourse. The argument for divine address assumes that biblical text addresses the faith community across time and space.[102] It presupposes the presence of the divine author and human author; it also holds that God has spoken and continues to do so through the Bible. To argue for divine action is to suggest that the text is constituted by divine action in the context of liturgy and practices of the church.[103] It recognizes that God is at work through Scripture toward a new life in and through the church, made possible through Jesus Christ. Divine discourse assumes

---

98 See, for example, Andrew Louth, *Genesis 1–11*, Vol. 1 (Downers Grove: IVP, 2001).

99 Thomas C. Oden, "General Introduction" in *Genesis 1–11*, x.

100 Robert Louis Wilken, *Isaiah: Interpreted by Early Christian and Mediaeval Commentaries,* trans. and editor, Angela Russel Christman and Michael J. Hollerich (Grand Rapids: Eerdmans, 2007), xi.

101 Wilken, *Isaiah*, xi.

102 Trevor Hart, "Tradition, Authority, and a Christian Approach to the Bible as Scripture," in *Between Two Horizons: Spanning New Testament Studies and Systematic Theology*, ed. Joel B. Green and Max Turner (Grand Rapids: Eerdmans, 2000),183–204.

103 Paddison, *Scripture*, 8.

that God speaks (i.e., when God speaks, it commands a response).[104] When God speaks, it results in speech action (i.e., expects obedience from the listeners). The *second* emphasis has to do with formation, especially in the ecclesial setting. Such reading of the Bible enables the readers to walk with God and others.[105] The goal of such reading is the transformation of the interpretative communities (i.e., God shapes them in the likeness of Christ through the work of the Spirit).[106] The *third* emphasis focuses on the final form of the biblical text: the canon or the narrative of the Bible.[107] The proponents of TIS recognize the final form of the Bible either as literary (e.g., narrative) or religious text (e.g., canon), which is "the prime theological witness."[108] For some, canonical reading of the Bible is the appropriate way of exploring the theological dimension of the biblical text.[109] It sees the need to connect the discipline of Bible and theology.[110] It also comes with the recognition of the canonicity of the OT and the NT.[111] For others, biblical interpretation ought to address the "theological issues" raised by the text in the contemporary context, whether ecclesial or social.[112] It argues for the primacy of theology within biblical interpretation; it also means arguing for a theological framework within biblical exegesis.[113] This theological framework may mean engaging in biblical interpretation concerning the question of God (i.e., the triune God).[114] It can also mean doing "justice to the perceived theological nature of the texts and embrace the influence of theology (corporate and personal; past and present) upon the interpreter's enquiry, context and method."[115]

Approaches of Theological Interpretation of Scripture

While focusing on divine authorship, reader, or text, TIS is trying to retrieve theology by engaging with two or more disciplines. Presently, most,

---

[104] See Kevin J. Vanhoozer, *First Theology: God, Scripture and Hermeneutics* (Downers Grove: IVP Academic, 2002).

[105] See Fowl, "Introduction" in *The Theological Interpretation of Scripture*, xii–xxx.

[106] Billings, *The Word of God for the People of God*, xiii.

[107] Vanhoozer, "Introduction," 23.

[108] Vanhoozer, "Introduction," 23.

[109] Childs, *Old Testament Theology in a Canonical Context*, 1.

[110] Brevard S. Childs, *Biblical Theology of the Old and New Testaments: Theological Reflections on the Christian Bible* (Minneapolis: Fortress Press, 1992), xvi.

[111] Christopher R. Seitz, *The Character of Christian Scripture: The significance of a Two-Testament Bible* (Grand Rapids: Baker, 2011).

[112] Watson, *Text, Church and World*, vii.

[113] Watson, *Text, Church and World*, 1.

[114] R. W. L. Moberly, *The Bible, Theology, and Faith: A Study of Abraham and Jesus* (Cambridge: CUP, 2000).

[115] Spinks, *The Bible and the Crisis of Meaning*, 7.

if not all, of the discussions are carried out by examining the relationship between biblical studies, systematic theology, or biblical theology. Here, the term *approach* is used referring to how biblical scholars and theologians engaged with theological disciplines to recover theology in biblical interpretation.

Biblical Studies and Systematic Theology

Over more than two centuries, there was little or no connection between biblical studies and systematic theology.[116] This disconnect is a result of the rise of modernity and the privileging of the original context and the eventual marginalization of theology in biblical interpretation. However, since the late twentieth century, some scholars have been trying to interface biblical studies and systematic theology to bring out a distinctive theological interpretation. As TIS constructively pursues such interests, there are also those who are apprehensive of such pursuits.[117] Yet, in the last few decades, there is a sense of growth in the study of the interfacing of the disciplines of biblical studies and systematic theology from both disciplines.[118] These scholars are searching for "a common ground,"[119] "dialogue,"[120] "reintegration,"[121] or "conversation"[122] between biblical studies and systematic theology.

The effort to bridge biblical studies and systematic theology came with urgency in the late twentieth century to include theology in biblical interpretation. An example from theologians trying to bridge these disciplines is evident in *The Bible for Theology*.[123] Gerald O'Collins and Daniel Kendall try to ascertain the question, "What effects should biblical texts produce in theology?"[124] They are interested in "how the Bible should ideally work in Christian theology" to come up with guiding principles for such theological engagement.[125] Their focus is to construct a framework,

[116] Max Turner and Joel B. Green, "New Testament Commentary and Systematic Theology," in *Between Two Horizons*, 1–22.

[117] Watson, *Text, Church and World*, 12.

[118] Richard Baukham, "Introduction" in *The Gospel of John and Christian Theology*, ed. Richard Bauckham and Carl Mosser (Grand Rapids: Eerdmans, 2008), x.

[119] O'Collins and Kendall, *The Bible for Theology*, 1.

[120] Watson, *Text, Church and World*, 12.

[121] Turner and Green, "New Testament Commentary and Systematic Theology" in *Between Two Horizons*, 1.

[122] Richard Bauckham, "Introduction" in *The Gospel of John and Christian Theology*, ed. Richard Bauckham and Carl Mosser (Grand Rapids: Eerdmans, 2008).

[123] See Gerald O'Collins and Daniel Kendall, *The Bible for Theology: Ten Principles for the Theology Use of Scripture* (New York: Paulist, 1997).

[124] O'Collins and Kendall, *The Bible for Theology*, 1.

[125] O'Collins and Kendall, *The Bible for Theology*, 1.

which will help theologians to "read, understand, interpret and apply the scriptures."[126] It comes with the assumption that the Bible is the witness of Christ, which came through the influence of the Holy Spirit. The Bible is seen "not merely *de facto* and based simply on the way they effectively function now in shaping life and teaching for the community of faith" but "a *de jure* authority that legitimately commands permanent loyalty and is derived from a foundational and authoritative past."[127] It acknowledges divine authority and revelation in the Bible; it also recognizes that the biblical text came through human authors. Collins and Kendall state that "the word of God came and comes to us in and through the words of human beings; that is to say, in a medium that is historically and culturally conditioned."[128] This understanding of the Bible requires careful attention to the biblical sense, i.e., the intended meaning(s) of the text by the human authors. It also needs to be done within the community of faith and with the presupposition that the Spirit "both inspired the writing of the scriptures and has guided their living interpretation."[129] To arrive at their stated task, Collins and Kendall suggest ten guiding principles. First, the principle of "faith hearing" requires the readers/interpreters to be "faithful and regular hearers of the inspired text."[130] Such an interpretative task orients toward the text instead of the readers, and responds to the meaning discovered in the text rather than the constructed meaning.[131] Second, the emphasis on "active hearing" requires the theologians to be "active, critically self-aware interpreters of the scriptures, appropriating them within the contexts of prayer, study and action."[132] Third, it focuses on the principle of "Community and its creeds" where theological appropriation is carried out in "the community of faith and in the light of its classical creeds."[133] The emphasis is to connect truth claims with "the Christian community's cumulative tradition of interpreting and 'performing' the scriptures."[134] Fourth, the principle of "biblical convergence" allows holding on to the theological questions examined by the readers/interpreters.[135] Fifth, the idea of "exegetical census" holds the understanding that "the consensus of centrist exegetes guides systematic theology."[136] Sixth, theological

[126] O'Collins and Kendall, *The Bible for Theology*, 1.
[127] O'Collins and Kendall, *The Bible for Theology*, 9.
[128] O'Collins and Kendall, *The Bible for Theology*, 14.
[129] O'Collins and Kendall, *The Bible for Theology*, 16.
[130] O'Collins and Kendall, *The Bible for Theology*, 6.
[131] O'Collins and Kendall, *The Bible for Theology*, 19.
[132] O'Collins and Kendall, *The Bible for Theology*, 6, 38.
[133] O'Collins and Kendall, *The Bible for Theology*, 6.
[134] O'Collins and Kendall, *The Bible for Theology*, 24.
[135] O'Collins and Kendall, *The Bible for Theology*, 6, 24.
[136] O'Collins and Kendall, *The Bible for Theology*, 6, 24.

appropriation of the Bible takes into account the "metathemes and metanarratives" of the divine.[137] It presupposes "the existence of patterns of divine activity and promise that recur in the Bible, yield an over-all picture, evoke varying human responses, and throw light above all, on Jesus' activity and identity."[138] Seventh, it recognizes the "continuity within discontinuity" in the theological events of the Bible.[139] A new event in the Bible, which entails new meaning, recognizes what has proceeded before the event. Eighth, the principle of "eschatological provisionality" regulates the theological use of the Bible.[140] The possibility of the fullness of glory in the future helps the readers to acknowledge "the partial, provisional, and anticipatory nature of even the best insights to be drawn from the scriptures about the tripersonal God and the world of grace in which we live today."[141] Ninth, the principle of "philosophical assistance" recognizes "the passage from the Bible to theology takes place in dialogue with philosophy."[142] It presupposes that philosophical reasoning sharpens theological reasoning in terms of sharpening "the questions to be asked, helps to organise the methods and material, partly illuminates the condition of human beings and their world, and brings conceptual clarity to bear on the biblical texts, which by and large are prephilosophical."[143] Tenth, the principle of "inculturation" helps in the theological appropriation of the Bible.[144] This principle recognizes the possibility of culture enriching the discussion of biblical testimony and theology.[145]

Collins and Kendall recognize the validity of these principles in the application of theological issues in systematic theology, such as Christology, soteriology, the doctrine of God, and ecclesiology. For instance, they suggest that when the ten principles are used to "monitor various moves from the scriptures to trinitarian theology, indicate that the three names of 'Father, Son and Holy Spirit' do not allow for substitutes."[146] Their contribution can be considered significant as there has been very little effort of such interpretative tasks. However, as they were keen to carry forward theological appropriation in biblical interpretation, it came with biases of the discipline of theology, but seeing this bias as a needed correction to bring about a more balanced theological appropriation.

---

[137] O'Collins and Kendall, *The Bible for Theology*, 7, 27.
[138] O'Collins and Kendall, *The Bible for Theology*, 28.
[139] O'Collins and Kendall, *The Bible for Theology*, 7.
[140] O'Collins and Kendall, *The Bible for Theology*, 7.
[141] O'Collins and Kendall, *The Bible for Theology*, 31.
[142] O'Collins and Kendall, *The Bible for Theology*, 7.
[143] O'Collins and Kendall, *The Bible for Theology*, 31–32.
[144] O'Collins and Kendall, *The Bible for Theology*, 7.
[145] O'Collins and Kendall, *The Bible for Theology*, 33.
[146] O'Collins and Kendall, *The Bible for Theology*, 92.

An example from biblical studies that tries to engage biblical studies with theology is seen in *Between Two Horizons*.[147] Joel B. Green and Max Turner try to answer the question: "What effects should theology produce in biblical interpretation?"[148] Their interest is the reinterpretation of "biblical exegesis with contemporary theology in the service of the church."[149] Their concern is to develop a constructive relationship between biblical studies and systematic theology of "the Christian church."[150] More specifically, their concern is "the relationship of biblical studies to the theological enterprise of the Christian church" and in developing "a biblical hermeneutics appropriate to doing theology."[151] This is to assume that most of the available exegetical resources leave the readers in the author's world with little or no information on *theology*. They argue for biblical interpretation that is theologically grounded in the ancient context and competent to the theological context of the twenty-first century.[152] They try to build a constructive relationship between biblical studies and theology dialogically by critically engaging with the text to avoid suppression of one discipline over the other.[153]

This is done by focusing on three key areas of biblical interpretation: the world "behind the text," the world "in the text," and the world "in front of the text."[154] As it stands, the contemporary biblical interpretation moves toward pluralistic interests; while resisting objective reading, there is prioritizing of a number of "in the text" and "in front of the text" approaches.[155] In light of this reality, interpreters come to the text with theological concerns, considering the meaning of "systematic theology" and what it entails.[156] This means considering a broader sense of systematic study of theological subjects, such as "Christology, atonement, creation, and the nature of personhood."[157] Turner and Green capture this prospect in light of the three requirements set by Colin Gunton: to be systematic in

---

147 Joel B. Green and Max Turner, eds., *Between Two Horizons: Spanning New Testament Studies and Systematic Theology* (Grand Rapids: Eerdmans, 2000).

148 Turner and Green, "New Testament Commentary and Systematic Theology" in *Between Two Horizons*, 1.

149 Turner and Green, "New Testament Commentary and Systematic Theology," 2.

150 Turner and Green, "New Testament Commentary and Systematic Theology," 1.

151 Turner and Green, "New Testament Commentary and Systematic Theology," 1–2.

152 Turner and Green, "New Testament Commentary and Systematic Theology," 3.

153 Turner and Green, "New Testament Commentary and Systematic Theology," 3.

154 Turner and Green, "New Testament Commentary and Systematic Theology," 4–6.

155 Turner and Green, "New Testament Commentary and Systematic Theology," 8.

156 Turner and Green, "New Testament Commentary and Systematic Theology," 9–10.

157 Turner and Green, "New Testament Commentary and Systematic Theology," 9–10.

theology is, first, to be consistent with one's theology in relation with the other; second, to be aware of the relation between "the content of a theology" and "the sources specific to the faith;" and third, to show awareness of the relationship between the content of a theology and "claims for truth in human culture in general, especially perhaps philosophy and science."[158] What could be added in this discussion is Webster's definition of TIS: "interpretation informed by a theological description of the nature of the biblical writings and their reception, setting them in the scope of the progress of the saving divine Word through time."[159] While recognizing that TIS can take several forms, it is seen as:

> A way of reading which is informed by a theologically derived set of interpretative goals, which are governed by a conception of what the Bible is: Holy Scripture, God ministering his Word to human beings through human servants and so sharing with them the inestimable good of knowledge of himself.[160]

In practice, the result of this effort came into fruition with the publication of the *Two Horizons Commentary* series.[161] This series pays careful attention to the difference between modern interpretation (i.e., regulated by semantics, linguistic, and social conventions of the ancient times), and pre-modern interpretation (i.e., regulated by theological concerns).[162] It prioritizes theological concerns over the historical concerns or the world behind the text. They are also interested in understanding how the theological concern ministers to the community of faith, "the Cathedra of Christ."[163] The result of such work is expected to have varied meanings, even within the constraint of "canonical context, the Rule of Faith, and the history of Christian interpretation."[164]

Both these books attempt to bring about theological appropriation in response to marginalization of theology in biblical interpretation. These books also carried forward some of the concerns raised by Watson. He warns that there are risks and dangers of interdisciplinary work: first, since the starting point is one discipline, the result may be superficial; second, there is the risk of taking the allegiance of one discipline to the other; and

---

158 Cf. Colin Gunton, "Historical and Systematic Theology" in *The Cambridge Companion to Christian Doctrine* (Cambridge: CUP, 1997), 11–18.

159 John Webster, *The Domain of the Word: Scripture and Theological Reason* (London: T&T Clark, 12), 30.

160 Webster, *The Domain of the Word,* 30.

161 See Stephen E. Fowl, *Philipians* (Grand Rapids: Eerdmans, 2005); Robin A. Parry, *Lamentations* (Grand Rapids: Eerdmans, 2010).

162 Fowl, *Philipians,* 1–5.

163 Parry, *Lamentations,* 3.

164 Parry, *Lamentations,* 3.

third, there is the question of the incompatibility between the two disciplines.[165] The concern is not so much about the inability to interface the discipline of biblical studies and theology, but it concerns one discipline dominating the other. Biblical scholars would carry forward the agendas and concerns of the discipline in its interpretative task (and vice-versa). If that is the case, such a project can take the form of biblical scholars or theologians taking up interdisciplinary tasks with departmental biases.

In response, a more integrated effort is seen in the book series *Scripture and Theology*.[166] It attempts to bring "biblical scholars and systematic theologians together in conversation around a biblical text that has played a formative role in Christian theology through the centuries."[167] This book series recognizes the discipline of biblical studies and systematic theology as "natural partners who have lost the means of effective communication with each other, so absorbed have they become in their own issues."[168] It suggests that "the critical task" of biblical interpretation is incomplete without association or relationship with Christian theology.[169] With it, there is an intentional conversation between biblical scholars on a given topic—in more than one way, and in different areas of concern. For example, in *The Gospel of John and Christian Theology*, both biblical scholars and theologians come together and converse on a given topic. Bauckham states,

> Both [Stephen C. Barton and Miroslav Volf] insist that to understand [Johannine] dualities properly they must be contextualized—whether in the narrative of the Gospel, in the Gospel's original historical context, or in the tradition of the church's reception of the Gospel, as well as in the pluralistic context of contemporary readers . . . [while] both authors also subject the concept of pluralism to analysis and critique.[170]

There are points of convergences, but the methodology of interfacing biblical studies and systematic theology is varied. In other words, TIS that emerges out of the dialogue between biblical studies and systematic theology is not monotone. It recognizes multiple methodologies, instead of

---

165 Watson, *Text, Church and World*, 12.

166 See Richard Bauckham and Carl Mosser, eds., *The Gospel of John and Christian Theology* (Grand Rapids: Eerdmans, 2008); Richard Bauckham et al., *The Epistle to the Hebrews and Christian Theology* (Grand Rapids: Eerdmans, 2009); Nathan MacDonald, et al., *Genesis and Christian Theology* (Grand Rapids: Eerdmans, 2012); Mark W. Elliot, et al., *Galatians and Christian Theology: Justification, The Gospel, and Ethics in Paul's Letter* (Grand Rapids: Eerdmans, 2014).

167 Bauckham, "Introduction" in *The Gospel of John and Christian Theology*, x.

168 Bauckham, "Introduction," x.

169 MacDonald, "Introduction" in *Genesis and Christian Theology*, xiv–xv.

170 Bauckham, "Introduction," xii.

a search for common methodology. It also creates the scope of multiple interpretations of the biblical text, while recognizing the final form of the text as a witness to the *divine*.

Though the above approach to bring about theological appropriation is important, there are concerns about whether systematic theology was tainted by modern concerns, like biblical studies. While attempting to incorporate theology in biblical interpretation, attempts of theological appropriation seem to presume that "systematic theology has not been subject to the same anti-theological disciplinary forces of the modern university as biblical studies has been."[171] John Milbank suggests that systematic theology that was developed in the modern period was dependent on modern social sciences and philosophy.[172] The critique is that the task of systematic theology is not entirely "a meta-discourse," but is also bound to the subject of "historical scholarship, humanist psychology or transcendental philosophy."[173] If this critique is to be considered, there is a need to reconsider or redefine the task of systematic theology and what it entails to interface the said discipline with biblical studies. In addition to the concerns of academic biases, most of these projects struggle to incorporate a whole view of the Bible. They are caught up with the question of how biblical text shapes and prescribes Christian theology.[174] What is being discussed along this direction is also context-bound and time-specific (i.e., it deals with issues and concerns that came with the dominance of biblical criticism in the modern period and in the Western context). The drawback of such emphasis is that other theological disciplines that did not emerge from this context and theological discussions that are not part of the attempt to recover theology are ignored. Since these discussions are either geographically bound or located to specific disciplines, the theological discussion that emerged from the Majority World is not a part of such discussions.

Biblical Theology and Systematic Theology

While attempting to bridge the distance between biblical studies and systematic theology, some have looked at the discipline of biblical theology as the answer.[175] Such pursuit would require an understanding of "how biblical

---

171 Fowl, *Engaging Scripture,* 23.

172 John Milbank, *Theology and Social Theory: Beyond Secular Reason,* Second Edition (Oxford: Blackwell Publications, 2006), 1.

173 Milbank, *Theology and Social Theory*, 1.

174 Markus Bockmuehl and Alan J. Torrance, eds., *Scripture's Doctrine and Theology's Bible: How the New Testament Shapes Christian Dogmatics* (Grand Rapids: Baker, 2008), 8.

175 See B. S. Rosner, "Biblical Theology" in *New Dictionary of Biblical Theology*, 3.

theology ought to be done and over its relation to systematic theology."[176] Such concern comes with the difficulty to define biblical theology and to ascertain the issues of interdisciplinary effort.[177] It anticipates "difficulties" of bringing together the subject of biblical studies and systematic theology.[178] This concern ought to be taken seriously, as there are different understandings of biblical theology[179] and as there are those who think that biblical theology cannot result in theological interpretation.[180] In spite of this reality, Brian Rosner suggests that the answer lies in looking at these disciplines as interdependent on each other.[181] While the task of biblical theology and systematic theology can be differentiated, these disciplines can be seen as complementary. This can be seen as the answer to the fragmentation of theological disciplines with the dominance of the critical approach.[182]

Since Gabler, the task of biblical theology moved in two distinct directions.[183] He differentiated between biblical theology and dogmatic theology. The first identifies biblical theology as historical and descriptive, while the latter is didactic and normative.[184] The first task was carried forward with much intensity and dominance in the modern period, while the latter was neglected. He tried to do away with dogmatic theology while studying the Bible (i.e., the NT) as a distinct historical discipline. Krister Stendahl sees the distinction between these two disciplines as a hermeneutical distinction between "what it meant" and "what it means."[185] Biblical theology that focuses on *what the text meant* gathers the original author and audience, while systematic theology that deals with *what the text means* gathers the contemporary context.[186]

---

176 See Kevin Vanhoozer, "From Canon to Concept: 'Same' and 'Other' in the Relation between Biblical and Systematic Theology," *SBET* 12 (1994): 96–124.

177 See also R. R. Reno, "Biblical Theology and Theological Exegesis" in *Out of Egypt*, 385–408.

178 Carson, "Systematic Theology and Biblical Theology" in *New Dictionary of Biblical Theology*, 89–104.

179 See Edward W. Klink III and Darian R. Lockett, *Understanding Biblical Theology: A Comparison of Theory and Practice* (Grand Rapids: Zondervan, 2012).

180 Fowl, *Engaging Scripture*, 1.

181 Rosner, "Biblical Theology," 3.

182 Watson, *Text and Truth*, vii.

183 See Gabler, "On the Proper Distinction between Biblical and Dogmatic Theology and the Specific Objectives of Each," 134–44.

184 See Kevin J. Vanhoozer, "Exegesis and Hermeneutics" in *New Dictionary of Biblical Theology*, 52–64.

185 Krister Stendahl, "Biblical Theology, Contemporary" in *The Interpreter's Dictionary of the Bible: An Illustrated Encyclopaedia*, George Arthur Buttrick, ed. (Nashville: Abingdon, 1960), 418–32.

186 See Treier, "Biblical Theology and/or Theological Interpretation of Scripture?" 16–31.

Because of these conflicting interests, integrating these disciplines anticipated difficulties. D. A. Carson suggests that any attempt to interface biblical theology with systematic theology should be done in recognition of the divergences of these disciplines.[187] While both disciplines share commonality in terms of their source of authority, over time they have grown apart because of the distinct discipline emphases.[188] Carson identifies the striking difference in the following manner:

> Although both are text based, the ordering principles of the former are topical, logical, hierarchical, and as synchronic as possible; the ordering principles of the latter trace out the history of redemption and are (ideally) profoundly inductive, comparative and as diachronic as possible.[189]

In his opinion, since systematic theology engages with the contemporary context, it is further away from the text; while biblical theology tends to be closer to the text as it is interested in the literary genre. In that sense, systematic theology tends to be "a culminating discipline," while biblical theology tends to be "a bridge discipline."[190]

Yet, there are those who see the relationship between biblical theology and systematic theology in a complementary sense. If it was not the case, Geerhardus Vos argues that,

> All attempts to show that the doctrines developed and formulated by the Church have no real foundation in the Bible, stand themselves without the pale of Theology, inasmuch as they imply that Christianity is a purely natural phenomenon, and that the Church has now for nineteen centuries been chasing her own shadow.[191]

He argues that "dogmatic theology is, when rightly cultivated, as truly a Biblical and as truly an inductive as its younger sister."[192] It can be made possible by endorsing systematic theology to be biblical by being more inductive, while biblical theology can be more constructive in its structuring of facts.[193] This is said with the assumption that one discipline is

---

187 Carson, "Systematic Theology and Biblical Theology," 89.

188 Carson, "Systematic Theology and Biblical Theology," 102.

189 Carson, "Systematic Theology and Biblical Theology," 102–3.

190 Carson, "Systematic Theology and Biblical Theology," 103.

191 Geerhardus Vos, "The Idea of Biblical Theology as a Science and as a Theological Discipline," in *Redemptive History and Biblical Interpretation: The Shorter Writings of Geerharddus Vos*, ed. Richard B. Gaffin, (Phillipsburg: Presbyterian and Reformed Publishing Co., 1980), 23.

192 Vos, "The Idea of Biblical Theology as a Science and as a Theological Discipline," 23.

193 Vos, "The Idea of Biblical Theology as a Science and as a Theological Discipline," 23.

"systematic and logical," while the other is "historical."[194] Vanhoozer is also of the view that the gulf that separates these two disciplines can be bridged "by better appreciating the contribution of the diverse biblical genres, and that a focus on literary genre could do much to relieve the ills currently plaguing both their houses."[195] The gulf that has emerged in the modern period has led to the demise of biblical theology.[196] People tend to approach the gap between biblical theology and systematic theology by emphasizing the "sameness" (i.e., content-oriented and form-oriented approach) or "otherness" (i.e., meaning other than Scripture).[197] The sameness approach sees interpretation as "an insignificant problem," while the otherness approach sees it "an insuperable problem"—where both these approaches fail to see interpretation as "a matter of work and prayer which approximates the text."[198] Instead, he calls for biblical theology that describes "the way in which biblical literary forms communicate content" (i.e., "a systematic study of the poetics of biblical literature").[199] If that is the case, then "biblical theology, to summarize, seeks to interpret the canonical forms on their own generic terms. Systematic theology then is the attempt to catch up and preserve the meaning of the various canonical discourses in a conceptual framework that will be intelligible for people today."[200] In another context, Vanhoozer puts this perceived predicament between biblical and systematic theology in the following manner:

> Biblical narrative gives rise to doctrine whenever we are puzzled by something in the story, such as, why Jesus had to die a bloody death. Story thus gives rise to systematic. More pointedly: *narrative raises questions that only ontology can answer.*[201]

Such conception of these disciplines helps us look at it in a complementary sense, instead of contrary terms. Such an approach is adapted to guide and direct biblical interpretation to strengthen and shape the community of faith, instead of dealing with *what the text meant*. Instead of juggling the tension between history and theology, a complementary approach between biblical theology and systematic theology brings a more constructive understanding of Scripture. It also helps contemporary

---

194 Vos, "The Idea of Biblical Theology as a Science and as a Theological Discipline," 23.
195 Vanhoozer, "From Canon to Concept," 96.
196 Vanhoozer, "From Canon to Concept," 98.
197 Vanhoozer, "From Canon to Concept," 106–10.
198 Vanhoozer, "From Canon to Concept," 110.
199 Vanhoozer, "From Canon to Concept," 112.
200 Vanhoozer, "From Canon to Concept," 114.
201 Kevin J. Vanhoozer, "Staurology, Ontology, and the Travail of Biblical Narrative: Once More unto the Biblical Theological Breach," *SBJT* 23.2 (2019): 7–33.

readers, including the church, to be aware of what the text holds and how/what it should address. Considering that all theology emerges from a context or addresses contextual concerns, a constructive interaction between these two disciplines gives us a way forward to bring together TIS and contextual theology as well.

Theological Interpretation of Scripture: Kevin J. Vanhoozer

Vanhoozer's TIS can be included in the previous approaches as he contributes to the interfacing of theological discipline.[202] As a systematic theologian, he converses with biblical scholars, but moves beyond them. While located in the discipline of (systematic) theology, he is interested in ascertaining "what does it mean to be biblical?"[203] This is said with the assumption that both biblical and systematic theology are in crisis, i.e., biblical theology (associated with critical approach) is devoid of theology, while systematic theology has moved away from Scripture. Yet, when Vanhoozer argues for TIS, he recognizes its task as "*the joint responsibility of all theological disciplines and of the whole people of God.*"[204] While taking the vantage point of situating to the discipline of systematic theology, contributions from other theological disciplines are recognized. He holds that "the study of church history can itself be a theological discipline insofar as it helps the present church to learn from previous ways of interpreting Scripture."[205] The current project makes a similar suggestion concerning the relationship between TIS and tribal theology (an example of contextual theology). The "redemptive" model or "theodrama" of Vanhoozer serves as "a lens or interpretative framework through which Christians think, make sense of their experience, and decide what to do and how to do it."[206] It can be the answer to the tension or crisis in the contemporary biblical interpretation. In the context of "the madness in method" of Western scholarship and the preoccupation of "orthopraxis" in the Majority World, *theodramatic proposal* is seen as an answer to the

---

[202] See Kevin J. Vanhoozer, "The New Testament and Theology," 401–18; Kevin J. Vanhoozer, "From Canon to Concept: 'Same' and 'Other' in the Relation between Biblical and Systematic Theology," *SBET* 12 (1994): 96–124.

[203] Vanhoozer, "From Canon to Concept," 96.

[204] *Emphasis* in original. Vanhoozer, "Introduction" in *Dictionary for Theological Interpretation of the Bible*, 21.

[205] Vanhoozer, "Introduction" in *Dictionary for Theological Interpretation of the Bible*, 21.

[206] Kevin J. Vanhoozer, "A Drama of Redemption Model: Always Performing?" in *Moving Beyond the Bible to Theology*, ed. Gary T. Meadors (Grand Rapids: Zondervan, 2009), 155.

crisis of contemporary biblical interpretation.[207] His theological method will be categorized under four principles: the core principle, canonical principle, catholic principle, and contextual principle.

The Core Principle

The core principle concerns the heart of Christianity—the gospel which is the "news about what the good God has done in the history of Israel that climaxes in Jesus Christ."[208] It is not the universal truth as some might have claimed, instead it is "an announcement of God's saving work in Christ."[209] It comes with the conviction that "God has spoken and acted in Jesus Christ and that God speaks and acts in the canonical Scriptures that testify to him."[210] Vanhoozer's *theodramatic* model is a redirection on two fronts: a "move from hermeneutical theology to theological hermeneutics (i.e., an approach to biblical interpretation informed by theology from the start)"[211] and a move "away from general hermeneutics informed by special hermeneutics" (what Vanhoozer calls a "*theological* general hermeneutic") toward "a *theological* special hermeneutic" that highlights the distinctive features of Christian biblical interpretation."[212] For Vanhoozer, coming to terms with the subject matter of theological method means asking the right *question*. It has to do with asking whether theology should "begin with God or with the Word of God?"[213] The answer lies in viewing God and Scripture together, instead of the background of the text. The subject matter of theology can be ascertained either through a theoretical framework or an objective-scientific inquiry. It requires a *faith seeking understanding*.[214] It requires viewing the gospel as *theodrama* (i.e., understanding "God as a communicative agent and Scripture as his communicative action").[215] It means speaking of the biblical text as "*a form of communicative act of a communicative agent fixed*

[207] Vanhoozer, "One Rule to Rule Them All," 85–126; Vanhoozer, "Theological Method," 894–98; Kevin J. Vanhoozer, "Theological Method" in *New Dictionary of Theology*, 901–3.

[208] Vanhoozer, "Theological Method" in *Global Dictionary of Theology*, 895.

[209] Kevin J. Vanhoozer, *Faith Speaking Understanding: Performing the Drama of Doctrine* (Louisville: WJK, 2014), 20–21.

[210] Vanhoozer, *The Drama of Doctrine*, 26.

[211] Putman understood it backwards when he said that it is a move "from hermeneutical theory shaped by theology (theological hermeneutics) toward a theology shaped by hermeneutics (hermeneutical theology)." Rhyne R. Putman, *In Defense of Doctrine: Evangelicalism, Theology, and Scripture* (Minneapolis: Fortress Press, 2015), 180.

[212] Putman, *In Defense of Doctrine*, 180.

[213] Vanhoozer, *First Theology*, 15.

[214] Vanhoozer, *Is There a Meaning in This Text?*, 15.

[215] Vanhoozer, *First Theology*, 35.

by writing" to move to an understanding of biblical interpretation where meaning of the text is a form of doing or performing.[216] This particular emphasis distinctly differentiates Vanhoozer from critical-modern scholars. While both talk about the author's intention, modern scholars locate the meaning back *then*, but Vanhoozer locates in the present as God is the communicating agent. Spinks finds this communicative ideal as shaping "meaning into a form of doing and allows Vanhoozer to continue to speak of the author and author's intentions without falling into the traps of much modernistic psychologising or the endless abyss of postmodern freeplay."[217] For modern scholars, the text, if it speaks, is the reconstructed meaning as shaped by the world *behind the text*; but for Vanhoozer, it is God speaking from the written text, prompting response from the readers. The difference in their interpretative task lies in their perception of the Bible: one reads the Bible like any ancient book, while the other reads the Bible as Scripture. One searches for historical information, while the other seeks divine instructions.

If the written text communicates, it calls for response from the readers.[218] It calls for a creative reading of the Bible. This need for response comes from the understanding that there is "real presence" in the written text.[219] Vanhoozer states, "In the Christian tradition, then, written words may mediate personal presence, just as Christ mediates the presence of God."[220] Reading the text, then, is not merely a reconstruction of historical events. However, if there is "something in the text prior to the act of reading—gaps, indeterminacies, instructions, flags, and signals," it calls for response from the readers/interpreters.[221] This makes sense as text, as written discourse, are "unfulfilled until they are appropriated or applied by readers' discourse ('someone saying something about something *to* someone') is incomplete without a recipient."[222]

Response from the readers is necessary as "reading is not merely a matter of perception but also of production; the reader does not discover so much to create meaning . . . Meaning is actualized not by the author at the point of the text's conception but by the reader at the point of the text's

216 *Emphasis* in original. Vanhoozer, *Is There a Meaning in This Text?*, 225.

217 Spinks, *The Bible and the Crisis of Meaning*, 82.

218 Kevin J. Vanhoozer, "The Hermeneutics of I-Witness Testimony: John 21:20–24 and the 'Death' of the 'Author,'" in *Understanding Poets and Prophets*, ed. A. Graeme Auld (Sheffield: JSOT, 1993), 366–87.

219 Vanhoozer, *Is There a Meaning in This Text?*, 87.

220 Vanhoozer, *Is There a Meaning in This Text?*, 87.

221 Kevin J. Vanhoozer, "The Reader in New Testament Study," in *Hearing the New Testament: Strategies for Interpretation*, ed. Joel B. Green (Grand Rapids: Eerdmans, 1995), 318.

222 Vanhoozer, "The Reader in New Testament Study," 309.

reception."[223] Such a task of interpretation is expressed in the following manner:

> The form of theology is 'dramatic' inasmuch as it concerns a word addressed by God to [humankind] and a response from [humankind] to God. The substance of theology is dramatic because it concerns what God has done in Jesus Christ. The task of theology, therefore is to enable hearers and doers of the gospel to respond and to correspond to the prior Word and Act of God.[224]

This is a corrective to critical interpretation emphasizing prescriptive theology, instead of descriptive theory/theology (i.e., of the critical approach).[225] Such an interpretative task holds that "The Triune God is the primary speaker and actor, but the people of God have been given the privilege and responsibility not only of thinking God's thoughts after him but of speaking God's words and of acting God's acts after him as well."[226] Reading the text is not just a theoretical exercise, instead it should result in action. It should result in a change of thinking and behavior.

In this *theodramatic* paradigm, "Bible is a script; doctrine as theatrical direction; and the church as part of the ongoing performance of salvation."[227] If the Bible is a script, canon is seen as a performance—and it serves as "normative specification of what God was saying and doing in Christ."[228] Tradition, then, is also a form of performance where it provides "a particular way of interpreting the script in life and thought."[229] Moreover, theology, with the help of dramaturgy (i.e., the working of drama), approximates a twofold task: making sense of the "subject matter (the speech and action of God)" and understanding the "function (interpreting and performing a script/Scripture)."[230] Vanhoozer argues that "theological dramaturgy, as a form of textual interpretation, involves both *scientia* and *sapientia*" (i.e., it entails exegesis, which helps people to know the meaning and perform them in the ecclesial community).[231] The goal of such an interpretative task is

223 Vanhoozer, "The Reader in New Testament Study," 301.

224 Kevin J. Vanhoozer, "The Voice and the Actor: A Dramatic Proposal about the Ministry and Minstrelsy of Theology," in *Evangelical Futures: A Conversation on Theological Method*, ed. John G. Stackhouse (Grand Rapids: Baker, 2000), 69.

225 Kevin J. Vanhoozer, "Scripture and Tradition" in *The Cambridge Companion to Postmodern Theology* (Cambridge: CUP, 2003), 151–52.

226 Vanhoozer, "The Voice and the Actor," in *Evangelical Futures*, 69.

227 Vanhoozer, "Theological Method" in *Global Dictionary of Theology*, 895; Vanhoozer, *The Drama of Doctrine*, 152.

228 Vanhoozer, *The Drama of Doctrine*, 152.

229 Vanhoozer, *The Drama of Doctrine*, 152.

230 Vanhoozer, *The Drama of Doctrine*, 245–47.

231 Vanhoozer, *The Drama of Doctrine*, 246–56.

"wise performance or performed wisdom."[232] In other words, reading the Word of God should result in doing what the Scripture says (i.e., live a life *like* Christ). This is enabled by the Holy Spirit. The Spirit illuminates the original meaning of the text intended by the author and helps the reader perform them.[233] While considering the Spirit's role in reading the Bible, Vanhoozer speaks of the Bible as "a species of divine communication action, consisting of three aspects."[234] First, the God's *locution*—the text as "the authorized words" of God/author; second, the *illocutionary* dimension—"what God *does* in Scripture is testifying, in various ways, to Christ," and; third, the God's *perlocution*—"what happens as a *result* of speaking."[235] The role of the Spirit is equated with God's perlocution, where readers are illumined to act on what has been said or heard. This is to say that "the Spirit convicts us that the Bible contains God's illocutions and enables us to respond to them as we ought."[236] In relationship to biblical interpretation, the Spirit's role can be identified in three areas: convicts the readers to accept the Bible as the human-divine Word of God (i.e., the locution), instills the Bible as commands, promises, etc. to the readers (i.e., the illocution), and persuades the readers to act/perform what the text says (i.e., the perlocution).[237]

Theodramatic interpretation privileges the performed wisdom absorbed in what God said/did and continues to do, especially in the community of faith. It is "*not simply a hermeneutic, a way of dealing with the text, but a way of life; a scripted and spirited performance, a way of wisdom generated and sustained by word and Spirit.*"[238] Yet, the performance in question is expected to be in line with Jesus (i.e., toward "Jesus' own example").[239] It needs to be accompanied by believing and acting on it—and in the local church. This is to affirm that "theology exists to serve the church. Its vocation is to help people think, imagine and understand how all areas of life relate to the God of the gospel made known in the Scripture."[240] It is in that sense believing ought to be "*action-oriented, situation-related*, and embedded in the *particularities and contingencies* of everyday living."[241]

---

[232] Vanhoozer, *The Drama of Doctrine*, 247, 252.

[233] Vanhoozer, *First Theology*, 224; Vanhoozer, *Is There a Meaning?*, 410.

[234] Vanhoozer, *First Theology*, 227.

[235] Vanhoozer, *First Theology*, 227.

[236] Vanhoozer, *First Theology*, 228; Vanhoozer, *Is There a Meaning?*, 410.

[237] Vanhoozer, *Is There a Meaning?*, 413–14.

[238] *Emphasis* in original. Vanhoozer, *The Drama of Doctrine*, 255.

[239] Vanhoozer, *Faith Speaking Understanding*, 18.

[240] Kevin J. Vanhoozer, *Pictures at a Theological Exhibition: Scenes of the Church's Worship, Witness, and Wisdom* (Downers Grove: InterVarsity Press, 2016), 9.

[241] *Emphasis* in original. Vanhoozer, *Faith Speaking Understanding*, 19–20.

It ought to be situated in a context. In addition, it ought to be located in the context of the local church, where "the rule of God breaks into and thus begins to change the world, through the lives of the disciples who have learned to enact God's world in fresh and compelling ways."[242] It should be the location where "the gospel of Jesus Christ gets performed, acted out by disciples who translate it into forms of life, worship, and works of love."[243] Focused on performing what God has said and is communicating, doctrine, as derived from the Scripture, serves the local church. While modern scholars are primarily located in the academy and unable to speak to the church, *theodramatic* reading of the text focuses on edification of the church.

The Canonical Principle

The text in question is the final canonical form of the Bible. It is the canonical principle that helps readers understand that "Scripture is the supreme authority for Christian faith, life and thought, the normative specification of the truth of Jesus Christ."[244] If Christian life is a performed wisdom, it needs something that measures the performance (i.e., the canon). For Vanhoozer, "The canon—the final form of 'Holy Scripture'—is the answer both to the problem to locate authority in the church and to the problem of how to preserve the identity of the gospel in the process of transmitting it."[245] This location of the authority of the Bible in the church validates the conception of biblical interpretation in the church. Canon, in that sense, is a criterion—not just of knowledge but a sapiential criterion.[246] It provides "a means of making judgements about how to speak and act in ways that best conform to Jesus Christ, the wisdom of God."[247] It is also "an instrument of nurture, a means of cultivating (not merely assessing) Christian wisdom."[248] It is not a mere listing of books of the Bible. It is "a measuring or even *divining* rod that enables us to discern what we should say and do today in order to continue and correspond to the way, truth, and life made known in Jesus Christ."[249] As it both measures and guides, canon helps Christian disciples live responsibly. It comprises

---

[242] Vanhoozer, *Faith Speaking Understanding*, xvi.

[243] Vanhoozer, *Faith Speaking Understanding*, 19–20.

[244] Vanhoozer, "Theological Method" in *New Dictionary of Theology*, 902.

[245] Vanhoozer, *The Drama of Doctrine*, 141.

[246] Vanhoozer, *The Drama of Doctrine*, 146; Vanhoozer, "One Rule to Rule them All," 112.

[247] Vanhoozer, *The Drama of Doctrine*, 146.

[248] Vanhoozer, "One Rule to Rule them All," 113.

[249] Kevin J. Vanhoozer, "Forming the Performers: How Christians Can Use Canon Sense to Bring Us to Our (Theodramatic) Senses," *Edification: Journal of the Society for Christian Psychology*, vol. 4.1 (2010): 12.

three elements: authority, interpretation, and community.[250] This constitutes and gathers the community of faith. It is not about what part of the book makes up the Bible, but the final form of it—and how that final text helps in performing wisdom. In addition, it is authoritative as the Bible is "a divine *covenant* document before it is an ecclesial constitution."[251] Vanhoozer states that,

> The canon, a divinely initiated covenant document, is quite unlike other human constitutions. Whereas human constitutions are indeed situated social constructs, Scripture is essentially theo-dramatic discourse whose authority originates not in a corporate will-to-power on the part of Israel or the church but in a *divine will-to-promise.*[252]

Biblical interpretation is not apart from the text, but with the existing Bible canon. This view of Vanhoozer's is somewhat like that of Brevard Childs's, who made a significant contribution to the theological reflection of the Christian Bible. For Childs, the final form of the biblical text that "marks the area in which the modern issues of life and death are defined in terms of what God has done and is doing, and what [God] demands as a response from [God's] people."[253] The canonical text speaks to the situation of the contemporary context; it moves from *description* to *witness* of the subject matter.[254] The canonical context is not limited to extrabiblical literature. Instead, it is the "means by which the readers engage the scriptures, namely an expectation of understanding through the promise of the Spirit."[255] It is through the Spirit that the readers can understand and apply what it teaches.[256] However, unlike Childs, Vanhoozer emphasizes on the performing aspect of the canon. Such use of the Bible can be differentiated from both modern and postmodern.

> Whereas modern biblical studies attended to Israel's religion, the tendency of postmodern theological studies is to attend to what the present church says, thinks, and does . . . But, the Christian canon is more than a chapter in the history of religions. Canonical-linguistic theology insists that the canon is the result of a divine covenantal initiative: canon and covenant are the form and content of the theodrama, respectively.[257]

---

[250] Kevin J. Vanhoozer, *Biblical Authority after Babel: Retrieving the Solas in the Spirit of Mere Protestant Christianity* (Grand Rapids: Brazos, 2016), 127.

[251] Vanhoozer, *The Drama of Doctrine*, 133.

[252] *Emphasis* in original. Vanhoozer, *The Drama of Doctrine*, 134–35.

[253] Brevard S. Childs, *Biblical Theology in Crisis* (Philadelphia: Westminster, 1976), 101–2.

[254] Childs, *Biblical Theology of the Old and New Testaments*, 80.

[255] Childs, *The New Testament as Canon*, 40.

[256] Childs, *Biblical Theology of the Old and New Testaments*, 724.

[257] Vanhoozer, *The Drama of Doctrine*, 146.

It is the covenant that *norms* the divine-human relationship. Similarly, it is the canon that "norms the meaning of the covenant."[258] The canon takes a pivotal role in the economy of redemption. However, as the church once set apart what was said and written by the apostles, it must move from the past to the present with the canon as the guide to the church. Yet, the church must move beyond the Scripture, beyond the written Word. This can be made possible by being faithful to the Spirit and by being attentive to the direction of Scripture.[259] Such emphasis recognizes that a canonical framework is made up of "not only stories but histories, prophecies, parables, and much more."[260] These events as recorded bear witness to who Jesus is (i.e., *the event of Jesus Christ*).[261] If the Word of God bears witness to the events of Christ, biblical interpretation would require a similar responsibility. It calls for ecclesial performance, which in turn requires "handing on performance practice from one generation to the next."[262] This takes us to the question of catholicity—the reading of the Scripture across space and time.

The Catholic Principle

The catholic principle (also "Pentecostal plurality"[263]) helps recognize the contribution of different interpreters in different places and times (i.e., the local and catholic context). This principle allows many readers in different locations (and contexts) to fully appreciate the rich divine/human authorial meaning. Vanhoozer suggests that "The canonic principle keeps us centered; the catholic principle . . . keeps us in bounds."[264] This principle can be better understood when church is seen at two distinct levels: "local and catholic" (i.e., there is "one church, with two aspects").[265] This distinction can be expressed in the following manner: "The one church is both seated in the heavenlies with Christ and located in particular places on earth. Similarly, the local church is wholly the church, but it is not the whole church."[266] If that is applied to contemporary biblical interpretation,

258 Vanhoozer, *The Drama of Doctrine*, 147.

259 See Kevin J. Vanhoozer, "'May We Go Beyond What is Written After all? The Pattern of Theological Authority and the Problem of Doctrinal Development," in *The Enduring Authority of the Christian Scriptures*, ed. D. A. Carson, 2 vols. (Grand Rapids: Eerdmans, 2016), 747–92.

260 Vanhoozer, *The Drama of Doctrine*, 148.

261 Vanhoozer, *The Drama of Doctrine*, 148.

262 Vanhoozer, *The Drama of Doctrine*, 152.

263 Kevin J. Vanhoozer, email message to author, November 23, 2020; Vanhoozer, *Is There a Meaning in the Text*, 419.

264 Vanhoozer, "One Rule to Rule Them All," 116.

265 Vanhoozer, *Biblical Authority After Babel*, 191.

266 Vanhoozer, *Biblical Authority After Babel*, 191.

it means "taking part in a worldwide conversation about how best to understand—to perform—the biblical text."[267] Here, we may ask: What would be the nature of biblical interpretation that takes seriously the catholic sensibility of the text? This question can be answered by considering the role of a pastor/interpreter (i.e., what they can do) in the context of church congregation and the role of *theology* (i.e., what it can do to the congregation and pastor).

The underlying concern addresses "the problem of doctrinal pluralism—*Which system? Whose confession?*—and its effect on the life of the church."[268] It addresses the postmodern problem of answering, "Whose interpretation counts and does not?" It answers the question of "*Whose direction* should the church follow and does any one set of directions provide reliable guidance for the church in each and every cultural situation?"[269] Answers to these questions (problems) can be given under the following categories: pastoral theology, creedal theology, confessional theology, and congregational theology. *First,* the emphasis for pastoral theology recognizes that the church needs direction—to witness Christ. According to Vanhoozer, "While the Holy Spirit is the primary director who oversees the global production, it is the pastor who bears the primary responsibility for overseeing local performance."[270] Pastor as a director is to communicate "to the actors about the meaning of the script and then indirectly through the actors, to the audience about the meaning of the play."[271] They are also responsible "for training the actors, and for getting the actors to work with one another."[272] Most of this communication should come through preaching the Word of God—an obedient act of listening.[273] The goal is to help "the congregation become better actors by helping them learn the script and understand how it should be performed in the present cultural scene."[274] *Second,* creedal theology is "an abbreviated, authorized, and adequate summary of both the biblical witness and the preaching and teaching of the universal church."[275] It serves the church as a guide to proper reading of the Bible. As a confession of the church, it provides "a binding and unifying" direction of the gospel to the local church.[276] It helps them

---

267 Vanhoozer, "One Rule to Rule Them All," 116.
268 Vanhoozer, *The Doctrine of Drama*, 446.
269 Vanhoozer, *The Doctrine of Drama*, 446.
270 Vanhoozer, *The Doctrine of Drama*, 447, 448.
271 Vanhoozer, *The Doctrine of Drama*, 448.
272 Vanhoozer, *The Doctrine of Drama*, 448.
273 Vanhoozer, *The Doctrine of Drama*, 448–49.
274 Vanhoozer, *The Doctrine of Drama*, 449.
275 Vanhoozer, *The Doctrine of Drama*, 449.
276 Vanhoozer, *The Doctrine of Drama*, 450.

retrieve the beliefs and practices of the ancient church and encourages them to do better. Vanhoozer suggests that it is creedal theology that "*direct*[s] *the local church into the way of Scripture and to relate the local church to previous great performances* . . . gives 'catholic direction': direction for understanding and participating in the theo-drama that the 'whole' church accepts."[277] *Third*, confessional theology is useful by way of "*mediating* between the universal (catholic) and particular (local)."[278] It is performed with the wisdom of a particular historical context that carries with it lessons for the church. Confessional theology can be differentiated in the following manner: "While they invariably affirm the ancient creeds, they also respond to further complications and questions concerning the best way to understand the theo-drama in specific cultural and intellectual contexts."[279] Though they are committed to the Bible, confessional theology displays "the signs of the times in which they were framed."[280] It carries with it local interests that are time and context specific. *Fourth*, congregational theology states the understanding that "the local church is fully the church" and "part of a larger church."[281] That means "*each concrete local church bears the responsibility of representing in its space and time the church as a whole.*"[282] As the parts of many make up the whole, the local church contributes to the catholic church. The relationship between the local and the catholic church is as follows: "There is a kind of 'hermeneutical circle' between the whole (*viz.*, the catholic church) conceived through the parts (*viz.*, local churches) that actualize it, and the parts conceived through the wholes—both the smaller 'regional' confessional wholes and the larger catholic whole—that guide them."[283]

This is to suggest that the local church needs to be associated with confessional or creedal theology—to stay faithful to the Christian gospel. At a concrete level, the pastor as assistant director should be "an itinerant preacher, able to move back and forth between the local, the regional, and the universal (catholic)."[284] They should be able to keep up with the time and context, but with a strong foundation of what has gone ahead in the church.

---

277 *Emphasis* in original. Vanhoozer, *The Doctrine of Drama*, 450.

278 Vanhoozer, *The Doctrine of Drama*, 452.

279 Vanhoozer, *The Doctrine of Drama*, 450, 453.

280 Vanhoozer, *The Doctrine of Drama*, 453.

281 Vanhoozer, *The Doctrine of Drama*, 454.

282 *Emphasis* in original. Vanhoozer, *The Doctrine of Drama*, 454.

283 Vanhoozer, *The Doctrine of Drama*, 454.

284 Vanhoozer, *The Doctrine of Drama*, 455.

The Contextual Principle

The contextual principle holds that the Christian faith is not separated from the everyday lives of the people. Instead, the theodramatic approach "encourages disciples to view everyday life as the stage upon which to pursue, and to demonstrate, faith's search for understanding."[285] Its task is to "continue the evangelical action by responding to the prompts of Word and Spirit in culturally appropriate manners."[286] In this case, mission is the operative word (i.e., "disciples are to embody the mind of Christ *here* and *now*, in this particular place and situation").[287] The contextual principle requires the disciple of Christ to develop a sense of improvisation in carrying forward the mission of the gospel. This task may take the form of "fittingness to the biblical text and to the cultural context, fidelity to the biblical language, yet intelligibility to the language of the day."[288] Yet, the task is not without difficulties or without problems. Interpreters must still deal with how theodrama will be played out in different cultural contexts. Here, Vanhoozer argues that:

> The challenge for the company of faith is to perform the *same* drama under radically *different* conditions, the same apostolic design for living in a post-Christendom scene, for there is no *other* gospel than the one associated with the 'one Lord, one faith, one baptism' (Eph 4:5).[289]

This reality calls for a faith seeking understanding in everyday life in different contexts. It would mean attempting to "grasp what is going on in ordinary situations (and why), and attempt to make sense of one's surroundings."[290] It means learning to read not just the biblical text but also the "cultural text and cultural trends."[291] This is a necessity as Christian disciples live in a concrete cultural context striving to find "Christian way through particular times and places, each with their own problems and possibilities."[292] According to Vanhoozer, this attempt to read cultural texts/trends requires a multiperspectival, multilevel, and multidimensional reading.[293] To suggest a multiperspectival reading of culture is to recognize the contribution of other disciplines, including theology; a multilevel reading "brings order in the plurality of possible methodological approaches by arranging hierarchically the various levels of

[285] Vanhoozer, "Theological Method" in *Global Dictionary of Theology*, 896.
[286] Vanhoozer, "Theological Method" in *Global Dictionary of Theology*, 896.
[287] Vanhoozer, *Faith Speaking Understanding*, 198.
[288] Vanhoozer, *Faith Speaking Understanding*, 198.
[289] Vanhoozer, *Faith Speaking Understanding*, 198.
[290] Vanhoozer, "What is Everyday Theology?" in *Everyday Theology*, 16.
[291] Vanhoozer, "What is Everyday Theology?" 16.
[292] Vanhoozer, "What is Everyday Theology?" 16.
[293] Vanhoozer, "What is Everyday Theology?" 45.

complexity that characterize cultural reality," and the multidimensional reading considers a distinct three-dimensional framework—reading "the biblical framework of creation-fall-redemption."[294] The goal is not to ascertain what the ancient writers were saying but to understand "what God is doing in Christ and 'context-sense' that discerns how to bear a creative yet faithful witness to the gospel in particular cultural and intellectual settings far removed from first-century Palestine."[295] If such a task still requires going back to the past, its goal is to bring ascertained meaning in context, primarily the local church context.

Observation and Conclusion

Before we can conclude, an effort will be made to draw out some observations and remarks on Vanhoozer, both pertaining to the task of TIS and of this project. Vanhoozer's theological method is seen as providing a holistic approach to TIS. While situated in the discipline of systematic theology, he acknowledges the contribution of other disciplines (i.e., TIS is considered a "joint responsibility of all theological disciplines").[296] In his view, interaction of theological disciplines is complementary, provided biblical interpretation is understood as theological. This is to suggest that readers with "a theological interest, whether in the academy or the church, will at least seek to go further than describing what *others* have said or thought about God."[297]

Amid the tension of theological disciplines over biblical interpretation, the perception of an interpreter's approach does not take priority over the role of Scripture. While recognizing the place and role of church in biblical interpretation, Vanhoozer does not allow the church or the catholic tradition to take priority over Scripture.[298] He values the theology and practices of the Christian past, but readers ought to have a proper presupposition about the subject matter of the Bible[299] (i.e., the saving work of God in Christ)[300]—and perhaps consider what that means in today's context. Such an interpretative process is guided by the Spirit, illuminating the readers to perform and communicate the text (i.e., live out the text in the day-to-day affairs).

[294] Vanhoozer, "What is Everyday Theology?" 45–48.
[295] Vanhoozer, "Theological Method" in *Global Dictionary of Theology*, 897.
[296] Vanhoozer, "Introduction," 21.
[297] Vanhoozer, "Introduction," 22.
[298] Vanhoozer, *The Drama of Doctrine*, 206.
[299] Vanhoozer, *The Drama of Doctrine*, 203.
[300] Vanhoozer, *Faith Speaking Understanding*, 20–21.

In addition, the core value of the Christian faith is confirmed by the canonical text. For Vanhoozer, the literal sense or the meaning of the text is refined by the canonical sense. The canon serves as the guide to arrive at the meaning of the text. It is not the reconstructed history or extrabiblical sources that shape its meaning. The canonical sense helps the interpreters/readers live out or perform what God said and did—corresponding with the work and person of Jesus. It is because of God's communicative emphasis in the text and canonical sense, Kevin Storer suggests that Vanhoozer's emphasis tends to remain in "a decidedly *past* event."[301] He seems to think that Vanhoozer speaks of God's action in the past tense, and as such, tends to stay there—and not necessarily in the present. However, this critique can be answered by his emphasis on the need to move beyond the text to the everyday lives of the people. He sees the disciples of Christ as living out their faith in their everyday affairs. Christians ought to operate their faith by means of demonstrating what God said and did in Christ—in different contexts and situations. Yet, what can be critiqued is that Vanhoozer still writes from a particular context with its own peculiar concerns and interests. While some of these concerns and issues may be shared with other contexts (e.g., tribal context), his work is still context-bound and time-specific. Though he addresses the need to consider the contextual concerns, this is said only in an implied sense when referred to other contexts. In other words, Vanhoozer speaks from a particular geographical-historical context/background (i.e., a place of privilege, unlike the place of neglect of the tribals). When one writes from a particular context, there is a need to come to terms with what is urgent and relevant to the tribal context in NEI. They still must come to terms with the culture and experience of the people. Interpreters must deal with the historical reality of the context (i.e., the tribal context in the state of oppression, suppression, and marginalization).

Though TIS partly addresses the tension between theological disciplines over biblical interpretation, it is yet to consider the tension between Western and Majority World. This is to say that TIS, as a movement, has shied away from interacting with contextual theology. Considering this reality, this project calls for such interaction in the NEI tribal context, bringing a relevant theological interpretation that is both biblical and contextual.

Taking cue from what might be considered a gap in the discussion of TIS and paying attention to the implied context of Vanhoozer, the next

301 Kevin Storer, "Theological Interpretation and the Spiritual Sense of Scripture: Henri de Lubac's Retrieval of a Christological Hermeneutics of Presence," *JTI* 7.1 (2013): 88.

chapter moves to the discussion of TIS that considers the tribal context in NEI (i.e., the local-tribal confessing community). *This is aimed toward a possible interfacing of TIS and tribal theology in NEI*. Here, it suffices to suggest that preoccupation with the discipline of biblical studies, biblical theology, and systematic theology in the reemergence of TIS is context-specific (i.e., Western scholarship) and time-bound (i.e., modern period). Hence, it is not enough to bring out a distinctive and relevant theological interpretation of Scripture in NEI without addressing and interacting with the concerns of tribal theology. Such a suggestion comes with the recognition of three perceived agendas. First, God's divine action is at work, both in the context of the catholic church and local church. Second, it recognizes that the *context* of the Western scholarship is different and unique, like the Majority World scholarship. Third, it acknowledges that Majority World scholarship brings unique insights in the discussion of TIS. Considering this reality, it will attempt to describe-prescribe a distinctive theological interpretation of Scripture that emerges from interaction with TIS and tribal theology.

What this chapter set out to achieve was to capture the development of TIS, the approaches of TIS, and Vanhoozer's theodrama as an answer to the perceived tension in the contemporary biblical interpretation. In the first part, an attempt was made to historically trace the development of TIS in the twentieth century, showing why retrieval of theology was necessary and favorable. This attempt to retrieve theology is a response to the marginalization of theology in the modern period. As theology is being retrieved, attempts are made to shift the location of interpretation from the academy to the church. The second part captures the approaches adopted by the advocates of TIS, revolving around the disciplines of biblical studies, biblical theology, and systematic theology. This is done showing the attempts to address the tension between theological disciplines over biblical interpretation. This section shows a time-bound and location-specific attempt to recover theology and address the tension of theological disciples over biblical interpretation. While the attempts of these approaches are appreciated, it is limited to the discussion of certain theological disciplines and their prioritized context. The third part looks at the work of Vanhoozer as encouraging attention to more than one context. His theodrama prioritizes the canonical context, encourages Bible reading in the context of the communion of saints, and calls for attention to the present context of the readers. While still limited, his theodrama is seen as helpful to address the tension in the contemporary biblical interpretation.

4

A CONSTRUCTIVE PROPOSAL OF THEOLOGICAL INTERPRETATION OF SCRIPTURE WITH CATHOLIC SENSIBILITY AND CONTEXTUAL SENSITIVITY IN NORTH EAST INDIA TRIBAL CONTEXT

Introduction

As the previous chapter indicated, the current discussions of TIS are preoccupied with the discipline of biblical studies, biblical theology, and systematic theology. As the discussion of TIS is limited to these disciplines, they avoided or neglected interaction with the discipline of contextual theology. On their part, this limitation can be considered valid as TIS is primarily related to retrieving theology because of the dominance of biblical criticism in the modern period—and as the discussion revolves around these disciplines. Hence, when efforts are made to recover theology in contemporary biblical interpretation, it is seen as conventional to limit the conversation to one or more of the above disciplines—perhaps a blind spot on the part of the proponents of TIS.

With the emergence of postmodern interpretation, it challenged the hegemonic position of the modern biblical interpretation. It brought a plurality of interpretative approaches with ideological concerns, along with other theological concerns. As it debunked some of the key claims of the critical approach, it brought a plurality of voices in biblical interpretation based on the location and identity of the readers/interpreters. In such interpretative tasks, there is no "independent standard or universal criteria" to determine the meaning of the text (i.e., there is no "right" or "true" interpretation).[1]

---

1 Vanhoozer, "Introduction," 21.

TIS emerged as a corrective, both to the modern and postmodern biblical interpretation. Part of this effort is an ushering of theology in the church, which was evidently deprived from the community of faith for over two centuries. An effort then is being made to bring back theology into the discussion of biblical interpretation from the academy to the church. The ecclesial setting is seen as the new-old location where TIS can be effectively performed.

While the correction of interfacing theological disciplines is needed in Western scholarship, such interactions may be seen differently in the Majority World. In the Majority World (and perhaps, parts of the West), engagement with *contextual theology* is seen as a necessity as indigenous-distinctive biblical interpretations are being developed. This theological direction comes from the affirmation that "all theology is ultimately 'contextual', that is it arises from a specific historical context and it addresses that context."[2] It also comes from the notion that the particularity of the historical context in the Majority World is different from the West. One can even argue that modern biblical interpretation as perceived or practiced in the West did not run its course in the Majority World, especially in the NEI tribal context.

As liberation theology was emerging in Latin America, similar contextual theologies developed in different parts of the Majority World. The emergence of contextual theologies influenced constructive and practical theology—and contextual interpretation of the Bible. Such a contextual approach (e.g., tribal biblical interpretation) emerged from integrating *tribal theology with tribal biblical interpretation*. Such initiative—like TIS—tries to bridge the gap between the discipline of biblical studies and theological studies. Like TIS, tribal theology is also a recovery of the enchanted worldview with attempts to retrieve tribal culture/heritage of the pre-missionary period.

As a part of such discussion, the current project attempts to contribute to the discussion of TIS: by providing *an entryway to the discussion between theological interpretation of Scripture and tribal theology*. As it engages TIS with tribal theology, it is critical of the tendency to reduce the relevant context to biblical interpretation or theologizing to only one context. What this chapter hopes to do is give some answers to the divide between the church and academia. It also hopes to provide some answers to the tensions between biblical studies and theology, between dominant and voices from the margin, and between different theological disciplines.

---

2 John Parratt, "Introduction" in *An Introduction to Third World Theologies* (Cambridge: CUP, 2004), 2.

Theological Interpretation of Scripture and Contextual (Tribal) Theology: The Stage

This section sets the stage for a constructive proposal of interfacing TIS with tribal theology with canonical sense, catholic sensibility, and contextual sensitivity. The next section attempts to construct an interface of the discipline of biblical theology with context theology (i.e., an interface that results in a constructive theological interpretation of the Bible). The term *interface* is used in dialogue/conversation, both sympathetically and critically. It is sympathetic to the concerns of TIS, but recognizes the neglect to interact with contextual theology. It is critical of the concerns of tribal theology, but affirms their effort to relate with context/culture. In doing so, the effort will be to move the location in the tribal ecclesial setting.

We begin by placing the current project in context: the hegemony of biblical criticism in the Western biblical scholarship and the hegemony of Western biblical scholarship as opposed to the Majority World. The first concern came with the privileging of the original context in biblical interpretation. The emergence and dominance of biblical criticism in the modern period is expressly described in chapter 1. Here, it suffices to suggest that the critical approach resulted in the marginalization of theology in biblical interpretation. More significantly, it caused a divide between academy and church where the concerns of the church or theology are ignored and marginalized. The second concern is evident with the continuing dominance of biblical criticism in the Majority World and continues with the neglect of Majority World biblical scholarship by mainline biblical scholarship.[3] Though biblical criticism did not run its course in NEI, its domineering influence cannot be denied in the Indian seminary, Bible colleges, and divinity schools. According to George Soares-Prabhu, until the late twentieth century, there was no evidence of indigenous or distinctive Indian biblical interpretation.[4] Most, if not all, interpretative efforts within the Indian subcontinent came with the influence of the critical approach. Scholars with Western education and missionary influence continue to operate within the framework of critical approach. It is only with the emergence and influence of Latin American liberation theology that there were emergences of liberation (theologies and) hermeneutics in different parts of Majority World; such discourse came with a sense of rigorousness and a strong emphasis to

---

[3] Tat-Siong Benny Liew, "When Margins Become Common Ground: Questions of and for Biblical Studies" in *Still at the Margins*, 40–55.

[4] Soares-Prabhu, "Interpreting the Bible in India Today," 70.

develop their interpretative "styles and strategies."[5] Such interpretative interests, which surfaced from different parts of the world (i.e., Asians, Africans, African Americans, and Native Americans), were dominated by the Eurocentric modes of interpretation and their inhospitality to their interpretative style.[6] Their interpretative approaches were sidelined or deemed inferior. As such interpretative interests move toward a pluralistic interest, biblical scholars from this part of the world, like the experience of Euro-American feminist biblical scholars,[7] face marginalization by the mainline biblical scholarship.[8] Western scholarship may question or be skeptical of the syncretistic tendencies of the interpretative task of the Majority World scholars, but they also have to answer the question of whether they can learn something from their works (i.e., as part of the catholic church). The question remains valid in terms of whether the dominant voice regards the church or their interpretative task as part of the catholic church.

If such neglect is not acknowledged, then there may be a question or two about the viability of this project: it proposes a constructive interface between TIS (i.e., West in orientation) and tribal theology (i.e., Majority World in orientation). To be truly an interface of two disciplines, two worlds, there is a need to recognize the voice of Majority World. If not, this project may never be launched to its desired/intended task.[9] That said, if the contribution of tribal theology should be acknowledged and received in the church, it should not be done uncritically. It may mean shifting its theological locale: *from academy to the ecclesial setting*. It should also come with an acknowledgement that advocates of TIS have something to say to the church, but with recognition of their neglect of contextual theology.

And we still must consider the nature of the *interface* of TIS and tribal theology. What is the nature of their relationship? Can TIS respond to the sociopolitical concerns of contextual theology? Can contextual theologians adhere to the principle and practice of *sola scriptura*?

---

5 R. S. Sugirtharajah, "Introduction" in *Voices from the Margin*, 1.

6 See, for example, R. S. Sugirtharajah, ed. *Still at the Margins: Biblical Scholarship Fifteen Years after the Voices from the Margin* (London: T&T Clark, 2008).

7 See, for example, D. C. Bass, "Women's Studies and Biblical Studies: An Historical Perspective" *JSOT* vol. 22 (1982): 6–22.

8 Sugirtharajah, "Introduction," 1–2.

9 See, for example, Christopher Rowland and Mark Corner, eds., *Liberating Exegesis: The Challenge of Liberation Theology to Biblical Studies* (London: SPCK, 1989).

Theological Interpretation of Scripture and Contextual Concerns

As indicated in chapter 3, there have been significant attempts in biblical interpretation with renewed theological interests. The following are some of the key features of TIS. First, a major contribution has been made to situate biblical interpretation in the church, instead of the academy. While emphasizing the concerns of the church, attempts are being made to interpret the Bible for/from the church. Second, as proponents of TIS react to the dominance of biblical criticism, there is much productivity in retrieving the pre-modern or precritical interpretation. In pursuit of the original context, critical interpreters neglected *theology*. With attempts to recover theology, TIS is seen as a corrective to the neglect of theology in the modern period. Third, the emergence of the critical approach left a lacuna between the church and the academy. Along with it, there was a division of theological disciplines with the dominance of the critical approach (e.g., biblical studies and dogmatic/systematic theology). As TIS reemerges, the division of theological disciplines are being addressed. This can be seen in the form of constructive interdisciplinary interaction in biblical interpretation.

While TIS makes advancements, several critiques are also being leveled at the TIS movement. These critiques of TIS, both from within and outside, need further consideration. Though reaction to TIS ranges from acceptance to dismissal, there is a need to deal with key critiques that are relevant to our discussion (i.e., the relationship between TIS and tribal theology). On the one hand, proponents of TIS have been attempting to locate the discussion of *theological interpretation* in the ecclesial context. Yet, most, if not all, of the discussions on TIS are still in the academy. Gregg R. Allison suggests that most of the discussions on TIS remain "scholarly and theoretical" (i.e., academy).[10] This is said referring to how there are very few concrete examples of theological interpretation—in practice. John Webster shared a similar opinion, where he suggested, "The most fruitful way of engaging in theological interpretation of Scripture is to do it."[11] He goes on to add that "we do not need much more by way of prolegomena to exegesis; we do need more exegesis."[12] On a certain level, the number of publications of theological commentaries can directly counter the above argument; these publications are directed toward the spiritual and practical needs of the church.

---

10 Gregg R. Allison, "Theological Interpretation of Scripture: An Introduction and Preliminary Evaluation," *SBJT* 14.2 (2010), 32.

11 Webster, "Editorial," 116–17.

12 Webster, "Editorial," 116.

While that may be the case, part of this critique remains valid, keeping in mind that most of the discussions in and around these theological commentaries are also in the academy. For instance, as Jaroslav Pelikan comments on the book of Acts in the *Brazos* commentary series, "in the transition from 'apostolic church' to 'church catholic' the church somehow continued to be 'apostolic,' as well as both 'one' and 'holy.'"[13] This is said with the assumption that the Nicene-Chalcedonian faith will provide an "a posteriori organizing principle for the exegetical task, perhaps above all and in a special way for the Acts of the Apostles."[14] Though the welfare of the church is the goal, the emphasis is still on developing *exegetical principles* to understand Acts. Simply put, most discussions on TIS are still located in the academy (i.e., books, book series, commentaries, or journals), instead of the ecclesial setting. The task remains, in terms of how *what is being said* are taken to the everyday life/experience of the community of faith. A glimpse of such effort is evident in the "Center for Pastor Theologians," where effort is being made to bring "together pastor-theologians dedicated to producing ecclesial theology—a theology born out of the context of the local church, and directed toward the ecclesial community."[15] If TIS ought to take shape in the context of tribal churches in NEI, such concern needs to be addressed. Tribal churches/scholars need to take up the mandate of theologizing for the church (i.e., address the concerns of the church).

While the proponents of TIS are attempting to prioritize the ecclesial location, there seems to be a sense of neglect concerning the role of Scripture in the world (i.e., the world outside the church).[16] The question of how/what the Scripture has to say to the world is not the primary focus. As it focuses on the ecclesial context, its reading of the Bible hopes to correspond with the needs of the ecclesial community. Addressing such neglect, Angus Paddison suggests that TIS has given less priority to "*theological* questions about the Bible's place and ministry in the world, questions derived from attention to God's action in the world and the appropriate postures the church should adopt in response to this determined presence in the world."[17] He argues for developing a healthy relationship between public theology and TIS and tries to ascertain what that may pertain. This critique needs consideration: since TIS privileges reading the Bible in, for, and by the community of faith, it struggles to find its

13 Pelikan, *Acts*, 28.
14 Pelikan, *Acts*, 28.
15 See https://www.pastortheologians.com/history (Accessed June 8, 2020).
16 Watson tried to bring the concerns of TIS with and in acknowledgment of the secular world. Watson, *Text, Church and World*, 236–40.
17 Paddison, "Theological Interpretation and the Bible as Public Text," 177.

place outside the church.[18] This is not just to recognize the authority of Scripture in the public square but to affirm that its reading should result in performing what it says beyond the church. One option is to address the *questions* that have emerged from contextual theology or to engage with the discipline of contextual theology. This is ideal as this is a community that reads the Bible as the Word of God[19] and engages with its sociopolitical context. Recognizing the significance of such a task may take the form of confrontation and acceptance. It remains to be seen in terms of what is *in* such engagement.

Tribal Theology and Theological Concerns

Tribal theologians are on target when they argue for situating in tribal culture/heritage and sociopolitical context. However, as they privilege them, the ecclesial setting is ignored in their theological discussion (see chapter 2). As they privilege the justice concerns, they neglect the discipling aspect of the Christian faith (i.e., the nurturing concerns of the church). This critique of tribal theology can be demonstrated in four areas of focus: *location*, *source*, *norm*, and *context* of tribal theology.

The *location* of tribal theological discussion is in the academy. Until recently, the ecclesial setting was not seen as a part of that discussion. Like biblical criticism, tribal theology is primarily an academic phenomenon. There is a divide between what is discussed and theorized in the academy and what is preached and practiced in the church. While reacting against dominant thinking (i.e., Western mission and its legacy and Indian Christian theology) and their state of oppression/marginalization, they focus on liberating the tribals from the dominant voice. Tribal church is perceived to be captivated by the theology and practice of Western missionaries. While their pursuit of social justice seems to address the concerns of the tribals, their task neglects the concerns of the local-tribal confessing community. Rosiamlian Tochhawng states that the present trend of tribal theology is "too theoretical, having little practical expressions."[20] As tribal theologians are preoccupied with recovering tribal culture/heritage, their theology has little to do with ecclesial experience (i.e., the practical expressions of theology). Moreover, as they formulate tribal theological tasks, it is not so much about church ministry or what the church needs. According to Daniel Tikhir, the tension between tribal theology and tribal church has to do with "the location" of tribal

18 Paddison, "Theological Interpretation and the Bible as Public Text," 176.

19 Vakha, "Jesus Christ in Tribal Theology," 64–81.

20 Rosiamlian Tochhawng, "Tribal Theology: Which Way Forward," in *Search for a New Society*, 56.

theology, i.e., it emerged from the seminaries (i.e., academy) from tribal theologians/scholars, who attempted to develop it from the perspective of "identity and liberation in the context of assimilation, human rights violation, etc."[21] This has to do with tribal theology being a phenomenon of the post-missionary period; the term "post-missionary" refers to the phenomenon *after* the arrival of Christianity or after the tribals in NEI had become Christians. Tribal theology emerged to address the perceived injustice that was prevalent against the tribals from NEI. While fighting for their sociopolitical concerns, the concerns to edify the church were put in the background (if not an afterthought). Such a task is primarily an academic phenomenon with its distinctive emphases—and particularly, with liberation/liberal concerns. In the meantime, the church or evangelistic concerns focus on custodianship or discipleship responsibilities. *This will be the point of disagreement or conflict with the current project.* Rather than retrieving tribal culture/heritage or responding to sociopolitical issues (while these concerns are also important), the current project places the context in the *ecclesial setting*, arguing that the local-tribal confessing community remains in the state of confessing (i.e., they continue to adopt and adapt their faith in different life situations and times since its emergence in the missionary period). It recognizes the historical particularities of the emergence of the tribal confessing community. The ecclesial setting in question places the local church in the context of catholic church. As it locates the discussion of theology in the ecclesial setting, it puts the church in direct confrontation with what tribal theologians are trying to achieve (i.e., the argument that tribal churches are living in the legacy of Western missionaries).

The concerns of *source*, *norm*, and *context* in tribal theology are interconnected. Like TIS, tribal theology is a kind of retrieval effort. It is a retrieval of the enchanted worldview of beliefs and practices before the arrival of Western missionaries. Both share a desire to retrieve, but primarily in the academy. TIS retrieves precritical interpretation, while tribal theology retrieves the tribal culture/heritage. What is required is to move their discussion in the ecclesial setting (i.e., address the needs and concerns of the church).

As tribal theologians retrieve their culture/heritage, they address sociopolitical concerns of the tribals in NEI. On the one hand, the *context* in question is the retrieving of tribal culture/heritage of the past. They use these reconstructed insights of tribal culture/heritage from the pre-missionary period for theologizing. This is an attempt to recapture the enchanted worldview before the arrival of the Christian faith. On the

---

[21] Tikhir, "Tribal Theology Now and Then: A Methodic Appraisal," 9–10.

other hand, they attempt to liberate the tribals from their state of captivity, which exists in the form of oppression, marginalization, etc. While privileging contemporary concerns, the experience of the tribals is not just a *source* of doing theology, but a *norm* for theologizing. Their experience becomes a defining criterion of doing theology. While scriptural authority and the importance of Christian tradition are acknowledged, the experience of the tribals has become the defining criteria of doing theology. It is now that which shapes the thinking about God vis-à-vis the captive experience of the tribal in the contemporary context. The tribal experience is allegedly put in equal standing with the Scripture when theologizing. Their experience in a particular historical period shapes the thinking and theological task of tribal theology. One can suggest that such a privileging of the human experience changes the story (i.e., tribal theological narrative emerges from the sociopolitical experience of the tribal from NEI). This reversal of priority seems to undermine what the church seeks to accomplish (i.e., God's dealing with God's creatures).[22] *This is also an area where the current project differs with tribal theology.* While retrieving tribal culture-heritage is important, making such an experience a norm to do theology is limited: it is limited to a particular tribal community or historical setting. It can be said that all Christian practice is a form of retrieval, but what is being neglected in the discussion of tribal theology is a recovery of Christian doctrine and practice that can help shape contemporary Christians. The current project focuses on retrieving Christian tradition (especially the solas of the Reformation) to reinforce not just the current theological discussion but also to offer answers to the plurality of interpretative/theological tasks. This comes with an emphasis on catholicity as a context to do theology. That means keeping track of the continuity of the confessing community of the Christian faith: from across space and time to the present tribal community (i.e., catholic sensitivity).

Theological Interpretation of Scripture and Contextual Theology: A Constructive Proposal

What the above sections did is to be both sympathetic and critical of the concerns of TIS and tribal theology. While sympathetic to the concerns of TIS, it analyzes and identifies areas of concern that can be further addressed or discussed. As they attempt to locate the discussion of TIS to church, it is observed that most discussions remain in the academy. As they try to address the concerns of the church, there is a tendency to neglect the public concerns or a failure to engage with context theology. While affirming the concerns of tribal theology (i.e., their dealing with

[22] See Vanhoozer, "A Drama of Redemption," 155.

the sociopolitical context), it is critical of its tendency to neglect the ecclesial context. As they retrieve tribal culture/heritage, they address the justice concern of the tribals placing their *experience* both as the *source* and *norm* of doing theology. In doing so, their theological task neglects the Christian tradition (i.e., neglects catholicity as a context of doing theology). This perceived gap would be addressed while engaging TIS with tribal theology.

The above critique suggests the need for the academy to engage with the church (i.e., tribal theology needs to gather to the concerns of the tribal church). This can take the form of bringing contextual sensitivity (i.e., the historical particularity of the emergence of the confessing community). Such a task will involve helping them understand not just what God said and did, but what God is speaking and doing in their current situation. Similarly, the tribal church needs to engage with the academy that deals with the sociopolitical concerns of the tribals. This means defining what this "engagement" involves: it may mean asking what the academy has to offer the church that the church cannot provide for itself (and vice-versa).

It may also mean asking the following question: What does it mean to locate the discussion of TIS in the church? It may mean discussion on TIS within the church, discussion by the church pastors/leaders, or discussion by Christians committed to the church and focusing on the implications for the church. In this case, it means the latter. Such engagement should take the shape of "critique" and "critical appropriation."[23] Tribal theology emerged, partly, as a critique to the continual presence of colonial dominance evident through the legacies of Western missionaries. The tribal church—its theology, along with the church building, hymn, and other ecclesial practices—largely remains a Western construct. They argue that the theology and practices of the tribal churches are alienated from the life of the tribals (i.e., the gospel brought by the Western missionaries failed to engage with the culture of the tribals).[24] Longchar argues that their theology tends to be "otherworldly, anthropocentric, and detached from the soil": their preaching focuses on "the second coming of Christ" (i.e., "otherworldly"), but neglecting "the soil-centered worldview" central to the tribals; while viewing God as absolute and transcendent from the human experience and creation, they talk about doctrine of God detached from creation, and; holding an anthropocentric view of "the salvific work of Christ," they prioritize the saving of human souls and neglected concerns

---

[23] Kevin J. Vanhoozer, email message to author, August 23, 2020.

[24] Longchar, "The Need for Doing Tribal Theology," in *Tribal Theology*, 6; Keitzar, "Tribal Perspective in Biblical Hermeneutics Today," 319–10.

of the world which inculcated dualistic thinking (e.g. between sacred and secular, etc.).[25] In light of such perceptions, tribal theologians argue that the churches in NEI need to engage with the tribal culture/heritage (i.e., its religious tradition, folklore, festivals, songs, dances, sacrifices, observances, and ethics). In doing so, they will address the contemporary concerns of the tribals. This is their *critique* against the tribal churches. This is an area where the tribal churches need to be sensitized (i.e., learn to engage with its sociopolitical concerns).

They carried forward the task of retrieving tribal culture/heritage and responding to social issues with the aim of liberating them from their state of oppression—but also with the hope of developing a distinctive tribal theology. In its earlier discussion, the church and its leaders saw the need to engage with the social change of the time. However, they gradually moved away from such discussions. One of the main reasons is the assumption that tribal theology was syncretizing the Christian faith with tribal tradition or religion. The other concern has to do with how tribal theology became the concerns of the ecumenical/liberals. Such theological pursuit was not found appealing to the church. It was not seen as addressing and meeting the needs of the church. Hence, they moved away from the agendas of tribal theology. Similarly, as tribal theology began to take a distinctive shape, they also avoided interaction with the church (i.e., vice-versa).[26] As the tribal church would suggest, their subject matter primarily became increasingly anthropological (i.e., the experience of the tribals in the contemporary context). As they privileged the human concerns in their theological task, they seemed to sideline the subject matter of the Bible and the Christian tradition. This is the *church's critique* of tribal theology. This is the area where tribal churches can contribute to the NEI theological discussion. It can be done by affirming that "theology is the *application of Scripture*, by persons, *to every area of life*."[27]

The *critical appropriation* can be in the area of experience or situation where the tribal community is learning and adapting to express its faith in Christ. This concern will be articulated in further detail in the later part of this chapter. At this point, it is important to note that "the context in question" is the local-tribal confessing community where local Christians are trying to live out their faith. Such a task recognizes the historical particularity of the emergence of the local-tribal confessing community. It argues that the local-tribal confessing community has been in the state of confessing (i.e., since confessing their faith in Christ, they have

---

25 Longchar, "The Need for Doing Tribal Theology," 6–7.

26 Tochhawng, "Tribal Theology: Which Way Forward," 41.

27 *Emphasis* in original. John M. Fame, *Systematic Theology: An Introduction to Christian Belief* (Phillipsburg: P&R Publishing, 2013), 8.

been adapting/applying their faith in their everyday affairs). It may mean helping the church to recognize the subject matter of the Bible where the kingdom of God is being realized in and through Christ. The subject matter is the message of salvation that recognizes what God is saying and doing in Jesus through the work of the Spirit "to renew minds and to make all things new."[28] If such concern is extended beyond the tribal ecclesial setting, it may mean asking what God is saying/doing in the experience of the tribals (e.g., oppression). What is God saying/doing in their state of oppression, suppression, or marginalization? Such reading of the Bible would affirm the biblical narrative that God suffers as Jesus suffered and walked with the suffering of the people.

The following constructive task will be carried forward at two levels: theoretical and practical. The theoretical level partly addresses the tensions that were described in the previous chapters, considering the concept of history, theology, and context (ideology); the practical level constructs a possible interfacing of biblical theology and contextual theology (i.e., construct a TIS that recognizes canonical sense, catholic sensibility, and contextual sensitivity).

A Constructive Theoretical Framework: History, Theology, and Context

As shown in chapter 1, the tension between biblical studies and theology can be seen as the tension between history and theology: one privileges history in terms of prioritizing the original historical context of the text, while the other privileges theology in terms of what God is speaking and doing in the lives of believers. It can also be seen as the tension between two rival conceptions of history: one that is "flat" (i.e., dismisses divine involvement) and one that has "depth" (i.e., recognizes divine presence and activity).[29] As shown in chapter 2, the tension between the dominant voice and voices from the margin can be seen as the tension between context and theology: it revolves around the question of which "context" should be privileged (i.e., the context of the biblical authors or contexts of the readers). While capturing the discussion of TIS in chapter 3, the importance of canonical context and catholic context is recognized, emphasizing the centrality of Scripture and the performing aspects of the biblical text. Considering this reality, this section explores how the terms history, theology, and context are used (or not used), and suggests how it should be used in NEI.

---

28 Kevin J. Vanhoozer, email message to author, August 23, 2020.

29 Kevin J. Vanhoozer, email message to author, July 7, 2020.

History

The relationship of history and theology has been a tricky issue since modernity: one is privileged, while the latter is neglected in biblical interpretation. Murray A. Rae suggests that the tension between history and theology has been in existence for over two centuries (i.e., unable to bring together).[30] It stems from the understanding that the realm of history is different from that of theology. It comes from a limited understanding of history and theology: history is defined as a record or documentation of events (i.e., related to the things of the human beings), while theology is defined as a study about the subject of God or religion (i.e., related to the things of the divine). This perceived tension has resulted in two camps: one camp privileges history, while the other privileges theology—in theologizing or interpretation.[31] To put it differently, there are two rival conceptions of history at stake: natural history and supernatural history. While recognizing this tension, an argument is made for an integrated understanding of history and theology in biblical interpretation. Such perception means moving away from a critically reconstructed history (i.e., what we know about the natural world) as the framework for reading Scripture. Instead, it means a theological reading of Scripture (i.e., the true story of the world) as the framework to read the biblical narrative. This means understanding the *why* and *how* of history in TIS: Why do we need history in theological interpretation? How do we use history in TIS in the NEI tribal context?

The answer to these questions is given by limiting the discussion in NEI. The first question gives the rationale of why history requires theologizing/interpretation. But the focus here is not pure history (i.e., the discipline of history), but history that helps recognize the presence of the divine and human contribution in Christian history. It primarily refers to,

> Every aspect of lived Christianity—worship, sacraments, daily godliness, private devotion, religiously inspired benevolence, preaching—and every major theme of Christian theology—the nature of God in relation to the world, the meaning of Christ, the character of salvation, the fate of the universe—directly or indirectly involves questions about how the present relates to the past.[32]

It recognizes the involvement of the divine in all aspects of life. More specifically, there is a tendency to relate and connect tribal biblical interpretation with tribal heritage/tradition and sociopolitical situation. As indicated earlier, the context in question is the oppressed state or experience of

---

30 Murray A. Rae, *History and Hermeneutics* (London: T&T Clark, 2005), 5–6.

31 Rae, *History and Hermeneutics*, 30–39.

32 Mark A Noll, "History" in *Dictionary for Theological Interpretation of the Bible*, 295.

the tribals and their search for justice (see chapter 2). Tribal theologians are interested in recovering tribal culture/heritage. To achieve that, they react against the dominant voice (e.g., Western mission and their legacy and Indian Christian theologians) as they develop a distinctive tribal theology or tribal biblical interpretation. Because of this tendency, their priority is to draw inward to its social, economic, or political situations (i.e., geographical *location*) and retrieve from its cultural and religious tradition (i.e., *identity*).

Meanwhile, the catholic understanding of Bible reading is ignored or taken for granted. Biblical interpretation, then, is about what the text means to *me* and *my* tribe—and less about what God is communicating to the contemporary tribal context and the larger Christian community. What is at stake in such discussion is "what the Bible is about, namely, God's actions in the past (e.g., exodus of Israel; resurrection of Jesus)."[33] In tribal biblical interpretation, there is an apparent departure from the "core principle" of Christianity. As history is neglected, it is the *now* aspect of the biblical text that shapes tribal biblical interpretation. In light of such reality, emphasis is being made to reconnect with the Christian traditions (i.e., history). This is to suggest that Christians—whether indigenous or traditional—should not live in isolation but in relationship with other Christian traditions (i.e., across space and time). Further suggestion is made to recognize precritical biblical interpretation to help contemporary readers hear God's Word and help shape their lives.

In addition, we also must deal with how to integrate history in biblical interpretation. We must ask: In a context where Christian tradition is neglected, how do we use history in a theological way (and not necessarily in conflict with it)? Better still, how do we use history in the discussion of TIS in NEI, where theological/interpretative tasks are dominated by modern and tribal biblical interpretation? Such a task would require an understanding of the meaning of history (i.e., what sort of history); it would require taking into consideration the questions surrounding the role of history in theology.

Taking up such mandate may mean asking the questions that Brent A. Strawn raised,

> Do history and theology go together? The prior question, of course, is: *can* they go together at all? Even more pointedly, can they go *together!* Or, is it the case that one must always go first with the other following? And, which would (or should) do which?[34]

Answers to these questions can be put in the following manner. History, in this case, is not seen in an abstract sense. Instead, it refers to

---

33 Kevin J. Vanhoozer, email message to author, July 7, 2020.

34 *Emphasis* in original. Strawn, "Docetism, Kasemann, and Christology," 162.

the events of the past related to the person of Jesus, the early church, the church in NEI, and church-Christianity at large (i.e., the presence of the divine in human history). It refers to the lived Christianity and Christian theology across space and time and how the past relates with the present (and vice versa). The history in question recognizes the Christian tradition as well as God's saving events in the past to which Scripture bears witness. It recognizes the catholicity of the church and its practices, i.e., it encourages the local church to live in "continuity which the church the Creed calls 'one, holy, catholic and apostolic.'"[35] *Such understanding of history is compatible with theology.* Such understanding of history allows a healthy interaction of the present with the past and vice versa. For example, Bible reading before the critical period can inform—reform, transform—the present community of faith. This point will be further discussed in the later part of the chapter. For now, it suffices to suggest that the kind of history or catholicity that is endorsed here is founded on the Bible. If we recall the promise of Jesus in John 16:13, it affirms that "the Spirit of truth" will guide the believers into all the truth: the Spirit will "not speak on his own, but will speak whatever he hears, and he will declare to you the things that are to come." This is to affirm that the Spirit continues to guide the community of faith. If history or catholicity is understood and received in this manner, it should enable the interpreters to look at events where the divine is present and active in human history.

Yet, as shown in chapter 1, critical interpreters shifted the narrative: from the divine narrative of the world to the natural world, from the enchanted to the disenchanted worldview. The result is placing theology like an *afterthought* in Bible interpretation. Consequently, the interface of history and theology is not well received by some proponents of TIS. There are those who reject history or historical criticism. This confusion needs some clarification as well as some direction. The rejection of history, as Charlie Trimm suggests, has to do with the downplaying of "historical criticism."[36] He argues that "While the rejection of the excesses of historical criticism is needed, some TIS interpreters (like some literary interpreters) have gone so far as to ignore history altogether—that is, the historical context of the text."[37] He is of the view that scholars tend to recognize some historical reconstructions more firmly (e.g., the patristic period), while other historical reconstruction may be ignored (e.g., the modern period). What needs recognizing is to see Christian faith as

35 Carl E. Braaten and Robert W. Jenson, eds., *The Catholicity of the Reformation* (Grand Rapids: Eerdmans, 1996), vii.

36 Trimm, "Evangelicals, Theology, and Biblical Interpretation," 318.

37 Trimm, "Evangelicals, Theology, and Biblical Interpretation," 319.

intrinsically connected with history, and not just theology.[38] While this emphasis of the importance of history is well-taken, there seems to be some confusion about what is perceived as *historical criticism* and *history*. The dismissal of historical criticism ought not to be equated with the rejection of history. TIS is critical of historical/biblical criticism and the privileging of the original context, but not necessarily history. It is also critical of the negligence or marginalization of theology in biblical interpretation. However, as proponents of TIS remain critical of biblical/historical criticism, there is a way in which the importance of history can be highlighted. D. A. Carson's recommendation on this matter may be of some help.[39] First, records of past events need not be seen entirely from a naturalistic historical point of view, but may recognize history as accessible by faith. Carson states, "In this sense, Jesus' resurrection *is* a historical event, and is accessible to historians in much the same way that all past events are accessible to historians—through witnesses of various sorts."[40] This is to say that theological facts or "revelatory claims about God" can be implicitly ascertained with historical grounding. Second, the NT writers' use of the OT is "a certain *historical* reading of the earlier biblical documents—and this *historical* reading is determinative for a great deal of *theological* interpretation."[41] While there are several hermeneutical approaches for such reading, the answers lie in reading the text "through the lens of the resurrected Christ" by underscoring "*historical* sequence".[42] This is to suggest that "New Testament readings of the Old Testament Scriptures turn on *historical* distinctions (not least sequence in time to establish continuity and discontinuity) in order to establish *theological* instruction."[43] The task is not just to identify theology of the past (i.e., historical context) but to recognize the theological ramification in the present as well.

The other clarification and direction that is needed is that TIS did not entirely reject the critical approach. While critical of modern interpretation, it did not reject everything about critical approach—but moved beyond them. As TIS privileges theology, they also recognize the contribution of critical tools.[44] While that may be the case, "their analyses do not omit mention of, and often highlight, the ways that the Bible informs and is expounded by the church's teaching."[45] According to Vanhoozer,

---

38 Trimm, "Evangelicals, Theology, and Biblical Interpretation," 319.

39 Carson, "Theological Interpretation of Scripture," 188–92.

40 Carson, "Theological Interpretation of Scripture," 190.

41 *Emphasis* in original. Carson, "Theological Interpretation of Scripture," 190.

42 Carson, "Theological Interpretation of Scripture," 190–91.

43 Carson, "Theological Interpretation of Scripture," 191.

44 Adam et al., *Reading Scripture with the Church*, 10.

45 Adam et al., *Reading Scripture with the Church*, 10.

this employing of critical tools—whether of modern or postmodern method—can be used for theological interpretation. He states,

> On the contrary, modern and postmodern tools and methods may be usefully employed in theological interpretation to the extent that they are oriented to illumining the text rather than something that lay "behind" it (e.g., what actually happened) or "before" it (e.g., the ideological concerns of an interpretative community).[46]

Such statements are helpful not just for its stated goal but to help others understand that TIS is not just about a simplistic interpretation of the Bible. It is instead equipped with critical tools and aims to help readers understand the text, which is hoped to shape them. The interest of this project is to keep the first thing *first* (i.e., "to keep God as our first thought" in biblical interpretation).[47] In that sense, history, if it is important to do theology, should lead in understanding the subject matter of the Bible in each context (in this case, the tribal context). It should provide the contextual sensitivity helping theologians/interpreters to understand the subject matter in a particular place and time with catholic sensibility. TIS of such persuasion, then, can be defined as *a reading of the Bible that seeks to understand the subject matter of the Bible with catholic sensibility and contextual sensitivity*. The catholic sensibility recognizes God's action across history, including the present tribal situation; the contextual sensitivity refers to the historical particularities of the emergence of the local-tribal confessing community in NEI.

Theology

This subsection takes into consideration the kind of theology that shapes TIS. It also considers the nature and role of theological disciplines: What sort of theological discipline (e.g., systematic theology, biblical theology, or contextual theology) should take up the role of TIS? It deals with the question of theology and suggests what it means to do theology—in a way that is biblical, but also contextual—in biblical interpretation.

As demonstrated in chapter 2, theologizing in NEI is done by drawing insights from the tribal culture/heritage; from the discussion of tribal theology, a distinctive tribal biblical interpretation is also being developed. Though it is at its exploratory stage, there are signs of moving toward a pluralistic interest. As tribal biblical interpretation is developing in the twenty-first century, most, if not all, of its interpretative approaches can be categorized as "ideological criticism" or "post-colonial criticism." Their consolidated interest is reading the Bible from the tribal perspective:

46 Vanhoozer, "Introduction" 22.

47 Vanhoozer, *First Theology*, 9.

retrieving tribal culture/heritage and responding to the sociopolitical situation of the tribals. The reading lens is "tribal perspective," and *theological concerns*. As they search for an appropriate method, their concern revolves around this question: What is the lens through which tribal scholars read the Bible? Their search is the kind of reading that suits the tribals and their sociopolitical context. Their concern is reading the Bible that hopes to liberate them from their state of oppression and marginalization. This is their lens: *reading the Bible with sociopolitical interests with the aim to liberate them and give justice*. For example, Zhodi Angami reads Matthew 1–2 by attempting to interact with the tribal context and the context of the text. This is done by taking an "interpretative clue from the tribal political context of military occupation, which is analogous to Matthew's setting of Roman imperial rule," and by taking into account "the tribal experience of being at the margins—socially, politically and academically."[48] The tribal perspective is the state of oppression that came through the military occupation of the Indian central government and the marginalization tribals experience in their day-to-day affairs. The governing interests of these approaches are the liberation concerns (i.e., liberation from oppression, suppression, marginalization, negligence, etc.). In doing so, the concerns of the tribal churches are neglected from the tribal theology and their interpretative tasks. As they privilege tribal experience, theological or spiritual concerns are neglected in their theological-interpretative tasks. While Scripture does recognize certain political concerns, there is a need for a more balanced reading of the text (i.e., with theological concerns).

In the above theological pursuit, there is an evident neglect of the theology or the concerns of the church. However, in this project, the *theology* that is being endorsed is located in the "doctrine of God [that] affects the way we interpret Scripture, while simultaneously acknowledging that our interpretation of Scripture affects our doctrine of God."[49] Vanhoozer calls this the *first theology*: a theology that "*concerns the nature of the relationship between God and Scripture*"[50] and the Word of God and the people of God.[51] Such understanding of the doctrine of God-Scripture (not either/or) is located in viewing the Bible as "a communicative agent, its ultimate author."[52] While recognizing the role of human authors, the communicative acts of the Bible are ascribed to God. The *what* of such theology is "God-centred biblical interpretation" (i.e., a trinitarian approach to biblical interpretation where God is "a triune communicative agent and

48 Angami, *Tribals, Empire and God*, xi.

49 Vanhoozer, *First Theology*, 10.

50 *Emphasis* in original. Vanhoozer, *First Theology*, 30.

51 Kevin J. Vanhoozer, email message to author, November 23, 2020.

52 Vanhoozer, *First Theology*, 34.

Scripture as the written locus of God's communicative action").[53] Biblical interpretation of such pursuit gives way to the creative work of the triune God in the text. The strength of such an interpretative approach is stated in the following manner:

> Its strength lies precisely in its ability to do justice to the many ways God is present and active in the Word: commanding, promising warning, comforting and so on. It also enables us to conceive of an integral unity between God and Scripture, without confusing them and without reducing one to the other. Finally, the notion of divine communication action highlights the importance of entering, via the imagination, into the many ways of seeing and thinking about God, the world and ourselves enacted by the divine Author for our benefit.[54]

The emphasis of such theological interpretation helps readers delve into the text, recognize the divine action, understand the integral relation between God and Scripture—and enter seeing and thinking about God, creation, and humanity (as attested by the biblical text). Such theological approach helps us with a way to look at the theologian as an interpreter. It gives us insights into theologians taking the role of an interpretation of the Bible. The modern approach tended to go back to the original historical context and remain there. The goal of such TIS, even if it means exploring the historical context, is to arrive at what it means today (i.e., what it means to live according to the Word). This means recognizing the effects of divine communicative action as the text is read in "Spirit and in truth."[55] Embracing the text as God's communicative action is to recognize the many ways in which God communicates, and in implication, the many ways of responding to the Word.[56] In terms of everyday experience, it may mean making it clear what the text means by way of teaching, preaching, or writing in different cultural and ecclesial contexts. In terms of practice, it means living out what the Word says (i.e., commands, instructions, promises, and calls for justice). This point can be a point of intersection between tribal biblical and theological interpretation: *an interpretation of the Bible, which calls the readers to perform or live out what it says.* Such intersection can be seen as the direction of God's communicative action, the kind of biblical interpretation that focuses on "a matter of performance knowledge, a matter of doing the Word, of *living*, as well as *looking*, along the text."[57] In other words, to consider the role of theologian as an interpreter of the Bible is much more than collecting information, *it ought to be a lived*

---

53 Vanhoozer, *First Theology*, 38.
54 Vanhoozer, *First Theology*, 39.
55 Vanhoozer, *First Theology*, 39.
56 Vanhoozer, *First Theology*, 39.
57 Vanhoozer, *First Theology*, 39.

performance. This lived performance as emerging from the triune God can be categorized in two levels: "First, there is the material of the theo-drama: God's word-acts from creation to consummation" and "Second, there is script, the *formal* principle of the drama of redemption."[58]

This emphasis takes into consideration the very nature of Scripture (i.e., it is in itself "a revelatory and redemptive word-act of the triune God").[59] If that is the case, there is a sense in which God continues to speak to the created order. Hence, the task of the theologian is to help the readers ascertain that ongoing task: How God is speaking in the *present*, including the tribal context? If this aspect of the ongoing speaking of God is not realized (i.e., if the Word is not "appropriated and acted on"), it will remain dormant. However, if it is acted upon, then it "leads to human flourishing abundant life."[60]

This, again, is not the mere learning of wisdom and performing that wisdom from any said perspective. Instead, the task is to see Christ (i.e., as readers attempt to live according to the text, they are expected to find Christ). It means the goal of interpretation is "a matter of becoming right with God."[61] According to Vanhoozer, "the ultimate purpose of biblical interpretation is to achieve right relationships: with God, with others, and with oneself."[62] And hence, opening possibilities for thinking (and doing something about) social justice. Living according to the Word is to live an orderly life, both with God and others. Part of such a task is to help bring an orderly life by helping people read the text to find and know Christ—and even move beyond it. To talk of first theology as an interpreter is to help others recognize the prospect the Word of God offers to the world, to the readers.

Context

The theology in question also needs to be translated in a *context* (i.e., the local-tribal confessing community). This local context/church "should represent both the catholic church and the cultural context" (i.e., the middle ground between "catholic" and "contextual").[63] So far, the focus of the tribal theologians is the liberation of the tribals from their state of oppression using tribal culture/heritage and responding to sociopolitical concerns—while located in the academy. However, it has failed to interact with the tribal churches and address the concerns of the church. The

58 Vanhoozer, *The Drama of Doctrine*, 176–77.
59 Vanhoozer, *The Drama of Doctrine*, 176–77.
60 Vanhoozer, *First Theology*, 40.
61 Vanhoozer, *First Theology*, 40.
62 Vanhoozer, *First Theology*, 40.
63 Kevin J. Vanhoozer, email message to author, August 23, 2020.

tribal ecclesial setting will be the focus of this section: the emergence of *the local-tribal confessing community* during the missionary period in NEI. For lack of knowledge and expertise, when referring to the historical particularities of the confessing community, it will be in the Tangkhul Naga community. This section contributes to the discussion that biblical interpretation should be local and catholic, like the church it serves.

In regard to the pre-missionary period, scholars of NEI studies (both Western ethnographers and local writers) argue that a sense of common or collective identity (such as, Naga, Khasi, Kuki, Mizo, etc.) was not apparent before the arrival of the colonials/Western missionaries.[64] They see the formation of the collective identity of tribals as a recent construct; the colonial-missionaries gave them the name. The sense of tribal commonality of the pre-missionary period can be narrowed down to common dialect, religious values, social norms, and practices of people living in a particular geographical area.[65] In those days this sense of a collective/ethnic identity was limited to family, clan, or village.[66] While that may be the case, within that social structure (i.e., of family, clan, or village), there was a strong sense of community, even communitarianism, which encouraged and motivated each member of the society to work toward "the common good" of the people.[67] While the selfish goal or desire of individuals were not absent, selfless acts for the benefit of the community was prominent. Their sense of belongingness within the given social structure spread across every facet of their lives. In addition, within this community-oriented society, there was an identifiable belief system or tribal religion (also *primal religion*—but not *animism*).[68] One can suggest that they had a high view of God, who is the creator and sustainer of all created beings. Their God (also *Supreme Being*) is related to human beings and creation through the benevolent spirits—associated with the house, fertility, and ancestor's spirits.[69] Their view of God (or spirituality)

---

64 T.C. Hodson, *The Naga Tribes of Manipur* (London: Macmillan and Co., Limited, 1911), 81; Mashangthei Horam, *Naga Polity* (Delhi: n.p., 1975), 25; S. M. Duby, "Inter-Ethnic Alliance, Tribal Movements and Integration in North-East India," in *Tribal Movements in India*, 4.

65 Downs, "Baptist and Tribal Identity in North East India," 64.

66 Duby, "Inter-Ethnic Alliance, Tribal Movements and Integration in North-East India," 4.

67 Thanzauva, *Theology of Community*, 107–8.

68 See Jonathan H. Thumra, "The Primal Religious Tradition" in *Religious Traditions of India*, ed. P. S. Daniel, David C. Scott, and G. R. Singh (Delhi: ISPCK, 1988), 45–76.

69 Yangkahao Vashum, "Jesus Christ as the Ancestor and Elder Brother: Constructing a Relevant Indigenous/Tribal Christology of North East India," *Journal of Tribal Studies* 13.2 (2008): 27.

is deeply intertwined with their social values and practices (i.e., there was no segregation of secular from sacred).[70] What was a religious/spiritual activity was related to their everyday affairs—primarily, their agricultural lifestyle. It can be argued that there was some sense of confessing community—but without Scripture or redeeming knowledge of Christ. This is to say that their confessing was limited to a belief in *Supreme Being* and appeasing/offering of sacrifice/worship to the malevolent and benevolent spirits/deities.[71] A strong element of this community orientation or community participation in socioreligious activities was carried forward when tribals became Christians (i.e., when they became a confessing community to the subject matter of the Bible).

In the missionary period, the sense of common identity amongst the tribes became more distinguished. The concept of common identity of a group of people—like Nagas, Khasi, Kuki, Mizos, etc.—was further shaped by the coming and influence of the missionaries.[72] Frederick S. Downs offers fours factors that shaped the tribal identity: first, translation of the Bible into the local language provided a marker of representing a group of people, especially within their established mission station; second, the institution of mission schools eventually contributed to bringing the community within a particular region; third, the introduction of "Christian ideology" relevant to all humankind helped shape their conceptual framework; and fourth, the formation of church structures contributed to tribal solidarity.[73] Such Western missionary influences came to the NE region through several missionary efforts. It was initially begun by the Serampore Mission (later merged with the Baptist Missionary Society); it was continued by American Baptist and Welsh Presbyterian Missions; Anglican and Lutheran presence was seen in the form of a few chaplains, primarily for the welfare of their European members; and the Roman Catholics engaged in missionary work in the NE region en route to Tibet (much like the American Baptist of Shah Mission).[74]

Tribal identity then was formatively shaped by the emergence of a distinctive confessing community during the missionary period—which continues to influence the thinking and practice of the tribal community.

---

70 Jonathan H. Thumra, "The Naga Primal (Traditional) Religion and Christianity: A Theological Reflection" in *In Search of Praxis Theology for the Nagas*, ed. V. K. Nuh (Delhi: Regency, 2003), 54.

71 Thumra, "The Primal Religious Tradition," 47–73.

72 Downs, "Baptist and Tribal Identity in North East India," 65.

73 Downs, "Baptist and Tribal Identity in North East India," 65–66.

74 Frederick S. Downs, *History of Christianity in India: North East India in the Nineteenth and Twentieth Centuries*, vol. 5.5 (Bangalore: CHAI, 2003), 65–93.

Within the Tangkhul Nagas, the birth of a confessing community can be located with the baptism of twelve people in the year of 1901.[75] This baptism event and the birth of the church[76] in the following year marked their faith in Christ—as it also provided a historical particularity of the emergence of the confessing community. It marked the bringing of the triune understanding of God: the redeeming act of God in Jesus and through the work of the Holy Spirit. The message of the Bible within the Tangkhul community was reinforced by a vision that was seen by the headman of the Hunphun village, three hundred years before the arrival of the missionary. In the vision the headman saw a certain white man telling him that "he was coming to give them light, and when the people receive the light, the leaves of the trees will speak and their day-to-day needs will be met from their pockets."[77] This vision helped the community receive the gospel. It helped them identify with the coming of the messiah that was foretold in Isaiah. It also helped them see the missionary (i.e., William Pettigrew) as "a real messenger of God to give light to the people in darkness."[78]

However, in the post-missionary period, some informed tribal theologians/scholars saw the confessing community as either too Western or missing contextual relevance. The local-tribal confessing community was not seen as rooted in the culture and worldview of the tribals. Instead, they were seen as living in the legacy of the Western missionaries. For our purposes and clarity, we will narrow down the tribal theological discussion to the doctrine of Christ (Christology) and church (ecclesiology). As they were attempting to indigenize Christian thinking, they sought answers from the tribal culture/heritage. For instance, as they searched for an indigenized understanding of Christ, L. H. Lalpekhlua argues for contextualization of the concept of *pasaltha*, referring to "a person who was regarded as an exemplary character, or a model for perceiving the meaning of a true human being."[79] Such theologizing was done with the assumption that the gospel must be received in and through the tribal perspective. This is to suggest that the message of Christ must be "incarnated in the culture of the tribal people."[80] He argues

[75] Y. K. Shimray, "William Pettigrew and The Hill People" in *Rev. William Pettigrew (A Pioneer Missionary of Manipur)* (Imphal: Fraternal Green Cross, 1996), 15.

[76] Yuimirin Kapai, "William Pettigrew: Mythicizing the Man and His Work," *International Bulletin of Mission Research* 43.4 (2019): 358–67.

[77] K. Prongo, "The Coming of Rev. William Pettigrew Foretold," 5.

[78] Prongo, "The Coming of Rev. William Pettigrew Foretold," 6.

[79] This book claims to be the first contextual effort on Christology from the tribal perspective. Lalpekhlua, *Contextual Christology*, 164.

[80] Lalpekhlua, *Contextual Christology*, 201.

for contextualization of Jesus as "a *pasaltha* who bravely fights unto death against the powers of evil that divide and oppress human beings and the world;" a *pasaltha-tlawmngai* as someone who selflessly was "born into the world and lived in the world for other," and to perceive the resurrection of Jesus Christ as "God's response to the person and works of Jesus and God's exaltation of him as the *Pasaltha-tlawmngai.*"[81] Lalpekhlua made further attempts to connect the kingdom of God by associating it with the communitarian society of the tribals. He sees *the kingdom of God* as resonating with the communitarian experience of the tribals and exhibiting "the qualities of life nurtured by *pasaltha* and *tlawmngaihna*."[82] This is done by connecting Jesus's message and activities with the tribal communitarian society (in this case, Mizo)—"a society in which people, along with other creature[s] and God, live together in close relationship with one another as a family."[83]

Such theologizing, while it has its benefits for the concerned tribe, is limited. First, it is limited to its conceptualization. We need a Savior, and not a moral exemplar. A complete picture of such conceptualization (i.e., example) cannot be found in any other tribe. Second, it is limited to a particular tribe. This limitation is also acknowledged by Lalpekhlua.[84] However, what has not been acknowledged is that, in such theological attempts, conceptual contextualization may not be found in other tribal communities. It cannot be transferred to other tribes, less beyond the NEI region (i.e., it lacks catholic sensibility). Moreover, what is unexplored in Lalpekhlua's work is that through the death of Jesus on the cross, "there is reconciliation in Jesus Christ, a 'new humanity' that breaks down ethnic (and presumably tribal) barriers."[85]

A similar effort is seen in developing contextualized ecclesiology. K. Thanzauva argues for the use of "community home," a form of social institution or dormitory meant for the security of the village, training of young men, recreation (fellowship), and discussing topics/issues.[86] Community home was an important aspect of the tribal community life. With the coming of Christianity—specifically, with the founding of the church building—the practice and tradition of community homes began to fade. The physical form of community home is no longer in existence. Nonetheless, Thanzauva argues, "the form or spirit of a community home

---

81 Lalpekhlua, *Contextual Christology*, 204–29.
82 Lalpekhlua, *Contextual Christology*, 229.
83 Lalpekhlua, *Contextual Christology*, 230.
84 Lalpekhlua, *Contextual Christology*, 203.
85 Kevin J. Vanhoozer, email message to author, August 23, 2020.
86 Thanzauva, *Theology of Community*, 134, 137.

was transformed into the Christian church and the educational hostels."[87] Though some essential features of community homes were lost, it needs to be recovered in the contemporary church. It can be in areas where the tribal churches are unable to add to or supersede the traditional form of community home. The recovery can be seen in how community homes helped build "the harmony, welfare and peace of the village community," which the current structure has failed to do because of its diverse denominational presence.[88] It holds the prospect of building a bridge to bring together nonbelieving tribals and Christian tribals. It assumes that the current tribal churches can be informed by practices and values that existed before Christianity. It also assumes that the tribal church is incomplete or unable to fulfill its task as a church. While such conception may be found in most of the tribes, it misses out on seeing Christ as a figure who mediates on behalf of humanity and the world. Moreover, on a practical front, it triggers some issues—primarily exclusion of other groups of people—in the practice of the Lord's Supper, which embraces "the people of God in all contexts (i.e., it is catholic)."[89]

Taking such critique into consideration, R. Zolawma attempts to integrate early Christian tradition with the tribal (Mizo) tradition using the concept of *zawlbuk*, the Mizo community home.[90] With insights from a select early Christian tradition, the author argues that Christianity has engaged with the local cultures, both shaping and influencing their thinking. He argues that the early church attempted to contextualize "the Christian message and communities amongst non-Jews."[91] In addition to the principle of community (*zawlbk*), Zolawma argues for the incorporation of *thawmngaihna* (i.e., community ethics): a concept that places "community over the self wherein self sacrifice for the needs of others was to come in spontaneously as a natural part of one's life" and the practice of egalitarian principle where people are treated equally with respect and dignity.[92] When these views are integrated with the early Christian tradition, it means incorporating the principle of self-sacrifice with the *kenosis* of Christ, an integration of the *koinonia* with the egalitarian principle of the tribal community, and advocating the tribal common house or *zawlbuk* church as "a communion of local Christian community that embraces all groups of people who follow Jesus Christ."[93] While it is ultimately

87 Thanzauva, *Theology of Community*, 140.
88 Thanzauva, *Theology of Community*, 141–42.
89 Kevin J. Vanhoozer, email message to author, August 23, 2020.
90 Zolawma, *Tribal Ecclesiology*, 259–68.
91 Zolawma, *Tribal Ecclesiology*, 230.
92 Zolawma, *Tribal Ecclesiology*, 106, 113, 117–31, 132–37
93 Zolawma, *Tribal Ecclesiology*, 259–68.

about the communion of the saints, it is more than "a matter of morality or (human) community."[94] It is a matter of the new humanity formed in Christ through the Spirit.

Theologizing is done by searching for concepts which were in practice before the arrival of the Western missionaries. However, theologizing through models or concepts can be limiting (i.e., it misses "the riches and complexity of the divine-human relationship").[95] While privileging the recovery of tribal culture/heritage, there is a sense of absence of Scripture—and in implication, a sense of neglect of the teachings associated with it. Such theologizing is done from a context where tribal theologians are increasingly becoming critical and skeptical of the colonial past and its continuing legacy—and indirectly, critical of the contemporary tribal church. The other concern has to do with how the privileging of tribal culture/heritage is seen as a norm to do theology, especially in the academy. However, such theological process is being imposed on the confessing community or church—which privileges the Scripture and its teachings and practices. The academic tribal theologizing tends to miss the contemporary concerns of the tribal church. Though they assume that the tribal churches are living in the legacy of the Western missionaries, in a sense, they have been adapting. This is to argue that the confessing community has been adapting since its emergence in the late twentieth century (or the early twenty-first century). This is also to argue that the confessing community is not passive, but it remains active responding to the situations of the church (i.e., remaining in the state of confessing).[96] John Webster argues that,

> Confession is a permanently occurring event; the church never reaches a point where the act of obedient confession can be put behind it as something which has been made, and which can be replaced by a text which will become the icon of the church as a confessing community.[97]

This confessing of the Christian faith is not a one-time event, rather, it is in continuation. Before it is a *document*, it is an "*act* or *event*."[98] This is to suggest that the tribal church continued to confess their faith in the triune God, long after the Western missionaries left the NEI region. They continue to confess their faith in the triune God in their own words and

---

94 Kavin J. Vanhoozer, email message to author, August 23, 2020.

95 Cf. Sallie McFague, *Metaphorical Theology: Models of God in Religious Language* (Philadelphia: Fortress, 1982), 144.

96 Otto Weber, *Foundations of Dogmatics,* trans and annotated by Darrell L. Guder, vol. 1 (Grand Rapids: Eerdmans, 1983), 21.

97 John Webster, *Confessing God: Essays in Christian Dogmatic II* (London: T&T Clark, 2005), 73.

98 Webster, *Confessing God*, 73.

in their day-to-day experience. Webster argues that the confessing event "*originates in revelation*," is "*responsive, not a spontaneous act*," and is "*an episode in the conflict between God and sin which is at the center of the drama of salvation.*"[99] The confessing community continues to receive what God is saying and doing through the Word of God, and they continue to respond or obey God's direction through the Spirit in different life situations. While some aspects of the Western missionaries were carried forward,[100] it cannot be denied that the tribal church continues to obey God's direction within the lives of the community (and beyond).

Along with the newfound faith in the triune God, Scripture now constitutes the confessing community. It is not just the source of doing theology but also the authority of preaching and practice in the church. One can argue that there was a shift from traditional religion to Christian faith. According to Thanzauva and Hnuni, the Bible became "a propositional truth about God and human" through Jesus and about how life is "supernaturally communicated to human beings by the Holy Spirit."[101] On a broader scheme of things, the tribals were able to transfer their high view of the *Supreme Being* to the God of the Bible. For them, the Scripture "became an important factor for the emergence of a new tribal identity."[102] In other words, it became a guide to the tribal churches as they adapt to new situations and circumstances. The confessional community is also constituted by the rich church tradition brought by the Western missionaries: seen constructively, it refers to the catholicity of the Christian faith; seen negatively, it refers to the introduction of plurality of Christian denominations. This is to suggest the following: while a part of this church tradition came with the recognition of divine presence across history, it also came with the plurality of denominations—*and it is this aspect of the Western mission that the tribal theologians are critical of.* As there are disadvantages, the advantage is that these rich church traditions are helping the tribal church come to terms in relationship with other groups of people and churches, both inside and beyond the tribal community.

A Constructive Theological Proposal: Biblical Theology and Contextual Theology

While setting the stage for a constructive interface of TIS and tribal theology, the above subsections suggest how the terms history, theology,

[99] *Emphasis* in original. Webster, *Confessing God*, 72–73.

[100] See, for example, William Pettigrew, *Jesuwui Lā: Hymns in Tāngkhul Naga* (Assam: ABMH, 1907).

[101] Thanzauva and Hnuni, "Ethnicity, Identity and Hermeneutics," 346.

[102] Thanzauva and Hnuni, "Ethnicity, Identity and Hermeneutics," 346.

and context should be used in theological interpretation in NEI. While pointing out the limited view of these terms or of its neglect, it suggests that Christian tradition should be remembered, recall God events that Scripture bears witness, and emphasizes the need to address the concerns of the church. While recognizing history as indispensable to theology, it is used as that which recognizes divine involvement or God's saving events that the Scripture bears witness; theology is that which concerns the relationship between God and Scripture and the Word of God and the confessing community, and while locating the theological discussion in the ecclesial setting (instead of the academic setting), the context recognizes the historical particularities of the emergence of the local-tribal confessing community.

Having set the stage, the current section proposes a constructive interface of the theological discipline of *biblical theology* and *contextual theology* that can result in theological interpretation of Scripture in NEI. The biblical theology in question can be seen as a combination of a redemptive model that recognizes canonical sense and constructive theology.[103] It refers to a theology of the Bible which concerns the relationship between God and Scripture and the Word of God and the community of faith. This is a renewed understanding of biblical theology used synonymously with TIS; this is the kind of biblical theology that is seen as complementary to the discipline of systematic theology (and not opposed to it). Part of this task is to address the tension between theological disciplines (i.e., between biblical studies, biblical theology, and systematic theology) by suggesting that interfacing of biblical theology with contextual theology can result in a constructive theological interpretation of the Bible. While the task at hand does not undermine the contribution from other theological disciplines (e.g., between biblical theology and systematic theology), it argues for a possible contribution from theological discipline that is conducive to the tribal community (i.e., contextually sensitive): a theological interpretation of Scripture that emerges from the interface of biblical theology and tribal theology. Yet, as suggested, the context in question is not the recovery of tribal culture/heritage or responding to sociopolitical issues but recognizing the confessing community as a context to do theology—and consequently, suggesting how contextual theology can be done in and from the church in NEI. The former contexts miss out on ecclesial needs and concerns of the tribals, while the latter context helps the tribal church to do theology constructively or perform the biblical text in the church and in their day-to-day affairs.

---

[103] This is an adaptation of a redemptive model, canonical approach, and theological construction. King III and Lockett, *Understanding Biblical Theology*, 22–25.

Biblical Studies/Theology and Contextual Theology

Before modernity, the Bible was not the sole property of the modern academy. The task of interpretation was carried forward by priests and laypersons, and not necessarily solely by professional biblical scholars. However, with the dominance of biblical criticism, biblical interpretation became the task of biblical scholars, especially in the academy. Interpreters outside the discipline of biblical studies (i.e., outside academia) are required to cross-check their work with the works of critical interpreters before they can arrive at their results. However, with the reemergence of TIS in the recent past, theology is reentering the discussion of biblical interpretation. Similarly, with the arrival of postmodernism (see chapter 1), some biblical scholars are engaging in the task of biblical interpretation with certain sociotheological assumptions (e.g., liberation theology, tribal biblical interpretation, etc.). Such discussion, while distinct from TIS movement, can be categorized as an interaction between biblical studies and contextual theology. In the latter part of the twentieth century, such tasks were carried out productively, both individually and corporately.

Relevant to our discussion is Norman K. Gottwald's *The Tribes of Yahweh*, which posed a challenge to traditional biblical scholarship (i.e., critical approach).[104] While employing a social critical study of the Bible, it opened pathways to several sociological readings of the Bible. *The Tribes of Yahweh* represents an integration of "biblical history and biblical sociology," which is an attempt to integrate biblical studies with social scientific studies.[105] Similar to the task of liberation theology, Gottwald integrates social theory in the area of biblical studies. As he relied on social theorists (such as Émile Durkheim and Max Weber), he positioned his theoretical framework in Marxism.[106] While he recognizes the difference between sociological and historical methods, he uses them in a compatible manner.[107] He saw the sociological method as inclusive of "all the methods of inquiry proper to the social science and aims at grasping the typical patterns of human relations in their structure and function," while the historical method was seen as "embracing all the methods of inquiry from the humanities, with the aim of grasping the sequential articulation of

---

104 Norman K. Gottwald, *The Tribes of Yahweh: A Sociology of Religion of Liberated Israel, 1250–1050 BCE* (Maryknoll: Orbis, 1979).

105 Gottwald, *The Tribes of Yahweh*, 4–7.

106 Roland Boer, "Introduction: On Re-reading *The Tribes of Yahweh*," in *Tracking the Tribes of Yahweh: On the Trail of a Classic*, ed. Roland Boer (London: Sheffield, 2002), 2.

107 Norman K. Gottwald, "Sociological Method in the Study of Ancient Israel" in *Encounter with the Text: Form and History in the Hebrew Bible*, ed. M.J. Buss (Philadelphia: Fortress, 1979), 69.

Israel's experience as reflected in its literature and religion."[108] Though this may be seen as a shift from historical criticism, the sociological approach relies on literary, historical, and archaeological sources. Scholars continue to recognize the relevance of *Tribes* in contemporary biblical studies with sociological and anthropological emphases.[109] Boer states,

> A book like *Tribes* has in many ways enabled the kind of critical work we do now. It is, then, an eye-opening experience to read *Tribes,* patiently for the first, second or third time, and witness this very process at work. For *Tribes* is very much *our* text, one that is a key player in contemporary debates.[110]

This recognition can be seen in two areas: on the one hand, there is a connection "between detailed, scholarly and informed analysis," and on the other, the connection is seen with "a distinct political passion" (i.e., liberation concerns).[111] *Tribes* worked as it encouraged attention to the reader's context that has been taken for granted by the modern critical approach. It also worked in a sense that the reader's context is seen as a contributing factor in constructing the meaning of the text. While that may be the case, the critical-analytical emphasis is primarily located in the academy (along with humanities studies in the universities), and the political interest is channeled toward sociopolitical concerns of the contemporary context. To put it differently, it still neglects the ecclesial context as a location to do theology or interpretation. While it pays attention to the readers, the ecclesial concerns are still neglected.

However, what can be seen as directly related to the experience of the oppressed or marginalized is the integration of social theory and theology. In the mid-twentieth century, liberation theology emerged in Latin America (along with parallel movements in the Majority World), where "experiences of oppression, vulnerability or marginalization have led to a sustained reflection on Christian tradition."[112] Liberation theology is seen as a form of theologizing/interpretation where social concern, text, and tradition are brought into dialogue with each other. Liberation theology,

---

[108] Walter R. Wifall, "The Tribes of Yahweh: A Synchronic Study with a Diachronic Title," *Zeitschrift für die alttestamentliche Wissenschaft* 95.2 (1983): 198.

[109] See also Frank S. Frick, "Norman Gottwald's *The Tribes of Yahweh* in the Context of 'Second-Wave' Social-Scientific Biblical Criticism" in *Tracking the Tribes of Yahweh*, 17–34.

[110] *Emphasis* in original. Boer, "Introduction: On Re-reading *The Tribes of Yahweh*," 5.

[111] Boer, "Introduction: On Re-reading *The Tribes of Yahweh*," 4.

[112] Christopher Rowland, ed. *The Cambridge Companion to Liberation Theology* (Cambridge: CUP, 1999), xiii.

in this case, is a form of theologizing or interpretation where the present context, or the world "in front" of the text, is taken into account. It "emerged as the result of the actions of committed Christians in social and political struggles, as well as the consequences for the pastoral ministry of such commitments."[113]

Specific to our interest is *Liberating Exegesis*, where an attempt was made to integrate biblical studies with liberation theology. The contributors tried to establish a threefold task: first, they offered a sample of biblical interpretation that emerged out of liberation concerns; second, they attempted to ascertain the impact of biblical interpretation with liberation concerns to the dominant interpretation of the Bible, especially the North American and European churches and academics; and the contributors sought to keep liberation theology in the context of the poor, not dismissed as just another theology that was once relevant in the academic debate.[114] The underlying argument of *Liberating Exegesis* is the assumption that the claimed objectivity of historical criticism is unattainable. Moreover, in response to the hegemony of historical criticism, Christopher Rowland and Mark Corner attempt to bring to light the interpretative approach that emerges with the influence of liberation theology. This project can be seen as an attempt by both Western and Majority World scholars to integrate the interpretative approach from the margin with the dominant voice. They argue that attention must be given to the present interpretative community; they argue for liberation interpretation that focuses on the "grassroots" interpretation, and they take into consideration the critique of liberation theology into their context, arguing to reconsider the dominant pastoral practices and their understanding of the Christian tradition.[115] Rowland and Corner argue that,

> Liberation exegesis is as appropriate to a First World as to a [Majority] World context. It is a method which sets out to awaken the exegete to the context of his or her reading of the Bible, and this by definition applies to all contexts and not simply to the ones within which the theology of liberation initially emerged.[116]

While liberation theology has been dismissed by many, there are some who argue that "liberation theology and its exegesis is as relevant—in some ways more relevant—to the rich nations as to the poor ones, and

[113] Pablo R. Andiñach and Alejandro F. Botta, "Introduction: The Bible and the Hermeneutics of Liberation: Worldwide Trends and Prospects" in *The Bible and The Hermeneutics of Liberation*, ed. Pablo R. Andiñach and Alejandro F. Botta (Atlanta: SBL, 2009), 2.

[114] Rowland and Corner, *Liberating Exegesis*, 2–3.

[115] Rowland and Corner, *Liberating Exegesis*, 32, 53.

[116] Rowland and Corner, *Liberating Exegesis*, 53.

also that it exists within a framework that is recognizable as traditionally Christian."[117] Such a task is seen as part of the ongoing evangelicals' attempts to come to terms with liberation theology. By the mid-1970s,[118] liberation theology had made significant advancements in Latin America and motivated other nations to develop similar theologies or interpretative tasks.[119] According to Samuel Escobar, "Though there had been antecedents of [liberation] theology in the Protestant circles of Church and Society in Latin America (ISAL), it was basically a Roman Catholic phenomenon."[120] This new theological pursuit redirected the source of theologizing to Scripture; while making abundant use of the Scripture, a new hermeneutical approach was proposed and practiced. However, since this new theological pursuit was predominantly within the Roman Catholic church, it invited response from the evangelicals.[121] A glimpse of this evangelical response suggests that liberation theology takes a threefold direction. The first direction offers a critical reading of the Catholic Church in light of colonialism and neocolonialism, the second gives a new direction of Bible reading where the concerns of the poor are taken into account, and the third direction takes into consideration what it means to be a Christian—the praxis aspect of faith—in Latin America.[122] Rowland and Corner's *Liberating Exegesis* can be seen as an attempt to give a new direction in the reading of the Bible in the West with liberation concerns.

While their task is seen as urgent, some saw their work as unsuccessful (i.e., it did not receive a constructive response from the West like they hoped for). Max Turner and Joel B. Green suggest it was unable to "(1) understand individual books theologically in their ancient context and (2) be able to interpret them competently into the theological contexts of the turn of the twenty-first century."[123] Their suggestion was to understand

117 Rowland and Corner, *Liberating Exegesis*, 53.

118 See, for example, Gustavo Gutierrez, *A Theology of Liberation: History, Politics and Salvation*, trans. and ed. Caridad Inda and John Eagleson (Maryknoll: Orbis, 1973).

119 Samuel Escobar, "Doing Theology on Christ's Road" in *Global Theology in Evangelical Perspective: Exploring the Contextual Nature of Theology and Mission*, ed. Jeffrey P. Greenman and Gene L. Green (Downers Grove: IVP, 2012), 67–85.

120 Escobar, "Doing Theology on Christ's Road," 76.

121 See, for example, J. A. Kirk, *Liberation Theology: An Evangelical View from the Third World* (Atlanta: John Knox, 1979); E. A. Nunez and W. D. Tayler, *Crisis in Latin America: An Evangelical Perspective* (Chicago: Moody, 1989); A. F. McGovern, *Liberation Theology and its Critics: Toward an Assessment* (Maryknoll: Orbis, 1989).

122 Escobar, "Doing Theology on Christ's Road," 77–78.

123 Max Turner and Joel B. Green, "New Testament Commentary and Systematic Theology: Strangers or Friends?" in *Between Two Horizons*, 3.

the ancient book theologically and also bring theological concerns (i.e., the concerns of the interpretative community) into the area of biblical interpretation. But as opposed to modern interpretation, biblical interpretation with liberation concerns is vying for an interpretation that speaks with and to the contemporary concerns (i.e., the location and identity of the readers/interpreters). Their theological task can be seen as preoccupying with only one concern or context. As they focus on the liberation concerns of the poor or the marginalized, the experience of the readers/interpretative community was prioritized. However, as Turner and Green pointed out, the theological concerns (i.e., what was seen as dogmatic) of the text are neglected, if not ignored. As they prioritize the concerns/context of the interpretative community (i.e., the present readers), the divine-human relationship appears to be ignored in their interpretative task.

Biblical interpretation with sociopolitical concerns in this part of the world (i.e., Majority World) and the West are taking manifold directions.[124] There is much productivity in the area of integration of social analysis and theology. Such productivity of interpretative interests in NEI, if not the same in all parts of the world, is analytically described in chapter 2. A closer look at tribal biblical interpretation will suggest that there is an integration of biblical studies and contextual theology. Their focus is to do biblical or theological interpretation by engaging with tribal heritage and sociopolitical context (i.e., limited to the struggles and experience of the readers/interpreters). In the search for contextual interests/concerns, tribal theology privileges the *tribal culture-heritage*, which functions as both source and norm of doing theology. Moreover, aiming for relevance in their theological engagement, they engage with contemporary issues of the tribals (i.e., sociopolitical situations that the tribals are facing). However, more recently, with the emergence of tribal biblical interpretation, there is a lot of borrowing of the interpretative approaches from the West, which can be categorized under ideological criticism or postcolonial criticism (see chapter 2). These interpretative approaches can be critiqued with a twofold concern. First, while the proponents of tribal biblical interpretation claim their interpretative task to be indigenous or distinctively tribal, their task is carried forward by way of borrowing methodology or approaches from the Western academy (i.e., not very different from the postmodern interpretation in the West). Such borrowing is not the only concern, but it is the claim of such interpretation. How indigenous is an interpretative task when its methodology is borrowed

[124] See, for example, Pablo R. Andiñach and Alejandro F. Botta, eds., *The Bible and The Hermeneutics of Liberation* (Atlanta: SBL, 2009).

from the Western academy? The result of such interpretation could not be distinctively indigenous or tribal. Whether it is acknowledged or not, there is already an interface of the West and the Majority World in the NEI theological discussion. In the tribal biblical interpretation, there is an engagement of two or more interpretative tasks—and from more than one region or geographical location. This is to suggest that any claims of biblical/theological interpretation could not be achieved without interaction with other Christian communities or traditions. Second, whether in conceptualization or methodology of tribal biblical interpretation, the dichotomy between the academy and the church is becoming increasingly evident. Their attempt to arrive at a distinctive or new tribal hermeneutical approach revolves around academia (i.e., within ecumenical or liberal colleges/universities). On the one hand, in addition to their failure to engage with the Church, evangelicals or theological colleges with evangelical emphases are not considered part of the conversation of tribal theology or tribal biblical interpretation.[125] On the other hand, in response to the increasing pressure on the church by the liberals, South Asian evangelicals are attempting to do theology by being rooted in the Bible and relevant to its context (i.e., the present context).[126] Such a response also reminds the evangelicals of the need to respond to the social issues that the church members are facing in their everyday affairs. While a part of this project recognizes the need to respond to such urgency, the other part also observes that evangelicals struggle to engage with the discussion of tribal theology and tribal biblical interpretation. If they do, they tend to speak dismissively of tribal theology, and they fail to constructively engage with tribal theology. They are yet to come to terms with what it means for the tribal church to do theology that is scripturally founded and contextually relevant.

These two concerns/critiques take us to the next section. If there should be interfacing of the West and the Majority World in biblical interpretation, what would that look like? If the Church should engage with tribal theologians (i.e., academy) or vice versa, what would be the shape of such theological construction?

Biblical Theology and Contextual Theology

This subsection is constructed in a threefold manner. The first part identifies with traditional evangelical use and understanding of biblical theology and contextual theology—and moves beyond them; the

125 Thomas, *Evangelising the Nation*, 185–86.

126 See, for example, Timoteo D. Gener and Stephen T. Pardue, eds., *Asian Christian Theology: Evangelical Perspective* (Cumbria: LGL, 2019).

second part further points out the areas of interface between TIS and tribal theology/biblical interpretation; and the third part constructs how a *multi-contextual biblical-theological interpretation of Scripture* is employed in the NEI tribal context.

The relationship between the discipline of biblical theology and contextual theology can take an interesting turn. The former primarily gathers the concerns of the biblical text (however, that is understood) and the latter addresses the social concerns (i.e., situation) of a particular sociohistorical context. Given how these two disciplines privilege the text and social context respectively, this invites an interesting opportunity to interface. As noted in the previous section, such discussion requires coming to terms with how these terms are used in this project. More significantly, the task is to arrive at a theological interpretation of Scripture that helps us understand what God said and did in the Bible and what God is saying and doing in the church with catholic sensibility and contextual sensitivity. As suggested, the term evangelical or biblical theology is used by identifying with how it is used by Asia Theological Association (here on, ATA), an accrediting body for theological institutions in Asia—but moves beyond what they prescribe. We show how this term is used and show how evangelicals do theology in this part of the world. Even by the end of the twentieth century, there was a sense of reluctance on the part of evangelicals in Southeast Asia to engage in theological reflection or theological scholarship. According to Saphir Athyal, the late twentieth century evangelical Christians in Asia either neglected scholarship or were increasingly influenced by "Western liberal theology."[127] While reacting against the liberals and responding to the needs of the church, their task focuses on the practical and spiritual concerns of the church. But they were not very keen on interacting with sociopolitical concerns or issues that were seen as secular; there was a strong sense of divide between the sacred and secular in their theological framework. The church and its task were limited to the sacred aspect, while the concerns of the world (or liberals) were seen as secular. According to Bong Rin Ro and Ruth Marie Eshenaur, neglect of scholarship has much to do with "distrust in intellectual concerns," and their tendency to over-prioritize church ministry and works related to church administration.[128] As they privileged the spiritual/practical concerns of the church, they also neglected the creative and constructive aspect of church ministry (i.e., church and theological scholarship). Consequently, their response or presence is found

---

[127] Saphir Athyal, "A History of Asia Theological Association" in *The Voice of the Church in Asia*, ed. Bong Rin Ro (Taiwan: ATA, 1975), 1.

[128] Bong Rin Ro and Ruth Marie Eshenaur, "Preface" in *The Bible and Theology in Asian Contexts*, vii.

to be slow in the public square. This reluctance or slow response comes with the assumption that "the question of the content of the evangelical message is settled, and have, therefore, focused on 'how to' question of evangelistic strategy."[129] They seem to have ready-made answers to potential questions. As a result, people tend to see evangelicals in this part of the world as "too Western" or irrelevant to the present context, especially when it comes to sociopolitical issues.[130] This is to suggest that theology or practice in the church appears to be captivated by Western mission and its legacy. In recognition of this reality and the increasing pressures of relativism, evangelicals in the late twentieth century focused on coming to terms with how to make the Christian gospel relevant to a particular historical context. In the 1982 ATA theological consultation, evangelicals "reconfirmed their loyalty to the Scriptures and to the person of Jesus Christ as the unique Savior of the world."[131] The contributors/participants also asked:

> How is the church in Asia to interpret, obey and present the message of the Bible in a variety of cultures in Asia Today? How is the Gospel of Christ to be proclaimed faithfully and effectively so that people and cultures may be transformed?[132]

Such concerns were taken up not just for theological tasks but to enable the church to grow and expand. But more significantly, the church was being encouraged to engage with its sociopolitical context. They were encouraged to respond to issues that were emerging out of their context. In this theological consultation, their view of the Bible (i.e., it speaks in any given context or culture) remained consistent even in the following decade (i.e., 1990s). Their attempt to engage with the reader's context came with the notion that "the reliable and authoritative Bible has something essential to say to a world that needs to hear God's message."[133] But it takes the form of translating the meaning of the text without necessarily interpreting the culture where the message is being delivered. Rin Ro calls this approach a "biblically oriented" theology, where there is a sense of rootedness in the Bible and recognition of the need to connect with the context.[134] As they focused on making the gospel relevant, the emphasis is on hearing the "Word of God" as convicted by the "Holy Spirit" so that

---

[129] Rin Ro and Eshenaur, "Preface," viii.

[130] Rin Ro and Eshenaur, "Preface," viii.

[131] n.a. "The Bible and Theology in Asia Today: Declaration of the Sixth Asia Theological Consultation" in *The Bible and Theology in Asian Contexts*, 3

[132] n.a. "The Bible and Theology in Asia Today, 4.

[133] Ken R. Gnanakan, "Introduction: Biblical Theology in Asia," in *Biblical Theology in Asia*, v.

[134] Bong Rin Ro, "Theological Trends in Asia: Asian Theology," *ATN* 13 (1987): 57.

hearers may come to "a deeper and more realistic understanding of themselves and their cultures."[135] As they emphasize the needs of the church, they recognize the authoritative role of the Bible and the role the Spirit plays in helping the readers hear what it says.

These evangelical attempts of the 1980s and 1990s to engage with the reader's context in Southeast Asia takes into consideration the context of Buddhist, Hindu, Muslim, and (Marxist) totalitarian contexts.[136] As they focus on making the gospel relevant to the dominant groups, they are uncritical of the presence of other contexts (i.e., indigenous groups, minority groups, etc.). They made the mistake of ignoring the concerns of the minority groups or voices from the margins, such as the tribals, Dalits, women, etc. In addition, their theologizing came with the notion that theology or the Christian gospel *confronts* particular local beliefs and practices. Culture or insights from a particular historical context were not seen as significant to the discussion of theology. A change in their view of the culture or engaging a particular context came only in the twenty-first century: *there was a shift from (mostly) confronting culture to constructively engaging with culture with the belief that it will enrich the Christian theological discussion*. This change in evangelical thinking came with the affirmation of the need to be "biblically rooted, historically aware, contextually engaged, and broadly evangelical."[137] What has remained constant (since the last century) is their emphasis on Scripture and awareness of the importance of culture/context. What has changed is their emphasis, their approach to context/culture, their historical awareness, and emphasis on what it means to be evangelical. First, the emphasis to engage with culture-context is not just about presenting the Christian message in an understandable manner but it means addressing "the pressing questions of a given context or culture."[138] It also means recognition of catholicity as a context where the concerns of the local church and the insights of the catholic church are taken seriously.[139] Second, though there has been a neglect of history in the past, there is now an intentional effort to gain or recover insights from the church across space and time. The history of the church is seen as helpful or beneficial for the functioning of the contemporary church. And third, recognizing that the term evangelical is in dispute, its definition is clarified by association with the work of John Stott: it is concerned with the trinitarian gospel with "the revealing work of the God the Father, the redeeming work of God the Son, and the

135 n.a. "The Bible and Theology in Asia Today, 4–5.

136 n.a. "The Bible and Theology in Asia Today, 13–19.

137 Gener and Pardue, "Introduction," 2.

138 Gener and Pardue, "Introduction," 3.

139 Gener and Pardue, "Introduction," 4.

transforming ministry of God the Holy Spirit."[140] This change in thinking is made not just in abstract terms, but also in their practice—and with the recognition that "evangelicalism is a specific, historical movement, birthed in the midst of the church's varying responses to modernity."[141] It is in itself a part of a movement that seeks to recapture the enchanted worldview where divine involvement is endorsed in its narrative.

While associating with the current discussion of the evangelicals in Southeast Asia, this project moves beyond them by specifying how and what is being retrieved from church history (i.e., catholicity as a context of doing theology). The key here is to reflect on the doctrine of the church where the local and catholic contexts are integrated. While there are those who prioritize the theoretical construct of ecclesiology,[142] there are others who privilege the practical and "concrete shape" of the church.[143] But in terms of approach, rather than being caught up in the dichotomy between what seems to be theoretical or practical, this project tries to inculcate both right thinking about the church and relevant-contextual living of the church. Such understanding stems from the doctrine of the church where the local church is seen as representing the universal church in a particular place[144]—in this case, the local-tribal confessing community. It also stems from the understanding that "the whole Catholic Church is present and operative in the local church."[145] This dynamic of representing and presence of the local and catholic church provides a fuller understanding of the divine-human relationship i.e., there is both divine presence and human involvement in the functioning of the church.[146] When this understanding is reflected in a particular context, the local-tribal confessing community is seen as relating to the community and context of the people.[147] *It is adapting to the situation and needs of the time.* It also suggests that the local church takes into consideration what the saints—past and

---

[140] Gener and Pardue, "Introduction," 4; John Stott, *Evangelical Truth: A Personal Plea for Unity, Integrity and Faithfulness*, Revised and edited (Carlisle: Langham, 2013), 11.

[141] Gener and Pardue, "Introduction," 5.

[142] Paul M. Collins, "Ecclesiology: Context and Community" in *Christian Community Now, vol. 2: Ecclesiological Investigations*, ed. Paul M. Collins et al. (New York: T&T Clark, 2008), 135–56.

[143] See Nicholas M. Healy, *Church, World and Christian Life: Practical-Prophetic Ecclesiology* (Cambridge: CUP, 2004).

[144] Vanhoozer, *The Drama of Doctrine*, 454.

[145] Dulles, *The Catholicity of the Church*, 23.

[146] Aloys Grillmeier, "Commentary on *Lumen gentium*," in *Commentary on the Documents of Vatican II*, vol. 1 ed. Herbert Vorgriller (New York: Herder and Herder, 1967), 167.

[147] Collins, "Ecclesiology: Context and Community," 136.

present, East and West—have agreed upon. When the term catholicity or catholic context is used in reference to biblical interpretation, it reflects the concerns of the local church and the practice of the catholic church.

Since the early attempt of the evangelical engagement with culture-context, the role of biblical theology (i.e., understood in this project as the theology of the Bible) was seen as foundational. They defined biblical theology as "theological reflection" that takes into consideration "the historical context in which various themes have been woven to make an integrated whole."[148] The historical context in question refers to the process of translation of the text from "what it meant" to "what it means" to the contemporary church. This is done holding a high view (supracultural) of the Bible (i.e., it speaks to all groups of people through the work of the Holy Spirit without necessarily interpreting the culture). Theologians were expected to pick some themes from the Bible that may be found relevant in a culture and expect the text to speak to them. They hoped that when the truth claims of Christ confront the listeners, it would result in a change of lives. Ken R. Gnanakan, one of the contributors of the 1982 ATA theological consultation, can be identified with such thinking. He equates evangelical theology with biblical theology (i.e., "a commitment to the totality of revelation contained within the Bible").[149] He speaks of biblical theology as containing "biblical truths which are universally valid," while maintaining that its outworking may differ from one context to another.[150] However, his use of the term "biblical theology" leans toward a biblicist understanding of biblical theology. His usage is not to be equated with how the term biblical theology is used in this project, i.e., this project *recognizes a specific history of redemption within the final form of the Bible canon and located in the preaching and practice of the confessing church.* Gnanakan's view of the Bible is motivated by "the concern of God" and the condition of humanity.[151] While hesitating to call theology that engages with context as "contextual theology," the focus is on making the message of the Bible as *actualizing* what God has to say to the context. Gnanakan states, "I prefer the word 'actualize' where the messenger['s] whole message lives out so that [they communicate] relevantly to [their] situation."[152] While privileging a certain theology of the Bible, a theology that emerges from the context is dismissed (without necessarily engaging with it). His view of the Bible can be located under four

148 n.a. "The Bible and Theology in Asia Today, 8.

149 Ken Gnanakan, "Introduction: Biblical Theology in Asia" in *Biblical Theology in Asia*, v.

150 Gnanakan, "Biblical Theology in the Indian Context," 205.

151 Gnanakan, "Biblical Theology in the Indian Context," 206.

152 Gnanakan, "Biblical Theology in the Indian Context," 206.

features. First, the emphasis is on the uniqueness of Christian revelation located in the person of Christ. Second, with the assurance of authority found in the name of Jesus, the biblical truth confronts the context. Third, he calls for an integrated view of God's call in all areas of life, instead of dichotomizing between the secular and sacred. Fourth, he argues for a dynamic understanding of the church where theology is "actualized in the work and witness" of the worship community.[153] However, what would be reverted from his perception, both in this project and by later evangelical scholars, is their view of context/culture or how one ought to approach context/culture. While affirming the role the Bible plays in the ministry of the church or mission, culture-context is seen as contributing and enriching theological discussion.

Now, taking note of the above evangelical theological development, as well as the prior research, four areas of interface between TIS and tribal theology are identified. First, as suggested, while reacting to the dominant voice, tribal theologians moved away from the concerns of the tribal church. As they emphasized the need to make theology relevant and contextual, they focused on recovering tribal culture/heritage (i.e., to theologize). In doing so, the Bible or the use/reading of the Bible in their theological task became marginal.[154] However, in the recent past, with the emergence of tribal biblical interpretation, the Bible or the Word of God is made the focus of theological inquiry (i.e., with exploratory attempts to read the Bible from the tribal perspective). This can be a key area of interface between tribal theology and TIS. Biblical interpretation, when seen from the concerns of tribal theology, the emphasis is on the experience of the tribals in the contemporary context (i.e., a tribal perspectival reading); when seen from the concerns of TIS, the emphasis is on the concerns or theology of the church. What is common in both the pursuits is the reader's context: tribal theology emphasizes on the sociopolitical context of the readers, recognizing the location and identity of the readers (situated in the academic setting); while TIS emphasizes the concerns or theology of the church, seeing the question of God, Scripture, and church together (situated in the church setting). Our concern here is to recognize and emphasize the role of the Spirit in such an interpretative task. The Spirit's role as suggested by Vanhoozer is to recognize the role the Spirit plays in accepting the Bible as the Word of God; how the Spirit instills the Word of God as God's command, promise, etc.; and how the Spirit persuades or illumines the readers to live out what the Word of God says. What might be further helpful is to recognize how the Spirit inspires the text in various

153 Gnanakan, "Biblical Theology in the Indian Context," 206–13.

154 Vakha, "Jesus Christ in Tribal Theology: A Critique" in *Perspectives*, 64-81.

genres so that "we who read the Bible can benefit from it in various ways, namely to imbed Scripture in our minds to know the will of God, to be creative and progressive in the expression of our faith, and to accomplish the perlocutionary effect of Scripture."[155] Such suggestion further takes us to the prospect of inquiring about the role of the Spirit in using the wisdom of the world, and how that can help the readers to understand the Word of God (i.e., provide insights from the tribal sociopolitical context). This is to ask (and anticipate) whether our worldly understanding can be used to understand the Word of God—which in turn could broaden our understanding of contextual sensitivity. Yet, as Keener suggested, such exploratory or creative efforts should be approached with some caution (i.e., while we recognize that the Spirit does illuminate the readers, along with some sense of ambiguity, one should not derail from "the originally Spirit-inspired design").[156]

Second, the above evangelical attempt to engage with culture-context comes with a strong commitment to the Bible. However, it also comes with a condescending view of culture and what it might offer. In the twenty-first century, the evangelical commitment to the Bible and its content is still endorsed. While recognizing the importance of divine revelation and inspiration of the Bible, they maintain a sense of authoritative status of the Bible for theologizing. However, there is a shift in their view of culture/context. In the present context, context-culture is seen as that which can offer insights in theologizing (i.e., as a resource, but not necessarily as a norm in it).[157] However, to *engage* with the context-culture can mean more than one thing. This is an area where evangelicals and tribal theologians can dialogue in their theological task (since both emphasize the need to engage with culture-context). When the term is used in the discussion of tribal theology, it is used in reference to recovering tribal culture/heritage and responding to the sociopolitical issues of the tribals. But when it is used in reference to evangelical theological discussion, it is less about "political correction" and more about affirming that "theology must be local—in that it makes sense to, and addresses the concerns of, its immediate community—while also being catholic—taking seriously the commitments and concerns of the wider body of Christ scattered across space, culture, and time."[158] The former prioritizes the sociopolitical concerns of the present tribal context, while the latter privileges the ecclesial concerns. Such an interface should recognize the prospect of tension, but

[155] Jones, "A Critique of Kevin Vanhoozer's Pneumatological Hermeneutics in Light of Selected Historical Figures on the Doctrine of Illumination," 345.

[156] Keener, *Spirit Hermeneutics*, 19, 250.

[157] Gener and Pardue, "Introduction," 4.

[158] Gener and Pardue, "Introduction," 4.

it should be approached with a way forward as well. In this case it may mean recognizing the critique of tribal theology that the tribal churches are partly living in the legacy of Western missionaries, but it also means that the local-tribal confessing community has been constructively *adapting* in the lives of the people. This adaptation is evidently present in a threefold sense. The first is seen in how the confessing community continues to communicate the Christian faith in the local language. Within the Tangkhul Naga community, the community or church continues to translate the Bible, hymns, and other church documents in the local language (i.e., Ukhrul/Hunphun dialect). While confessing the truth claims of the Bible, the Word of God is performed within the groups of people who speak the same language. Having said that, this translation attempt should also be seen critically. There is a possibility that Tangkhul Bible translation is captivated by Western missionary theological framework and hymnal books are still translated from English hymns. There is very little room for creative or indigenous composition. The second is seen in how the confessing community continues to adapt to the situations and the needs of the time and people. As indicated, they adapted to the vision/dreams that were foretold to them about a certain white man bringing light to them. They saw Pettigrew as a bringer of light as the dream foretold. Moreover, their confession to the newfound faith invited reaction in the form of expelling them from the existing community. They had to learn to maneuver in and around this newfound faith as they were segregated from their old faith and community. This is to suggest that the local-tribal confessing community has been in the state of confessing (i.e., they have been adapting, formulating, and developing—and not necessarily devoid of actual contextual-cultural interaction). And the third can be seen both positively and negatively. It has to do with how leadership structure is carried forward from the post-missionary cultural practice to the current ecclesial setting. As the custom law is withheld, controlled, and shaped by men (i.e., patriarchal system),[159] similarly, the current church structure is controlled and dominated by men—and with very little room for women involvement or women leadership. This point is to suggest that not all adaptation by the confessing community was good. It also came with some cultural packages, which are not necessarily constructive for the church.

The third is in how the term community is perceived. There is a strong sense of community within the tribal society, both in the pre-missionary period and in the post-missionary period. The tribal theologians see this communitarian aspect as a liberative key. Critical of the colonial

[159] Ikrormi Konghay, comp. *The Tangkhul Naga Community of Past, Present and Future* (Imphal: Development of Human Potential, 2016), 31.

influence, they tend to go back to the pre-missionary period to re-inform or reform the present context. This tendency to go back to tribal culture/heritage is not their only source but it has become some sort of norm. Their experience of oppression or marginalization is a defining criterion to do theology and the lens to read the Bible. This emphasis on *a strong sense of community* can be an area of interface. However, this project confronts the underlying assumption that this strong sense of community existed only in the pre-missionary period. Instead, it argues that the sense of community continues to exist during the missionary and post-missionary period within the local-tribal confessing community. The essence of tribal communitarianism was never lost. Instead, it continues to grow beyond where members of the church sacrificially show care and concern for one another. The outlook of this communitarian aspect of the tribal society may have changed—from *community house* to *church* building—but it continues to grow with different facets and input (e.g., Scripture, church tradition, etc.). The pre-missionary communitarianism existed within the bond of family, clan, and village. However, in the post-missionary period, with the emergence of a confessing community, the sense of community now extends beyond a said tribe *to* different races or tribes and across the world (i.e., beyond a geographical location). This sense of community is reinforced by their faith in Christ and being rooted in Scripture. This is also to acknowledge that they continue to receive guidance from the Spirit, both in the reading of the Bible and in the growth of the church. This sense of community continues to grow as the confessing community adapts to their newfound faith. Such a view is possible when the church is seen with catholic sensibility (i.e., it is both local and catholic). The tribal confessing community exists in harmony and unity with other churches across space and time.

The fourth area is located in how liberation concern is understood. Here, the suggestion is made that liberation concern is both biblical and contextual. Tribal theologians focus on liberation concerns that integrate with social theory. Hence, their focus is to liberate the tribals from their state of oppression by the dominant voice—in this case, Western mission and their legacies and the advocates of Indian Christian theology. They argue for tribal concerns in the face of adversity from a dominant voice that either neglects their voice or mistreats them. This struggle for liberation can be another area where tribal theologians and tribal churches can interface. While tribal theologians were addressing the sociopolitical concerns, they neglected the practical and spiritual concerns of the church. In fact, their theological discussion became a predominantly academic enterprise. The need is to recognize not just the academic context but also the tribal ecclesial context where liberation concerns can be addressed.

While tapping on the liberation concerns of the Bible (i.e., liberation from the captivity of tyranny, power, sin, etc.), some key questions can be raised in terms of how God can liberate them from their state of helplessness or oppression. It would mean demonstrating that the liberation concerns are biblical as much as they are contextual i.e., it is an ecclesial/theological concern of the Bible. This is the kind of theological concern that will help Bible readers find Christ, instead of social theory or a perspective of the said method. It is the kind of interpretation where readers find God who liberates them from their state of captivity. Such a task can take the form of embracing and confronting tribal theological concerns. The tribal church ought to *confront* the direction tribal theology is taking. It needs to confront the pluralistic direction it is taking, as they are preoccupied with methods of theologizing or interpretation. In addition, it needs to confront the tendency of tribal theology where it focuses only on contemporary sociopolitical concerns while neglecting not just the tribal church but also the catholic sensibility of the Christian faith. The tribal church needs to *embrace* the prospect of liberation concerns for the welfare of the believers. This means taking into consideration what God is saying and doing in the sociopolitical situations of the tribals, instead of just limiting to the spiritual concerns of the church. In other words, they should move beyond their tendency to dichotomize the secular from sacred (i.e., ecclesial concerns).

Yet, the above said interface ought to answer the question: What does a biblical-theological-contextual liberation look like? It ought to be governed and shaped by canonical sense, catholic sensibility, and contextual sensitivity. With this note, an effort is made to adapt Vanhoozer's theological method. This effort is seen as an answer to the issue of plurality of biblical interpretation: a *multi-contextual biblical-theological interpretation of Scripture.*[160] It is an approach that maintains evangelical ethos (i.e., the solas of the Reformation), recognize canonical sense (i.e., the measuring and guiding criteria), assert catholic sensibility (i.e., value the contribution of the local and catholic church), and affirm contextual sensitivity (i.e., the local-tribal confessing community). These are the contexts that enable Christians to read the Bible as what it is, namely, human and divine discourse in NEI.

The biblical theology in question refers to the kind of theology that integrates the redemptive model that recognizes canonical sense and constructive theology, while the contextual theology in question refers to theology that emerges out of tribal ecclesial context with the emergence

[160] The name of this approach was suggested by Vanhoozer. Kevin J. Vanhoozer, email message to author, November 23, 2020.

of the local-tribal confessing community as a point of reference. Biblical theology that is endorsed here recognizes canon as a measuring and guiding principle to the church (as opposed to biblicist or modern understanding of biblical theology); while contextual theology that is proposed here recognizes the situation of the church, where believers are trying to live out their lives by faith. The contextual theology in question (for this project) is a faith seeking understanding of the context:[161] *the kind of theology that attempts to understand the emergence of a confessing community amongst the tribals in NEI and its continuing influence in the tribal community.* This is the kind of interface of theological discipline (between biblical theology and contextual theology) that considers the subject matter of the Bible (the triune God), canon as a guiding and measuring criterion, the tradition of the church (catholicity), and the situation of the tribal church (contextual sensitivity). This is possible when biblical theology is viewed as a discipline, which seeks to help the readers/interpreters understand a particular redemptive history shaped by the category of canon and located within the confessing community. This is also to prescribe "the gospel [as] the good news that God the Father has said and done things in Jesus Christ through the Holy Spirit for the salvation of the world."[162] When the church tries to understand and live out this wisdom in a particular context, it takes the form of "*practical* reasoning about what to say and do in particular situations in light of the gospel of Jesus Christ; practical reasoning about what to say and do in order to 'present [ourselves] to God as one approved, a worker who . . . correctly handles the word of truth' (2 Tim 2:15)."[163] In other words, the meaning of the biblical text does not stop in the saying and doing of the past but reinvigorates the present confessing community. Rather than focusing on the reconstructed history of "what it meant," the biblical theology (i.e., synonym to TIS) in question focuses on "what it means" in the present context (e.g., tribal ecclesial setting). In other words, such reading/interpretation of the Bible is geared toward performing the text, both within the confessing community and in the world. The text refers to the final form of the text with the *canon* as the defining category. The biblical canon is not just a list of books but *a sapiential criterion that measures the conduct of believers who conform to the person of Jesus Christ.*[164] It is "the way properly to identify Jesus Christ and to understand Christian identity;" such discipling takes the form of participating in the life and death

161 See Vanhoozer, "What is Everyday Theology?" 16.

162 Vanhoozer, "A Drama-of-Redemption," 155.

163 Vanhoozer, "A Drama-of-Redemption," 156.

164 Vanhoozer, *The Drama of Doctrine*, 146; Vanhoozer, "One Rule to Rule them All," 112; Vanhoozer, "Forming the Performers," 12.

of Jesus Christ.[165] Such conviction is founded on the understanding that "God has spoken and acted in Jesus Christ and that God speaks and acts in the canonical Scriptures that testify to him."[166] Yet, this theodrama of the triune God is not only limited to a particular history or geographical region (e.g. West). The triune God continues to speak in and transcend different parts of the world—and not just with the inclusion of the tribals in NEI—but also by fully participating in this theodrama as they confessed their faith in Christ. Yet again, this is not to argue for a *new* theology. However, it is to associate oneself with the learning of the previous Christians, while affirming the insights drawn from a particular history (i.e., the tribal ecclesial context).[167]

Whether acknowledged or not, the local-tribal confessing community is associated with other confessing communities in the world and across space and time. In addition to what has been said, this concern further takes us to the question of what it means to emphasize catholic sensibility in biblical interpretation. As we situate ourselves in the local church, it is imperative that we keep track of theological discussion across space and time. It means we ought to be aware of the situation of the local church-context, but also address the question of which confession the local-tribal churches are associated with. Our preference is the kind of confessing community that is rooted in Scripture and that which is locally embodied in Christ. One of the defining criteria and contributions of TIS is the attempt to recover the interpretative/theological task of the pre-modern period. Our task here is to clarify the confession that we are associated with and suggest what it would look like: Christian faith came to the NE region primarily through Protestant missionaries (e.g., Baptist, Presbyterian, Anglican, etc.). Suggestion can be made that our Christian heritage goes back to the sixteenth-century Reformation of the West. Consequently, back to the early church as the Reformers themselves saw the importance of affirming the Nicene formula concerning the doctrine of the Trinity. For our purposes and clarity, further attempt is being made to retrieve the *solas* of the Reformation seen as compatible with how this project perceives and addresses the issue of plurality of interpretative approaches. According to Vanhoozer, the Reformation was "a *retrieval*, first and foremost of the biblical gospel, particularly the Pauline articulation, but also, secondarily, of the church fathers."[168] This act of retrieval passes on what was received—and not repetitively but "to reform"—according to

---

165 Kevin J. Vanhoozer, email message to author, July 7, 2020.

166 Vanhoozer, *The Drama of Doctrine*, 26.

167 Gener and Pardue, "Introduction," 2–3.

168 Vanhoozer, *Biblical Authority After Babel*, 22–23.

"the living and active Word of Scripture."[169] As the local church remains in the state of confessing, retrieving the solas will help shape and transform the lives in the present context. This emphasis on the living Word will help us hear and perform what it says. The interpretative authority is retrieved to the confessing community: back to the church, from the academy. Vanhoozer sees retrieving the Reformation as essential to translate the gospel into a new cultural context. He argues that,

> *retrieving the five Reformation solas [will help] to address the contemporary problem of pervasive interpretative pluralism, and that retrieving the priesthood of believers (ecclesiology) helps to address the problem of the authority of interpretative communities.*[170]

The five solas, namely "grace alone, faith alone, Scripture alone, Christ alone, for the glory of God alone," are seen as reflecting the "core Reformation theological reflection" or "the *first theology* of mere Protestant Christianity."[171] As it presupposes the triune God, the solas' function is to "preserve the integrity of the triune economies of revelation and redemption."[172] The triune economy, in this case, refers to the work of the triune God: God, Jesus Christ, and Spirit. The *grace alone* concerns the way God, Jesus Christ, and Spirit operate: to God, "the ontology of grace, the giving of *love* that creates (originating grace);" to Jesus Christ, "the economy of grace, the giving of the *life* that redeems (saving grace);" and to the Spirit, "the teleology of grace, the giving of the *light* that sanctifies (illuminating grace)."[173] Retrieving the grace alone allows the readers to connect with how God shares love, life, and light with the world "in Jesus Christ and through the Spirit."[174] Such understanding allows the readers/interpreters of the Bible to participate in "the economy of grace"[175] (i.e., Bible interpretation is talking about God, and in implication, how humans correspond with God-talk). This takes us to the concern of *faith alone*, which recognizes "*the ontological inability of the sinner and the epistemological priority of the Holy Spirit.*"[176] To put it differently, this is to understand that at "a key moment in the story of how God forgives sin and restores right relations with fallen human creatures."[177] This faith consists of "testimonial rationality and public trust, the trust in God's people in the testimony of God's Spirit

[169] Vanhoozer, *Biblical Authority After Babel*, 23.
[170] *Emphasis* in original. Vanhoozer, *Biblical Authority After Babel*, 25.
[171] Vanhoozer, *Biblical Authority After Babel*, 26.
[172] Vanhoozer, *Biblical Authority After Babel*, 28.
[173] Vanhoozer, *Biblical Authority After Babel*, 36.
[174] Vanhoozer, *Biblical Authority After Babel*, 71.
[175] Vanhoozer, *Biblical Authority After Babel*, 71.
[176] *Emphasis* in original. Goldsworthy, *Gospel-Centered Hermeneutics*, 50.
[177] Vanhoozer, *Biblical Authority After Babel*, 73.

to the reliability of God's Word."[178] The emphasis is on the reliability of the Word of God, which takes us to the concern of *Scripture alone*. It directly confronts the understanding of reading the Bible like any other book. Keeping in mind that there have been some disagreements concerning how Scripture alone is understood, it is important to note that it does not mean Scripture without "the economy of grace," "the community of faith," or "church tradition."[179] But it is to suggest that Scripture is "the *primary*" in theology, and not the only source of it.[180] Hence, as one emphasizes on Scripture alone in the area of biblical interpretation, one ought to affirm "*prima facia* the catholic tradition as a *Spirit-guided embodiment of right biblical understanding*."[181] This is to say that even when we recognize the importance of context—whether the immediate context or the catholic context—Scripture remains primary. The next *solas,* Christ alone, affirms "Jesus Christ as the only mediator between God and humanity."[182] Yet again, this is not devoid of or absence of church. Rather, it is to recognize that "the body of believers in the midst of which the risen Christ exercises his rule on earth as it is in heaven."[183] It is to recognize the following: "The church is the domain where Christ's rule becomes flesh, embodies in the royal priesthood."[184] All of these are to be directed toward *the glory of God alone*. To glorify God is to make God known publicly. It is to show "the world the goodness of [God's] attributes and the goodness of [God's] gospel, including our unity in Christ."[185] In practice, this may mean the coming together of the catholic church "from east and west, Anglican and Baptist, Pentecostal and Presbyterian, to 'recline at table in the Kingdom of God' (Luke 13:29), and there to feast on the unsearchable riches of Christ (Eph 3:8)."[186] Moreover, pertinent to this project, it means a constructive interaction between West and Majority World in the area of biblical interpretation.

Like the canonical criterion, the solas are to be seen as guides that "generate and govern mere Protestant theology" (i.e., it provides "a pattern for reading Scripture theologically that enables Protestant unanimity on theological essentials, and thus the possibility of genuine fellowship in spite of secondary and tertiary doctrinal differences").[187] The solas, while revealing the triune economy of the gospel, provide a hermeneutical key

[178] Vanhoozer, *Biblical Authority After Babel*, 107.
[179] Vanhoozer, *Biblical Authority After Babel*, 111.
[180] Vanhoozer, *Biblical Authority After Babel*, 111.
[181] *Emphasis* in original. Vanhoozer, *Biblical Authority After Babel*, 146.
[182] Vanhoozer, *Biblical Authority After Babel*, 147.
[183] Vanhoozer, *Biblical Authority After Babel*, 148.
[184] Vanhoozer, *Biblical Authority After Babel*, 179.
[185] Vanhoozer, *Biblical Authority After Babel*, 180.
[186] Vanhoozer, *Biblical Authority After Babel*, 182.
[187] *Emphasis* in original. Vanhoozer, *Biblical Authority After Babel*, 28.

to "arbitrate the conflict of interpretations."[188] Instead of prioritizing the meaning of *back then* or of the theoretical perspective, it brings back the meaning of the text where it matters (i.e., the church). As suggested, the church, in this case, refers not just to the protestant church but is inclusive of other denominations (i.e., including Roman Catholic) where there is confession of Christ as their savior. This hermeneutical correction is further located in affirming the priesthood of all believers:

> The royal priesthood of all believers—briefly, the notion that all church members are ministers of God's Word—is actually part of a pattern of authority, indeed, part of a triune economy of authority. *"Royal" signals authority; "priesthood" signals interpretative community; "all believers" signals that individuals are not autonomous agents but citizens of the gospel.*[189]

While recognizing that the triune God speaks in and from the Scripture, readers/interpreters are required to cross-check their interpretation with the confessing community that they are part of—and not at the doorsteps of critical approach. Such accountability keeps them in check and helps them avert themselves from all sorts of interpretative ideas. When Bible interpretation/reading is done with this reality in focus, interpreters/readers cannot help but prioritize performing their reading within the community of faith. They cannot help but locate their reading/interpretation within the community of faith, the tribal ecclesial setting.[190] This is to affirm, "The church is the domain where Christ's rule becomes flesh, embodied in the royal priesthood."[191] If that is the case, and as suggested earlier, we have to come to terms with the question of the church: the church in question is when "two or more people, gathered in Jesus' name, that sets itself apart by its new-covenant ordinances (baptism and Lord's Supper), preaching of the gospel, and exercise of the keys, in order to be a parable of the kingdom, an embassy of Christ's rule."[192] As indicated, this church in question can be further categorized as the local and catholic church: "a communion *within* a church and a communion *between* churches."[193] Biblical interpretation when received in this manner, then, is not just what the text means in the local church but what it means in the catholic church.

The categorization of church into local and catholic further affirms the two convictions of the protestant church: the appeal to the authority

[188] Vanhoozer, *Biblical Authority After Babel*, 29.
[189] Vanhoozer, *Biblical Authority After Babel*, 29.
[190] Vanhoozer, *Biblical Authority After Babel*, 29.
[191] Vanhoozer, *Biblical Authority After Babel*, 179.
[192] Vanhoozer, *Biblical Authority After Babel*, 191.
[193] Vanhoozer, *Biblical Authority After Babel*, 191.

of the Bible and the catholicity of the church.[194] The first conviction keeps the church grounded on what God said and did in the Bible, and by implication, what God is saying and doing in the contemporary world. The second conviction helps the local church recognize the wealth of resources that are there across Christian history (i.e., across space and time). Retrieving the solas is not to romanticize what was said and done back then, but to recover what it means to the church and to help shape the present church. Yet, we do not carry out such tasks on our own nor address only human concerns but carry forward the theological concerns of the confessing community through the help of the Spirit. The confessing community is "accompanied by the Spirit (Acts 9:31, 10:44, 19:6), it convicts and persuades its hearers of its truth, thereby forming a community of believers."[195] The continuing influence of the confessing community corresponds with the work of the Holy Spirit. Believers act or respond to God's direction through the conviction of the Spirit. This is to say that the triune God is at work in the confessing community: "As with truth, so with life: [God] communicates each in [Jesus] through the Spirit."[196] While local theological expression needs to be acknowledged, it also needs criteria to make sure that the same gospel is preached across geographical regions. This is to call for "theodramatic correspondence" where "sanctified persons, persons whose minds and hearts and imagination are captive to the Word."[197] It means that it should lead them to a similar *direction*: "In the way of the truth and life as these are defined by the story of God's words and deeds that culminate in Jesus Christ."[198] To put it differently, it should result in reformed truth and life, instead of the methodological perspective or outcome of some social theory.

Conclusion

This final chapter contributes to the discussion of TIS: by providing *an entryway to the discussion between theological interpretation of Scripture and tribal theology*. The said task is carried out in three sections: the first part is a critique, the second part sets the stage, and the third is the construction part.

In the first part, this project shows that it is both sympathetic and critical to the concern of TIS and tribal theology. It is sympathetic to TIS's emphasis to gather the concerns of the church, but it is critical of its neglect

194 Vanhoozer, *Biblical Authority After Babel*, 198–99.
195 Vanhoozer, *Remythologizing Theology*, 267.
196 Vanhoozer, *Remythologizing Theology*, 265.
197 Vanhoozer, "One Rule to Rule them All," 124.
198 Vanhoozer, "One Rule to Rule them All," 124.

to address contextual concerns or failure to engage with contextual theology. It is sympathetic to tribal theology's emphasis to relate and engage with context, but it is critical of its neglect of the ecclesial context (i.e., tribal church).

The second part sets the stage for a constructive relationship between TIS and tribal theology by way of suggesting how the terms history, theology, and context should be used in theological interpretation in NEI. While noting how these terms are used in a limited sense (or neglected) in the NE region, the suggestion is made to remember Christian tradition (i.e., divine involvement in human history), identify Scripture as bearing witness to God events (i.e., God, Scripture, and church), and address the concerns of the church (i.e., the emergence of the local-tribal confessing community).

The third part proposes a constructive interface of the theological discipline of *biblical theology* and *contextual theology* that can result in the theological interpretation of Scripture in NEI. This part is further divided into two subsections. First, it shows early attempts to integrate contextual concerns with biblical interpretation. While identifying the limitation of the earlier initiative, it projects the likely direction of such interpretative tasks in NEI (i.e., interpretative tasks that pay attention to multiple contexts). Second, it shows how the discipline of biblical and contextual theology is used, identifies areas of interface between TIS and tribal theology, and lays out the constructive proposal of TIS in the NEI tribal context. Drawing from Vanhoozer's theological method, an argument is made for a *multi-contextual biblical-theological interpretation of Scripture* that maintains evangelical ethos (i.e., the solas of the Reformation), recognizes canonical sense (i.e., the measuring and guiding criteria), asserts catholic sensibility (i.e., value the contribution of the local and catholic church), and affirms contextual sensitivity (i.e., the emergence of the local-tribal confessing community). This proposed reading of the Bible is further reinforced by affirming the priesthood of all believers (i.e., Bible reading that remains accountable to the confessing community).

CONCLUSION

The current project is an attempt to answer the question: Is a multi-contextual approach to reading the Bible desirable, or even possible? The answer: yes and yes. That a multi-contextual approach is desirable should be evident. We have seen that the meaning of Scripture is located in the original context, if it is understood from the perspective of modern biblical scholars. Then, we have seen how meaning is situated in the reader's context if it is seen from postmodern or Majority World scholars. While making many evangelicals nervous, it is still an important consideration, especially when trying to read the Bible in a unique non-Western context. Meaning is also grounded in the canonical and catholic context, when read theologically or from an ecclesial perspective. This, we saw, was crucial to locate biblical interpretation in biblical and systematic/dogmatic theology. But we also observed the dangers when only one context is highlighted, or unduly privileged. In this project, I proposed that TIS has challenged this unnecessary privileging and offered a more holistic paradigm for interpretation and practice. That a multi-contextual approach is possible can be said through a twofold statement. First, as TIS recommends, we need to read the Bible with multiple contexts in mind: the original historical context, the canonical context, the context of catholic tradition, and the cultural context. Second, through our focus on contextual readings, we need to locate the multiplex contextual reading of the Bible more intentionally in the local-tribal confessing community which aims to be biblical, catholic, and contextual.

The emergence and dominance of biblical criticism in the modern period resulted in a conflict between critical and (allegedly) objective reading and theological reading of the Bible that created a sense of preoccupation with two different constructs of the original context. A sense of preoccupation with the readers or appropriate methods of interpretation were created between modern interpreters and postmodern interpreters. While privileging the original context, the theological or ecclesial concerns of the text were neglected and eventually, theology was marginalized in biblical interpretation in the Western context.

Chapter 1 showed the trajectory of biblical interpretation in the eighteenth and nineteenth-century West. Here, we showed the shift in the use of Scripture in modern biblical interpretation from using Scripture, the true story of the world, as the framework for understanding everything else, to using a critically reconstructed history (and what we know about the natural world) as the framework for reading (and criticizing) the biblical narrative. Such reading of the Bible, which is the privileging of the original historical context with a reconstructed history, neglects theology in their exegesis/interpretation. It results in a tension between biblical studies and systematic theology, between exegesis and theology. Moreover, it brought about a division between what is preached in the church and what is discussed in the academy.

Though the modern biblical interpretation in the West was the primary focus of this chapter, it also highlighted the kind of interpretative approaches that began in the later modern period. It also highlighted postmodern interpretation of the Bible and the churchly reading of the Bible. Postmodern interpreters saw the objective-scientific reading of the Bible as a failure as all knowledge claims reflect the knower's situation and power interest. As they emphasized the reader's context, there were attempts to appropriate an interpretative approach, which eventually resulted in the multiplication of interpretative methods. As suggested earlier, it also resulted in a tension between modern interpreters and postmodern interpreters. Churchly reading of the Bible responded to the dominance of the critical approach as it constructively engaged in biblical interpretation by developing the church's theology and addressing the concerns of the church. Such a task began to address the divide between academy and church.

Much like the kind of biblical interpretation that began to take shape in the late modern period, a plurality of interpretative interests began to take shape in the Majority World. Like postmodern interpretation, the task of biblical interpretation is carried forward by privileging the context of the readers. In the case of NEI, the tension between the dominant voice and voices from the margin is evident in the emergence of tribal theology and tribal biblical interpretation (see chapter 2). Here, an argument was made that tribal theology emerged as a reaction to the dominant voice (i.e., against Indian Christian theology and Western mission and its legacy). Tribal theology emerged as a reaction to Indian Christian theology and to the church in NEI, which they believe is captivated by the Western missionaries. To bring about a relevant theology and in pursuit of justice, tribal theologians interacted with their culture/heritage and sociopolitical situation considering the experience of the tribals in the contemporary context. It is out of this theological pursuit that the tribal biblical interpretation emerges, where each tribe or community seeks their distinctive voice. In doing so, tribal theology in NEI has moved away or ignored the concerns of the church. Moreover, their interpretative task is moving toward a pluralistic interest—in this case, the concerns of ethnic groups or tribes. The result is another legitimation crisis in biblical interpretation where there is no shared value or governing interest. As each tribe reads the Bible from their own perspective, they come up with their distinctive claims—which is exclusive to the said tribe, and not necessarily shareable with other tribes. One's particular social and historical experience shapes the meaning of the text—and not the canonical or catholic context.

Whether in the privileging of the original context or reader's context in the West and Majority World, theology was (and is being) neglected in biblical interpretation. In their claim to be context-free or context-bound, it created tension between biblical studies and theology, and between dominant voices and voices from the margins. More significantly, it created a lacuna between the academy and church: there was a divide between what was taught and discussed in the academy and what was preached and practiced in the church. This shift in biblical interpretation invited a distinct movement called the *theological interpretation of Scripture* from the early twenty-first century (see chapter 3). What TIS tries to fulfill is recovering *theology* in biblical interpretation—and shifting the discussion from the academy to the church, addressing the concerns of the church, while appealing the canonical and catholic context. As an answer to the tensions in the West and Majority World, TIS is seen as an answer to the disoriented preoccupation of the original context and preoccupation of appropriate methods of interpretations or plurality of interpretative interests. What we hoped to accomplish in chapter 3 was to recognize the strides that TIS is making in the contemporary context, and give a deeper glimpse of Vanhoozer's contribution to the discussion of TIS. What is fascinating and helpful to this project is his theodramatic model, which encourages attention to various contexts: it prioritizes the canonical context, encourages reading in the context of the communion of saints (catholic sensibility), and calls attention to the present context of the reader. His theodramatic model is not just a constructive lens to address the tensions in the contemporary context, but it is an interpretative approach for Christians to make sense of their faith and live/perform it.

As proponents of TIS try to bring about a distinctive understanding of TIS, they have been instrumental in bringing the discussion of biblical interpretation to the church. They can bring the concerns of the church in biblical interpretation. They have been able to build a more constructive relationship between theological disciplines over the issues of biblical interpretation. Specifically, they have been able to make a significant improvement to retrieve the contribution of precritical interpretation. However, as TIS makes its own strides, it is limited to disciplines that have been traditionally associated with biblical interpretation before the arrival of critical approach i.e., biblical studies, biblical theology, and systematic theology. While rebuilding the divide between the theological disciplines, conversation with contextual theology has been largely ignored or neglected. Considering this perceived gap, an attempt is made to contribute to the discussion of TIS: by providing *an entryway to the discussion between theological interpretation of Scripture and contextual theology* (i.e., tribal theology). In the Majority World, indigenous or contextual biblical interpretation emerges out of the discussion of contextual theology. Though such a task is not a straightforward one, it is seen as a necessity to dialogue with contextual theology if someone seeks to contribute to the discussion of biblical interpretation in this part of the world—in this case, dialogue TIS with tribal theology. Given this reality, this project gives a constructive proposal of TIS, offering canonical sense, catholic sensibility, and contextual sensitivity.

This constructive proposal of TIS in NEI tribal context takes the form of critique and critical appropriation. It is sympathetic and critical of TIS and contextual theology (i.e., tribal theology). The task at hand is carried out in a threefold manner. The first part sympathizes with the ecclesial concern of TIS and contextual concern of tribal theology, but it is critical of TIS' neglect to engage with contextual theology and tribal theology's neglect to engage with the ecclesial context. The second part explores how the terms history, theology and context have been used and suggests how they should be used in the NEI tribal context. This section sets the stage to bring about an entryway to the discussion between TIS and contextual theology. The history in question refers to lived Christianity and Christian theology across space and time, how the past relates to the present (and vice versa). As it recognizes the present aspect of a particular history, it also recognizes what God said and did in biblical times and across space and time. Theology in question refers to our understanding of God (i.e., the subject matter of the Bible) that influences our reading of the Bible but also recognizes that our reading of the Bible shapes our understanding of God. Such a view of God recognizes the role of human authors and the communicative aspect of the Scripture, which is ascribed to God. Moreover, the context in question refers to the local context or church—in this case, the local-tribal confessing community, where the meaning of the text is being interpreted or read. The local context ought to represent both the cultural context and the catholic context (i.e., the middle ground between catholic and contextual sensitivity). And the third part attempts to interface TIS with contextual theology by interfacing biblical theology with tribal theology. Instead of focusing on the tribal theological discussion in the academy (i.e., the sociopolitical concerns), an effort is made to bring back the discussion to the church (i.e., the local-tribal confessing community). Instead of taking a limited biblicist view of biblical theology, it considers a specific history of redemption within the final form of the Bible canon and the preaching and teaching of the confessing church (i.e., the catholic church). The biblical theology in question endorses the canon as the measuring and guiding principle of the church, while the contextual theology in question considers the situation of the church where believers are trying to live out their faith. While the basis is biblical, catholic, and contextual-cultural, the supreme authority lies in Scripture. The canon in question refers to the final form of the biblical text, where it is the defining criterion that measures the ways of people who confess their faith in Jesus Christ. The catholic principle helps believers come to terms with what God is saying and doing. This transcends a given tribe/ethnicity to different parts of the world across space and time. The contextual sensitivity corresponds with catholicity as a context of doing theology where it helps believers recognize the scope of their faith, within both the local confessing and catholic community.

In addition, further research to retrieve the *solas* of the Reformation were seen as compatible with how this project perceives and addresses the issue of plurality of interpretative approaches. Like the canon criterion, the *solas* can guide Christians with a sense of unanimity of theological essentials, instead of the exclusive claims of a particular tribe or community. Recognizing such unanimity can further bring about genuine fellowship between groups of believers (i.e., genuinely move beyond the local-tribal confessing community to other Christian confessing communities). Moreover, with claims of the priesthood of all believers, it corrects the tendency to move toward pluralistic directions in biblical interpretation. Interpreters or readers do not function on their own terms. Instead, they correspond with one another as belonging to one confessing community (i.e., the local-tribal confessing community corresponds with the Catholic Church).

By attempting to dialogue biblical theology with tribal theology, this project has contributed to the perceived gap in the discussion of TIS. While emphasizing on the need to address the divide between academy and church (both in the West and Majority World), it addressed the concerns of the tribal church (i.e., the local-tribal confessing community) by relating them with other confessing communities (i.e., the catholic confessing community). By implication, as this thesis is from the Majority World, and from a neglected geographical region, it contributes to the discussion of TIS, which is a predominantly Western discussion. Yet, in the end, this project remains theoretical. Its practice is only implied. It is a project for the church (i.e., it only gathers the concerns of the tribal church). The ideal goal is to move toward writing from/with the church. The project is limited by a constructive interface of biblical theology and contextual theology that can result in TIS. It remains to be seen what it would look like to incorporate canonical sense, catholic sensibility, and contextual sensitivity in the actual *theological interpretation of biblical text* in the NEI tribal context.

BIBLIOGRAPHY

Adam, A. K. M. *Faithful Interpretation: Reading the Bible in a Postmodern World*. Minneapolis: Fortress Press, 2006.

———. *What Is Postmodern Biblical Criticism?* Minneapolis: Fortress Press, 1995.

Adam, A. K. M., Stephen E. Fowl, Kevin J. Vanhoozer, and Francis Watson. *Reading Scripture with the Church: Toward a Hermeneutic for Theological Interpretation*. Grand Rapids: Baker, 2006.

Allen, R. Michael, ed. *Theological Commentary: Evangelical Perspectives*. London: T&T Clark, 2011.

Allen, Michael and Scott R. Swain. *Reformed Catholicity: The Promise of Retrieval for Theology and Biblical Interpretation*. Grand Rapids: Baker, 2015.

Anderson, Janice Capel, and Jeffrey L. Staley, *Taking it Personally: Autobiographical Biblical Criticism*. Atlanta: SBL, 1995.

Angami, Zhodi. *Empire and God: A Tribal Reading of the Birth of Jesus in Matthew's Gospel*. London: Bloomsbury, 2017.

Barr, James. *The Bible in the Modern World*. London: SCM, 1990.

———. *The Concept of Biblical Theology: An Old Testament Perspective*. Minneapolis: Fortress Press, 1999.

Barth, Karl. *The Epistle to the Romans*, Sixth edition. Translated by Edwyn C. Hoskyns. Oxford: OUP, 1968.

Bartholomew, Craig G. *Introducing Biblical Hermeneutics: A Comprehensive Framework for Hearing God in Scripture*. Grand Rapids: Baker, 2015.

Bartholomew, Craig G. and M. Goheen. *Christian Philosophy: A Systematic and Narrative Introduction*. Grand Rapids: Baker, 2013.

Bartholomew, Craig G., Colin Greene, and Karl Moller. *Renewing Biblical Interpretation*. Cumbria: Paternoster, 2000.

Bartholomew, Craig G., Scott Hahn, Robin Parry, Christopher Seitz, and Al Wolters, eds. *Canon and Biblical Interpretation*. Milton Keynes: Paternoster, 2006.

Bartholomew, Craig G., Mary Healy, Karl Möller, and Robin Parry, eds. *Out of Egypt: Biblical Theology and Biblical Interpretation*. Carlisle: Paternoster, 2005.

Bartholomew, Craig G. and Heath A. Thomas, eds. *A Manifesto for Theological Interpretation*. Grand Rapids: Baker, 2016.

Barton, John. *The Nature of Biblical Criticism*. Louisville: WJK, 2007.

Bauckham, Richard and Carl Mosser, eds. *The Gospel of John and Christian Theology*. Grand Rapids: Eerdmans, 2008.

Bauckham, Richard, Daniel R. Driver, Trevor A. Hart, and Nathan MacDonald. *The Epistle to the Hebrews and Christian Theology*. Grand Rapids: Eerdmans, 2009.

Bauspiess, Martin, Christof Landmesser, and David Lincicum, eds. *Ferdinand Christian Baur and The History of Early Christianity*. Translated by Robert F. Brown and Peter C. Hodgson. Oxford: OUP, 2017.

Becker, Carl L. *The Heavenly City of the Eighteenth-Century Philosophers*. New Haven: YUP, 1932.

Beiser, F. C. *The German Historicist Tradition*. New York: OUP, 2012.

Bendangjungshi, *Confessing Christ in the Naga Context: Towards a Liberating Ecclesiology*. Zurich: LIT, 2011.

Benedict XVI, *Verbum Domini: The Word of the Lord*. Boston: Pauline Books & Media, 2010.

Bevans, Stephen B. *Model of Contextual Theology*, Revised and Expanded Edition. Maryknoll: Orbis Books, 2002.

Billings, J. Todd. *The Word of God for the People of God: An Entryway to the Theological Interpretation of Scripture*. Grand Rapids: Eerdmans, 2010.

———. *Union with Christ: Reframing Theology and Ministry for the Church*. Grand Rapids: Baker, 2011.

Bloesch, Donald G. *Essentials of Evangelical Theology: Volume One: God, Authority, and Salvation*. New York: Harper & Row Publishers, 1978.

Bockmuehl, Markus. *Seeing the World: Refocusing New Testament Study*. Grand Rapids: Baker, 2006.

Bockmuehl, Markus and Alan J. Torrance, eds. *Scripture's Doctrine and Theology's Bible: How the New Testament Shapes Christian Dogmatics*. Grand Rapids: Baker, 2008.

Boer, Roland. *Last Stop Before Antarctica: The Bible and Postcolonialism in Australia*. Sheffield: SAP, 2001.

Bowald, Mark Aland. *Rendering the World in Theological Hermeneutics: Mapping Divine and Human Agency*. Hampshire: Ashgate, 2007.

Boyd, Robin. *An Introduction to Indian Christian Theology*. Delhi: ISPCK, 2009.

Braaten, Carl E. and Robert W. Jenson. *The Catholicity of the Reformation*. Grand Rapids: Eerdmans, 1996.

Burnett, Richard E. *Karl Barth's Theological Exegesis*. Grand Rapids: Eerdmans, 2004.

Burns, J. Patout. *Romans: Interpreted by Early Christians and Medieval Commentators*. Grand Rapids: Eerdmans, 2012.

Buschart, W. David and Kent Eilers, *Theology as Retrieval: Receiving the Past, Renewing the Church*. Downers Grove: IVP, 2015.

Buss, Martin J. *Criticism in its Context*. Sheffield: SAP, 1999.

———. *The Changing Shape of Form Criticism: A Relational Approach*. Sheffield: SPP, 2010.

Cabton, William. *A History of the British and Foreign Bible Society: With Portraits and Illustrations*, vol. 1–5. London: John Murray, 1904.

Calvin, John. *Institutes of Christian Religion*. Edited by John T. McNeil. Translated by Ford Lewis Battles. Philadelphia: Westminster, 1960.

Carson, Rachel. *Silent Spring*. Penguin Classics; London: Penguin, 2000.

Castleman, Robbie, Darian Lockett, and Stephen Presley, eds. *Explorations in Interdisciplinary Reading: Theological, Exegetical, and Reception-Historical Perspectives*. Eugene, Oregon: Pickwick, 2017.

Chhungi, Hrangthan, ed. *Theologizing Tribal Heritage: A Critical Re-Look*. Delhi: CWM/ISET/ECC/PCI/ISPCK, 2008.

Chhungi, Hrangthan, M. M. Ekka, and Wati Longchar, eds. *Doing Indigenous Theology in Asia: Towards New Frontiers*. Nagpur: NCCI/GTC/SCEPTRE, 2012.

Chhungi, Hrangthan, Raj Bharath Patta and P. Mohan Larbeer, eds. *Building Theologies of Solidarity: Interfacing Feminist Theology with Dalit Theology and Tribal/Adivasi Theologies*. Bangalore: BTESSC/NCCI/SCMI, 2012.

Childs, Brevard S. *Introduction to the Old Testament as Scripture*. Philadelphia: Fortress Press, 1979.

———. *New Testament as Canon: An Introduction*. Philadelphia: Fortress Press, 1984.

———. *Old Testament Theology in a Canonical Context*. Philadelphia: Fortress Press, 1985.

———. *Biblical Theology of the Old and New Testaments: Theological Reflections on the Christian Bible*. Minneapolis: Fortress Press, 1992.

———. *Biblical Theology: A Proposal*. Minneapolis: Fortress Press, 2002.

Collins, Anthony. *A Discourse of the Grounds and Reasons of the Christian Religion*. London: n.a., 1724.

Collins, John J. *Encounters with Biblical Theology*. Minneapolis: Fortress Press, 2005.

———. *The Bible After Babel: Historical Criticism in a Postmodern Age*. Grand Rapids: Eerdmans, 2005.

Cronin, Vincent. *A Pearl of India: The Life of Robert de Nobili*. New York: E. P. Dutton, 1959.

Davis, Ellen F. and Richard Hays. *The Art of Reading Scripture*. Grand Rapids: Eerdmans, 2003.

Derrida, Jacques. *Of Grammatology*, Corrected Edition. Translated by Gayatri Chakravorty Spivak. Baltimore: John Hopkins, 1974.

———. *Limited Inc*. Edited by Gerald Graff. Translated by Samuel Weber and Jeffrey Mehlman. Evanston: NWUP, 1988.

De Man, Paul. *Allegories of Reading: Figural Language in Rousseau, Nietzsche, Rilke, and Proust*. New Haven: YUP, 1979.

———. *Blindness and Insight: Essays in the Rhetoric of Contemporary Criticism*, Second Edition. Minneapolis: UMP, 1983.

De Spinoza, Benedict. *Theological-Political Treatise*. Edited and translated by Michael Silversthorne and Jonathan Israel. Cambridge: CUP, 2007.

Descartes, Rene. *Discourse on Method and Meditation*. Translated by Elizabeth S. Haldane and G. R. T. Ross. Mineola: Dover, 2003.

Downs, Frederick S. *History of Christianity in India: North East India in the Nineteenth and Twentieth Centuries*, vol. 5.5. Bangalore: CHAI, 2003.

Dube, Musa W. *Postcolonial Feminist Interpretation of the Bible*. St. Louis: Chalice, 2000.

Dulles, Avery. *The Catholicity of the Church*. Oxford: Clarendon, 1985.

Eagleton, Terry. *Literary Theory: An Introduction*, Second Edition. Malden: Blackwell, 1983, 1996.

Elliot, Mark W., Scott J. Hakemann, N. T. Wright, and John Frederick, eds. *Galatians and Christian Theology: Justification, The Gospel, and Ethics in Paul's Letter*. Grand Rapids: Eerdmans, 2014.

Elliott, Neil. *Liberating Paul: The Justice of God and the Politics of the Apostle*. Maryknoll: Orbis, 1994.

Ellis, E. Earle. *History and Interpretation in New Testament Perspective*. Atlanta: SBL, 2001.

Erb, Peter C., ed. *Pietists: Selected Writings*. New York: Paulist, 1983.

Fame, John M. *Systematic Theology: An Introduction to Christian Belief*. Phillipsburg: P&R Publishing, 2013.

Farkasfalvy, Denis. *Inspiration and Interpretation: A Theological Introduction to Sacred Scripture*. Washington: CUAP, 2010.

Farley, Edward. *Theologia: The Fragmentation and Unity of Theological Education*. Philadelphia: Fortress Press, 1983.

Fish, Stanley. *Is There a Text in this Class? The Authority of Interpretative Communities*. Massachusetts: HUP, 1980.

Florenza, Schuller. *But She Said: Feminist Practices of Biblical Interpretation*. Massachusetts: Beacon Press, 1992.

———. *In Memory of Her: A Feminist Theological Reconstruction of Christian Origins*, Tenth Anniversary Edition. New York: Crossroad, 1994.

Ford, David and Graham Stanton, eds. *Reading Texts, Seeking Wisdom: Scripture and Theology*. Grand Rapids: Eerdmans, 2003.

Fowl, Stephen E., ed. *The Theological Interpretation of Scripture: Classic and Contemporary Readings*. Cambridge: Blackwell, 1997.

———. *Engaging Scripture: A Model for Theological Interpretation*. Massachusetts: Blackwell, 1998.

———. *Philippians, The Two Horizons New Testament Commentary*. Grand Rapids: Eerdmans, 2005.

———. *Theological Interpretation of Scripture*. Eugene: Cascade, 2011.

Fowl, Stephen E. and L. Gregory Jones. *Reading in Communion: Scripture and Ethics in Christian Life*. Grand Rapids: Eerdmans, 1991.

Frei, Hans W. *The Eclipse of Biblical Narrative: A Study in Eighteenth and Nineteenth Century Hermeneutics*. New Haven: YUP, 1974.

Frye, Northrop. *The Great Code: The Bible and Literature*. New York: Harcourt Brace Jovanovich, 1982.

Frykenberg, Robert Eric. *Christianity in India: From Beginnings to the Present*. Oxford: OUP, 2008.

Gadamar, Hans-George. *Truth and Method*. Revised and translated by Joel Weinsheimer and Donald G. Marshall. London: Continuum, 1975.

Gallagher, Susan VanZanten, ed. *Postcolonial Literature and the Biblical Call for Justice*. Jackson: UPM, 1994.

Gangel, K. and W. S. Benson, *Christian Education: Its History and Philosophy*. Chicago: Moody, 1983.

Gener, Timoteo D. and Stephen T. Pardue, eds. *Asian Christian Theology: Evangelical Perspective*. Cumbria: Langham, 2019.

Gnanakan, Ken., ed. *Biblical Theology in Asia*. Bangalore: Theological Book Trust, 1995.

Go, Khup Za. *A Critical Historical Study of Bible Translations among the Zo People in North East India*. Churachandpur: Chin Baptist Literature Board, 1996.

Goldsworthy, Graeme. *Gospel-Centered Hermeneutics: Foundations and Principles of Evangelical Biblical Interpretation*. Downers Grove: IVP, 2006.

Goodall, Norman, J.E. Lesley Newbigin, W. A Visser 'T Hooft, and D.T. Niles, eds. *A Decisive Hour for the Christian Mission, The EACC 1959 and the John R. Mott Memorial Lectures*. London: SCM, 1960.

Gottwald, Norman K. *The Tribes of Yahweh: A Sociology of Religion of Liberated Israel, 1250–1050 BCE*. Maryknoll: Orbis, 1979.

Grafton, A. *Defenders of the Text: The Traditions of Scholarship in an Age of Science, 1450–1800*. Cambridge: HUP, 1991.

Green, Garrett. *Theology, Hermeneutics, and Imagination: The Crisis of Interpretation at the End of Modernity*. Cambridge: CUP, 2000.

Green, Joel B. *Seized by Truth: Reading the Bible as Scripture*. Nashville: Abingdon, 2007.

———. *Reading Scripture as Wesleyans*. Nashville: Abingdon, 2010.

———. *Practicing Theological Interpretation: Engaging Biblical Texts for Faith and Formation*. Grand Rapids: Baker, 2011.

Green, Joel B. and Max Turner, eds. *Between Two Horizons: Spanning New Testament Studies and Systematic Theology*. Grand Rapids: Eerdmans, 2000.

Green, Gene L. Stephen T. Pardue, and K. K. Yeo, eds. *Jesus Without Borders: Christology in the Majority World*. Cumbria: Langham, 2015.

Gregory, Brad S. *The Unintended Reformation: How a Religious Revolution Secularized Society*. Cambridge: Belknap, 2012.

Grett, Mark G., ed. *Ethnicity and the Bible*. Leiden: E. J. Brill, 1996.

Grondin, Jean. *Introduction to Philosophical Hermeneutics*. Translated by Joel Weinsheimer. New Haven: YUP, 1994.

Grotius, Hugo. *Annotationum in Novum Testamenturn II*. Paris: n.a. 1646.

Gundry, Stanley N., ed. *Four Views on Moving Beyond the Bible to Theology*. Grand Rapids: Zondervan, 2009.

Gutierrez, Gustavo. *A Theology of Liberation: History, Politics and Salvation*. Translated and edited by Caridad Inda and John Eagleson. Maryknoll: Orbis, 1973.

Harrison, Peter. *The Bible, Protestantism, and The Rise of Natural Science*. Cambridge: CUP, 2001.

Harrisville, Roy A. *Pandora's Box Opened: An Examination and Defense of Historical-Critical Method and Its Master Practitioners*. Grand Rapids: Eerdmans, 2014.

Harrisville, Roy A. and Walter Sundberg, *The Bible in Modern Culture: Baruza Spinoza to Brevard Childs*, Second Edition. Grand Rapids: Eerdmans, 1995, 2002.

Haynes, Stephen R. and Steven L. McKenzie, eds. *To Each its Own Meaning: An Introduction to Biblical Criticism and Its Application*, Revised and Expanded. Louisville: WJK, 1999.

Hobbes, Thomas. *Leviathan: With Selected Variants from the Latin Edition of 1668*. Edited, with Introduction and Notes by Edward Curley. Indianapolis: Hackett, 1994.

Hodgson, Peter C. *The Formation of Historical Theology: A Study of Ferdinand Christian Baur*. New York: Harper and Row, 1966.

Hodson, T. C. *The Naga Tribes of Manipur*. London: Macmillan,1911.

Holsinger-Friesen, Thomas. *Irenaeus and Genesis: A Study of Competition in Early Christian Hermeneutics*, Journal of Theological Interpretation Supplements 1. Winona Lakes: Eisenbrauns, 2009.

Horam, Mashangthei. *Naga Polity*. Delhi: n.p., 1975.

———. *Social and Cultural Life of Nagas*. Delhi: B. R. Publishing Corporation, 1977.

Hort, Fenton John Anthony. *The Way, The Truth, The Life: The Hulsean Lectures for 1871*. London: Macmillan, 1893.

Howard, Thomas Albert. *Religion and the Rise of Historicism: W. M. L. de Wette, Jacob Burckhardt, and the Theological Origins of Nineteenth-Century Historical Consciousness*. Cambridge: CUP, 2000.

———. *Protestant Theology and The Rise of Modern German University*. Oxford: OUP, 2006.

Hunt, J. *Religious Thought in England in the Nineteenth Century*. London: n.p., 1896.

Hutton, Charles. *A Philosophical and Mathematical Dictionary, Vol. II: Containing an Explanations of Terms, And an Account of Several Subjects, Comprised Under the Heads Mathematics, Astronomy, and Philosophy Both Natural and Experimental*. London: S. Hamilton, 1815.

Iggers, George G. *The German Conception of History: The National Tradition of Historical Thought from Herder to the Present*, Revised Edition. Middletown: WUP, 1983.

Imchen, Narola., ed. *Weaving New Patterns of Ministry for Women in North East India*, Women Study Series No. 3. Jorhat, Assam: WSD, 2004.

Jeanrond, Werner G. *Theological Hermeneutics: Development and Significance*. Hampshire: Macmillan, 1991.

Jenkins, Philip. *The Next Christendom: The Coming of Global Christianity*. Oxford: OUP, 2002.

———. *The New Faces of Christianity: Believing the Bible in the Global South*. New York: OUP, 2006.

Keener, Craig S. *Spirit Hermeneutics: Reading Scripture in light of the Pentecost*. Grand Rapids: Eerdmans, 2016.

Keener Craig, and M. Daniel Carroll, *Global Voices: Reading the Bible in the Majority World.* Massachusetts: Peabody, 2013.

Keitzar, Renthy, ed. *Good News for North East India: A Theological Reader.* Assam, India: CLC, 1995.

———. *In Search of a Relevant Gospel Message: Introducing Contextual Christian Theology for North East India.* Guwahati: CLC, 1995.

Kermode, Frank. *The Genesis of Secrecy: On the Interpretation of Narrative.* Cambridge: HUP, 1979.

Kirk, J. A. *Liberation Theology: An Evangelical View from the Third World.* Atlanta: WJK, 1979.

Kitzberger, Ingrid Rosa, ed. *The Personal Voice in Biblical Interpretation.* London: Routledge, 1999.

Klink III, Edward W. and Darian R. Lockett. *Understanding Biblical Theology: A Comparison of Theory and Practice.* Grand Rapids: Zondervan, 2012.

Kostenberger, Andreas J. and Richard D. Patterson. *Invitation to Biblical Interpretation: Exploring the Hermeneutical Triad History, Literature, and Theology.* Grand Rapids: Kregel, 2011.

Krentz, Edgar. *The Historical-Critical Method.* Philadelphia: Fortress Press, 1975.

Kumar, Nigel Ajay. *What is Religion? A Theological Answer.* Bangalore: SAIACS, 2014.

Kümmel, Werner Georg. *The New Testament: The History of the Investigation of its Problems.* Translated by S. McLean and Howard C. Kee. London: SCM, 1978.

Lalpekhlua, L. H. *Contextual Christology: A Tribal Perspective.* Delhi: ISPCK, 2007.

Larson, Timothy and Daniel J. Treier. *The Cambridge Companion to Evangelical Theology.* Cambridge: CUP, 2007.

Laseto, Razouselie, ed. *Garnering Tribal Resources for Doing Tribal Christian Theology.* Jorhat: ETC, 2008.

Laseto, Razouselie and Yangkahao Vashum, eds. *Tribal Christian Theology: Methods and Sources for Constructing a Relevant Theology for the Indigenous People of North East India.* Jorhat, Assam: ETC, 2007.

Lawrence, Michael. *Biblical Theology in the Life of the Church: A Guide for Ministry.* Wheaton: Crossway, 2010.

Law, David R. *The Historical Critical Method: A Guide for the Perplexed.* New York: T&T Clark, 2012.

Legaspi, Michael C. *The Death of Scripture and the Rise of Biblical Studies.* Oxford: OUP, 2010.

Levering, Matthew. *Participatory Biblical Exegesis: A Theology of Biblical Interpretation*. Notre Dame, Indiana: UNDP, 2008.

Liew, Tat-siong Benny. *Politics of Parousia: Reading Mark Inter(con)textually*. Leiden: Brill, 1999.

Lightfoot, J. B. *Saint Paul's Epistle to the Galatians*. London: Macmillan, 1884.

———. *The Apostolic Father, Part II: S. Ignatius, S. Polycarp*, Second Edition. London: T&T Clark, 2007.

Lincoln, Andrew T. and Angus Paddison, eds. *Christology and Scripture: Interdisciplinary Perspectives*. London: T&T Clark, 2007.

Lineman, Eta. *Historical Criticism of the Bible: Methodology or Ideology?* Translated by Robert W. Yarbrough. Grand Rapids: Baker, 1990.

Locke, John. *The Reasonableness of Christianity, as delivered in the Scriptures*, Edited with an Introduction, Notes, Critical Apparatus and Transcriptions of Related Manuscripts by John C. Higgins-Biddle. Oxford: Clarendon, 1999.

Long, D. Stephen. *Hebrews: Belief: A Theological Commentary on the Bible*. Louisville: WJK, 2011.

Longchar, A. Wati, ed. *An Exploration of Tribal Theology*. Jorhat: TSC, 1997.

———. *An Emerging Asian Theology: Tribal Theology Issues, Method and Perspective*. Jorhat: TSC, 2000.

———. *Returning to Mother Earth: Theology, Mother Earth, and Theological Education*. Kolkata: PTCA, 2012.

———. *Encounter between God and Tribal Culture*. Jorhat: TSC, 1999.

Longchar, A. Wati and Larry E. Davis, eds. *Doing Theology with Tribal Resources: Context and Perspective*. Jorhat: TSC, 1999.

Longkumer, Limatula, ed. *No More Sorrow in God's Garden of Justice: Tribal Women Doing Theology*. Jorhat: WSD, 2007.

Louth, Andrew. *Genesis 1–11*. Downers Grove: IVP, 2001.

MacDonald, Nathan, Mark W. Elliott, and Grant Macaskill. *Genesis and Christian Theology*. Grand Rapids: Eerdmans, 2012.

Maier, Gerhard. *The End of the Historical-Critical Method*. Translated by Edwin W. Leverenz and Rudolph F. Norden. Missouri: Concordia, 1974.

Marlow, Hilary. *Biblical Prophets and Contemporary Environmental Ethics: Re reading Amos, Hosea, and First Isaiah*. Oxford: OUP, 2009.

Marshall, I. Howard. *Beyond the Bible: Moving from Scripture to Theology*. Grand Rapids: Baker, 2004.

McFague, Sallie. *Metaphorical Theology: Models of God in Religious Language*. Philadelphia: Fortress Press, 1982.

McGovern, A. F. *Liberation Theology and its Critics: Toward an Assessment.* Maryknoll: Orbis, 1989.

Milbank, John. *Theology and Social Theory: Beyond Secular Reason*, Second Edition. Oxford: Blackwell, 2006.

Mildert, W. Van. *An Enquiry into the General Principles of Scripture-Interpretation*. Oxford: n.p., 1815.

Miller, Randolph Crump. *The Clue to Christian Education*. New York: Charles Scribner's Sons, 1950.

Minz, Nirmal. *Rise Up, My People, and Claim the Promise: The Gospel Among the Tribes of India*. Delhi: ISPCK, 1997.

Moberly, R. W. L. *The Bible, Theology, and Faith: A Study of Abraham and Jesus*. Cambridge: CUP, 2000.

———. *The Theology of the Book of Genesis*. Cambridge: CUP, 2009.

———. *Old Testament Theology: Reading the Hebrew Bible as Christian Scripture*. Grand Rapids: Baker Academic, 2013.

Morgan, Robert and John Barton, *Biblical Interpretation*. Oxford: OUP, 1998.

Moore, Stephen D. *Literary Criticism and the Gospels: The Theoretical Challenge*. New Haven: YUP, 1989.

———. *Mark and Luke in Poststructuralist Perspectives: Jesus Begins to Write*. New Haven: YUP, 1992.

Moore, Stephen D. and Fernando F. Segovia, eds. *Postcolonial Biblical Criticism: Interdisciplinary Intersections*. London: T&T Clark, 2005.

Morrow, Jeffrey L. *Three Sceptics and the Bible: La Peyrère, Hobbes, Spinoza, and The Reception of Modern Biblical Criticism*. Eugene: Pickwick, 2016.

Moulaison, Jane Barter. *Thinking Christ: Christology and Contemporary Critics*. Minneapolis: Fortress Press, 2012.

Mullens, Joseph. *A Brief Review of Ten Years Missionary Labour in India*. London: James Nisbet, 1863.

n.a. *Report of Third Decennial Missionary Conference held at Bombay, 1892–93*, vol. 1. Bombay: ESSP, 1893.

n.a. *A Collection of Papers Connected with the Movement of the National Church of India*. Madras: 1893.

Neil, Stephen. *A History of Christianity in India: The Beginnings to AD 1707*. Cambridge: CUP, 1984.

Neil, Stephen and Tom Wright, *The Interpretation of the New Testament, 1861–1986*, Second Edition. Oxford: OUP, 1988.

Neuhaus, Richard John, ed. *Biblical Interpretation in Crisis: The Ratzinger Conference on Bible and Church*. Grand Rapids: Eerdmans, 1989.

Newbigin, Lesslie. *The Reunion of the Church*, New and Revised. London: SCM, 1960.

Nicholson, E. W. *The Pentateuch in the Twentieth Century: The Legacy of Julius Wellhausen*. Oxford: OUP, 1998.

Noel, Bradley Truman. *Pentecostal and Postmodern Hermeneutics: Comparisons and Contemporary Impact*. Eugene: WIPF & Stock, 2010.

Nuh, V. K. *In Search of Praxis Theology for the Nagas*. New Delhi: Regency, 2003.

Nunez, E. A. and W. D. Tayler. *Crisis in Latin America: An Evangelical Perspective*. Chicago: Moody, 1989.

O'Collins, Gerald and Daniel Kendall. *The Bible for Theology: Ten Principles for the Theology Use of Scripture*. New York: Paulist, 1997.

Okello, Joseph B. Onyango. *A History and Critique of Methodological Naturalism: The Philosophical Case for God's Design of Nature*. Orlando: WIPF & Stock, 2015.

Okihiro, Gary Y. *Margins and Mainstreams: Asians in American History and Culture*. Seattle: UWP, 1994.

Osborne, Grant R. *The Hermeneutical Spiral: A Comprehensive Introduction to Biblical Interpretation*, Revised and edited. Downers Grove: IVP, 2006.

Ott, Craig and Harold Netlands, eds. *Globalizing Theology: Belief and Practice in an Era of World Christianity*. Grand Rapids: Baker, 2006.

Pachuau, Lalramliana, P. Mohan Larbeer, and A. Wati Longchar, eds. *Contours of Tribal Theology: Issues and Perspectives*. Kolkata: BTESSC, 2015.

Paddison, Angus. *Scripture: A Very Theological Proposal*. New York: T&T Clark, 2009.

Parkinson, Thomas. *A System of Mechanics, Being the Substance of Lectures upon That Branch of Natural Philosophy*. Cambridge: J. Archdeacon, 1785.

Parratt, John, ed. *An Introduction to Third World Theologies*. Cambridge: CUP, 2004.

Parry, Robin A. *Lamentations*. Grand Rapids: Eerdmans, 2010.

Pelikan, Jaroslav. *Acts*. Grand Rapids: Brazos, 2005.

Pennock, Robert R. *Tower of Babel: The Evidence Against the New Creationism*. London: MIT, 1999.

Pettigrew, William. *Jesuwui Lā: Hymns in Tāngkhul Naga*. Assam: ABMH, 1907.

———. *Varivarāwui Lairik: The New Testament in Tangkhul Naga*. Calcutta: BFBS, 1927.

Piper, Ronald Allan, ed. *The Gospel Behind the Gospel: Current Studies on Q*. Leiden: E. J. Brill, 1995.

Prabhakar, M. E., ed. *Towards a Dalit Theology*. Delhi: ISPCK, 1989.

Pratt, J. H., ed. *The Thought of the Evangelical Leaders: Notes of the Discussions of the Eclectic Society, London, During the years 1798–1814*. London: n.p., 1856.

Preus, J. Samuel. *Spinoza and the Irrelevance of Biblical Authority*. Cambridge: CUP, 2001.

Prior, Michael. *Jesus the Liberator: Nazareth Liberation Theology (Luke 4:16–30)*. Sheffield: SAP, 1995.

———. *The Bible and Colonialism: A Moral Critique*. Sheffield: SAP, 1997.

Putman, Rhyne R. *In Defense of Doctrine: Evangelicalism, Theology, and Scripture*. Minneapolis: Fortress Press, 2015.

Radhakrishna, Meena, ed. *First Citizens: Studies on Adivasis, Tribals, and Indigenous People in India*. New Delhi: OUP, 2016.

Rae, Murray A. *History and Hermeneutics*. London: T & T Clark, 2005.

Ragui, Taimaya. *An Analysis of Calvin's Hermeneutics with Implications for North East Indian Context*. Bangalore: SAIACS Archive, 2016.

Räisänen, Heikii, Elisabeth Schussler Fiorenza, R. S. Sugirtharajah, Krister Stendahl, and James Barr, eds. *Reading the Bible in the Global Village: Helsinki*. Atlanta: SBL, 2000.

Reardon, B. M. G. *From Coleridge to Gore: A Century of Religious Thought in Britain*. London: n.p., 1971.

———. *Religion in the Age of Romanticism: Studies in Early Nineteenth Century Thought*. Cambridge: CUP, 1985.

Redford, Shawn B. *Missiological Hermeneutics: Biblical Interpretation for the Global Church*. Eugene: Pickwick, 2012.

Reumann, John, Samuel H. Nafzger, and Harold H. Ditmanson, eds. *Studies in Lutheran Hermeneutics*. Philadelphia: Fortress Press, 1979.

Reventlow, Henning Graf. *The Authority of the Bible and the Rise of the Modern World*. London: SCM, 1980.

———. *History of Biblical Interpretation, vol. 4: From the Enlightenment to the Twentieth Century*. Translated by Leo G. Perdue. Atlanta: SBL, 2010.

Ro, Bong Rin and Ruth Eshenaur, eds. *The Bible and Theology in Asian Context: An Evangelical Perspective on Asian Theology*. Taiwan: ATA, 1984.

Rogerson, John W. *Old Testament Criticism in the Nineteenth Century: England and Germany*. London: SPCK, 1984.

———. *W. M. L. de Wette: Founder of Modern Criticism—An Intellectual Biography*. Sheffield: SAP, 1992.

Rolston, M. A. Z. *The United Church of Northern India Survey 1968*. Nagpur: UCNI: 1970.

Rosner, Brian S., ed. *The Consolidation of Theology*. Grand Rapids: Eerdmans, 2008.

Rowland, Christopher, ed. *The Cambridge Companion to Liberation Theology*. Cambridge: CUP, 1999.

Rowland, Christopher and Mark Corner, eds. *Liberating Exegesis: The Challenge of Liberation Theology to Biblical Studies*. London: SPCK, 1989.

Runions, Erin. *Changing Subjects: Gender, Nation and Future in Micah*. Sheffield: SAP, 2001.

Sandys-Wunsch, John. *What have they Done to the Bible? A History of Modern Biblical Interpretation*. Minnesota: Liturgical, 2005.

———. *Theology, History and Biblical Interpretation: Modern Readings*. London: Bloomsbury, 2015.

Sanneh, Lamin. *Translating the Message: The Missionary Impact on Culture*, Revised and Expanded. New York: Orbis, 2015.

Sarisky, Darren. *Scriptural Interpretation: A Theological Exploration*. West Sussex: Blackwell, 2013.

Schleiermacher, Friedrich. *Hermeneutics: And Criticism and Other Writings*. Translated and edited by Andrew Bowie. Cambridge: CUP, 1998.

———. *Constructing Local Theologies*. Maryknoll, New York: Orbis Books, 1985.

Scholder, Klaus. *The Birth of Modern Critical Theology: Origins and Problems of Biblical Criticism in the Seventeenth Century*. London: SCM, 1990.

Schreiter, Robert J. *The New Catholicity: Theology Between the Global and the Local*. Maryknoll: Orbis, 1997.

Schweitzer, Albert. *The Quest of the Historical Jesus: A Critical Study of its Progress from Reimarus to Wrede*. Translated by W. Montgomery. London: A. & C. Black, 1910.

Segovia, Fernando F. *Decolonizing Biblical Studies: A View from the Margins*. Maryknoll: Orbis, 2000.

Segovia, Fernando F. and Mary Ann Tolbert, eds. *Reading from this Place, vol. 1–2: Social Location and Biblical Interpretation in Global Perspective*. Minneapolis: Fortress Press, 1995.

Segovia, Fernando F. and R. S. Sugirtharajah, eds. *A Postcolonial Commentary on the New Testament Writings*. London: T&T Clark, 2009.

Seitz, Christopher. *The Character of Christian Scripture: The significance of a Two Testament Bible*. Grand Rapids: Baker, 2011.

Seitz, Christopher R. and Kathryn Greene-McCreight, *Theological Exegesis: Essays in Honor of Brevard Childs*. Grand Rapids: Eerdmans, 1999.

Shimray, Shimreingam, ed. *Tribal Theology: A Reader*. Jorhat: TSC, 2003.

Simon, Richard. *A Critical History of the Old Testament*. London: Davis, 1678.

———. *A Critical History of the New Testament*. Translated, introduced and annotated by Andrew Hunwick. Leiden: Brill, 2013.

Simson, Graham. *The Pastoral Epistles: 1–2 Timothy, Titus: An Exegetical and Contextual Commentary*. Bangalore: Primalogue, 2016.

Smalley, Beryl. *The Study of the Bible in the Middle Ages*. Notre Dame, In.: Notre DUP, 1964.

Smart, James D. *The Teaching Ministry of the Church: An Examination of the Basic Principles of Christian Education*. Philadelphia: Westminster, 1954.

———. *The Strange Silence of the Bible in the Church*. Philadelphia: Westminster, 1970.

Smith, Christian. *Bible Made Impossible: Why Biblicism is Not a Truly Evangelical Reading of Scripture*. Grand Rapids: Brazos, 2011.

Smith, George. *The Life of William Carey: Shoemaker and Missionary*. London: John Murray, 1885.

Sparks, Kenton L. *God's Word in Human Words: An Evangelical Appropriation of Critical Biblical Scholarship*. Grand Rapids: Baker, 2008.

Spener, Philipp Jakob. *Pia Desideria*. Translated and edited by Theodore G. Tappert. Philadelphia: Fortress Press, 1964.

Spinks, D. Christopher. *The Bible and the Crisis of Meaning: Debates on Theological Interpretation of Scripture*. New York: T&T Clark, 1998.

Spurgeon, Andrew B. *1 Corinthians: An Exegetical and Contextual Commentary*. Bangalore: Primalogue, 2011.

Staley, Jeffrey. *Reading with a Passion: Rhetoric, Autobiography, and the American West in the Gospel of John*. New York: Continuum, 1995.

Strauss, David Friedrich. *The Life of Jesus, Critically Examined*. Translated by George Eliot. London: Swan Sonnenschein, 1902.

Storer, Kevin. *Reading Scripture to Hear God: Kevin Vanhoozer and Henri de Lubac on God's Use of Scripture in the Economy of Redemption*. Cambridge: James Clark, 2015.

Storr, V. F. *The Development of English Theology in the Nineteenth Century, 1800 1860*. London: n.p., 1913.

Stott, John. *Evangelical Truth: A Personal Plea for Unity, Integrity and Faithfulness*, Revised and edited. Carlisle: Langham, 2013.

Stuhlmacher, Peter. *Historical Criticism and Theological Interpretation of Scripture*. Translated by Roy A. Harrisvile. Philadelphia: Fortress Press, 1977.

Sugirtharajah, R. S. *Asian Biblical Hermeneutics and Postcolonialism: Contesting the Interpretations*. Sheffield: SAP, 1988.

———, ed. *Voice from the Margin: Interpreting the Bible in the Third World*. London: SPCK, 1991.

———. *The Bible and the Third World Countries: Precolonial, Colonial, and Postcolonial Encounters*. Cambridge: CUP, 2001.

———. *Still at the Margins: Biblical Scholarship Fifteen Years after the Voices from the Margin*. ed. R. S. Sugirtharajah. London: T&T Clark, 2008.

Swain, Scott R. *Trinity, Revelation, and Reading: A Theological Introduction to the Bible and its Interpretation*. London: T&T Clark, 2011.

Takatemjen. ed. *Bible Reading from the Northeast India Context*. Makokchung, Nagaland: CTC, 2014.

Taylor, Edward B. *Religion in Primitive Culture*. New York: Harper and Brothers, 1958.

Thanzauva, K., ed. *Towards a Tribal Theology: The Mizo Perspective*. Aizawl, Mizoram: MTC, 1989.

———. *Theology of Community: Tribal Theology in the Making*. Aizawl, Mozoram: MTC, 1997.

———. *Transforming Theology: A Theological Basis for Social Transformation*. Bangalore: ATC, 2002.

Thiselton, Anthony C. *New Horizons in Hermeneutics: The Theory and Practice of Transforming Biblical Reading*. Grand Rapids: Zondervan, 1992.

———. *The Hermeneutics of Doctrine*. Grand Rapids: Eerdmans, 2007.

Tillard, Jean-Marie-Roger. *Church of Churches: The Ecclesiology of Communion*. Translated by R. C. De Peaux. Minnesota: Liturgical, 1992.

Thomas, John. *Evangelising the Nation: Religion and the Formation of Naga Political Identity*. New Delhi: Routledge, 2016.

Thomas, M. M. and Richard W. Taylor, eds. *Tribal Awakening: A Group Study*. Bangalore: CISRS, 1965.

Tompkins, Jane P., ed. in *Reader-Response Criticism: From Formalism to Post Structuralism*. Baltimore: JHUP, 1980.

Treier, Daniel J. *Introduction to Theological Interpretation of Scripture: Recovering a Christian Practice*. Nottingham: Apollos, 2008.

Vanhoozer, Kevin J. *Biblical Narrative in the Philosophy of Paul Ricoeur: A Study in Hermeneutics and Theology*. Cambridge: CUP, 1990.

———. *Is There a Meaning in This Text: The Bible, the Reader, and the Morality of Literary Knowledge*. Grand Rapids: Zondervan, 1998.

———. *First Theology: God, Scripture, and Hermeneutics*. Downers Grove: IVP, 2002.

———. *The Drama of Doctrine: A Canonical Linguistic Approach to Christian Theology*. Louisville: WJK, 2005.

———, ed. *Theological Interpretation of Scripture of the Old Testament: A Book-By Book Survey*. Grand Rapids: Baker, 2005.

———, ed. *Theological Interpretation of Scripture of the New Testament: A Book-By Book Survey*. Grand Rapids: Baker, 2005.

———, ed. *Dictionary for Theological Interpretation of the Bible*. Grand Rapids: Baker, 2005.

———. *Remythologizing Theology: Divine Action, Passion, and Authorship*. Cambridge: CUP, 2010.

———. *Faith Speaking Understanding: Performing the Drama of Doctrine*. Louisville: WJK, 2014.

———. *Biblical Authority After Babel: Retrieving the Solas in the Spirit of Mere Protestant Christianity*. Grand Rapids: Brazos, 2016.

———. *Pictures at a Theological Exhibition: Scenes of the Church's Worship, Witness, and Wisdom*. Downers Grove: IVP, 2016.

Vanhoozer, Kevin J., Charles A. Anderson, and Michael J. Sleasman, eds. *Everyday Theology: How to Read Cultural Texts and Interpret Trends*. Grand Rapids: Baker, 2007.

Vanhoozer, Kevin J. and Owen Strachan, eds. *The Pastor as Public Theologian: Reclaiming a Lost Vision*. Grand Rapids: Baker, 2015.

Vanhoozer, Kevin J. and Daniel J. Treier. *Theology and the Mirror of Scripture: Mere Evangelical Account*. Downers Grove: IVP, 2015.

Vashum, Yangkahao, ed. *Tribal Theology and The Bible: A Search for Contextual Relevance*. Jorhat, Assam: TSC, 2011.

———. *Christology in Context: A Tribal-indigenous Appraisal of North East India*. New Delhi: CWI, 2017.

Vashum, Yangkahao, Peter Haokip, and Melvil Pereira, eds. *Search for a New Society: Tribal Theology for North East India*. Guwahati: NESRC, 2012.

Vidyarthi, L. P. and B. K. Rai, *The Tribal Culture in India*. Delhi: Concept Publishing Company, 1977.

Volf, Miroslav. *After Our Likeness: The Church as the Image of Trinity*. Grand Rapids: Eerdmans, 1998.

Walls, Andrew. *The Missionary Movement in Christian History: Studies in the Transmission of Faith*. Maryknoll: Orbis, 1996.

Watson, Francis. *Text and Truth: Redefining Biblical Theology*. Edinburgh: T&T Clark, 1997.

———. *Text, Church and World: Biblical Interpretation in Theological Perspective*. Grand Rapids: Eerdmans, 1994.

———. *Paul and Hermeneutics of Faith*. London: T&T Clark, 2014.

———. *Gospel Writing: A Canonical Perspective*. Grand Rapids: Eerdmans, 2013.

———. *The Fourfold Gospel: A Theological Reading of the New Testament Portraits of Jesus*. Grand Rapids: Baker, 2016.

Weber, Otto. *Foundations of Dogmatics*. Translated and annotated by Darrell L. Guder. vol. 1. Grand Rapids: Eerdmans, 1983.

Webster, John. *Word and Church: Essays in Christian Dogmatics*. Edinburgh: T&T Clark, 2001.

———. *Holy Scripture: A Dogmatic Sketch*. Cambridge: CUP, 2003.

———. *Confessing God: Essays in Christian Dogmatics II*. London: T&T Clark, 2005.

———. *The Domain of the Word: Scripture and Theological Reason*. London: T&T Clark, 2012.

Westcott, Brooke Foss. *Introduction to the Study of the Gospels, With Historical and Explanatory Notes*. Boston: Gould and Lincoln, 1866.

———. *The Bible in the Church, A Popular Account of the Collection and Reception of the Holy Scriptures in the Christian Churches*. London: Macmillan, 1866.

Whiston, William. *An Essay Towards Restoring the True Text of the Old Testament, and for Vindicating the Citations thence Made in the New Testament*. London: n.a., 1722.

Williams, David M. *Receiving the Bible in Faith: Historical and Theological Exegesis*. Washington: CUAP, 2004.

Willimon, William H. *Pastor: The Theology and Practice of Ordained Ministry*. Nashville: Abingdon, 2002.

Wink, Walter. *The Bible in Human Transformation: Toward a New Paradigm for Biblical Study*. Minneapolis: Fortress Press, 1973.

Wintle, Brian, ed. *South Asia Bible Commentary: A One Volume Commentary on the Whole Bible*. Udaipur: Open Door, 2015.

Wolterstorff, Nicholas. *Divine Discourse: Philosophical Reflections on the Claim that God Speaks*. New York: CUP, 1995.

Wrede, William. *The Origin of the New Testament*. Translated by James S. Hill. London: Harber & Brothers, 1909.

———. *Paul*, Translated by Edward Lummis. London: Philip Green, 1907.

Zimmermann, Jens. *Recovering Theological Hermeneutics: An Incarnational Trinitarian Theory of Interpretation*. Grand Rapids: Baker, 2004.

Zizioulas, John D. *Being as Communion: Studies in Personhood and the Church*. New York: St. Vladimir's Seminary Press, 1985.

Zolawma, R. *Tribal Ecclesiology: A Critical Synthesis of Early Christian Traditions and Cultural Traditions of Northeast India*. New Delhi: CWP, 2016.

INDEX

academy, xi, xii, 2, 3, 4, 5, 6, 7, 8, 9, 10, 42, 50, 53, 54, 55, 58, 67, 71–73, 81, 88, 91, 117, 119, 122–30, 140, 149, 150, 154, 167, 174, 175, 177

Angami, Zhodi, 58, 71

Asia Theological Association, 4, 155, 159

Baptist, 4, 62–63, 66, 69, 141, 142, 166, 168, 183

Barth, Karl, 51, 83

Barthes, Roland, 46

believing criticism, 37

biblical criticism, 1, 3, 7–10, 12–13, 17–19, 21–24, 27–31, 36, 42, 44, 47–48, 51, 55, 81, 83–84, 87–88, 91, 121, 123, 125, 149, 173

biblical interpretation, v, vi, x, 1, 2, 4–13, 17–19, 23, 25–26, 29–30, 33, 35, 44, 47, 50–55, 57–58, 74–93, 95–96, 98, 99–102, 105–14, 117–19, 121–25, 133–34, 136–39, 141, 149, 151, 153–55, 159–60, 164, 166, 168–69, 171, 173–77

biblical scholars, xii, 8, 26, 30, 37, 42–43, 46, 49–52, 84, 86–88, 96, 101, 106, 123–24, 149, 173

biblical studies, v–vii, 1, 3, 6–7, 12, 31, 48, 50, 54, 81–82, 84, 86–87, 96, 99, 101–3, 112, 119, 121–22, 125, 132, 148–51, 153, 174–76

biblical theology, vi–vii, 4, 6, 28–29, 81–82, 88, 90, 96, 102–6, 112, 119, 121–23, 132, 137, 148, 154–55, 159, 164–65, 171, 176–78

canon, 4, 27, 29, 37, 50, 55, 90, 94, 95, 109, 111–13, 118, 159, 165, 177

canonical (principle), vi, xii, 4–6, 27, 42, 74, 90–92, 94–95, 100, 105, 107, 111–13, 118–19, 123, 132, 148, 164, 166, 168, 171, 173, 175–76, 178

Carson, D. A., 104, 113, 136

catholic principle, vi, 106, 113, 177

Christian response, 60

Christian theology, xii, 57–58, 62, 64, 66–68, 88, 96, 101–2, 127, 133, 163, 174

church, v–xii, 1–10, 14–15, 18–19, 24, 29, 37, 39–41, 44, 50–55, 57–58, 60–62, 64–67, 71–73, 78–86, 88, 90–94, 99, 101, 104, 106, 109–13, 115, 117, 119, 122–31, 135, 136, 138, 140–48, 152, 154–71, 174–78

Collins, Anthony, 19, 21
confessing community, 3–4, 119, 127–31, 137, 140–43, 146, 147–48, 158, 162–67, 169–71
context, v–vii, 1–10, 17, 21–24, 37, 44, 46–47, 49–50, 52, 55, 57–58, 60, 62–63, 65–82, 85–86, 89–92, 94, 95–96, 99–106, 111–13, 115–19, 121–23, 125–36, 138–40, 145–46, 148, 150–68, 171, 173–78
contextual principle, vi, 55, 106
contextual theology, vii, 3–6, 64, 66, 68, 82, 106, 118, 122–24, 127, 129, 132, 137, 147–49, 153–55, 159, 164, 165, 171, 176–78
core principle, vi, 107, 134
criticism, v, 1, 3, 7–10, 12–13, 16–19, 21–37, 42–51, 55, 74, 76–77, 81, 83, 84, 87, 92, 102, 121–23, 125, 135–37, 151, 153, 173
culture, 2, 30–32, 45, 50, 57, 59, 63–67, 69–70, 74–75, 77–79, 89, 91, 98–100, 116, 118, 123, 127–31, 137–38, 140, 143–46, 148, 153, 156–57, 159–61, 163, 174

de Wette, W. M. L., 31, 32
demarcation, 7, 67, 86, 88
Derrida, 47, 48
Descartes, Rene, 13, 14
disenchanted, 7–8, 10, 21, 25, 34–135
divine, 7–11, 13–14, 17–18, 22, 24–28, 34–35, 37, 41, 52, 54–55, 66, 89, 94–95, 97–98, 100, 102, 108, 110, 112–13, 119, 132–33, 135, 139, 147–48, 153, 158, 161, 164, 171
dominant, v, 2, 17, 42, 52, 57–59, 61–62, 64, 69, 72, 79, 122, 124, 127, 132, 134, 151–52, 160, 163, 174–75, 178

enchanted, 7–8, 10–11, 13–14, 21, 24–25, 34, 37–38, 54, 57, 64, 67, 122, 128, 135, 158
English Deist, 19

Fowl, Stephen E., 82, 86, 93, 100

Gabler, J. B., 25, 28–29, 103
German liberals, 19
Gottwald, Norman K., 149

Hobbes, Thomas, 13–14

Jesus Christ, 5, 21, 63, 65, 94, 107, 109, 111, 113, 127, 141, 144–45, 160, 165–68, 170, 177
justice, 59, 70, 72, 78–79, 95, 127, 130, 134, 138–40, 174

Keitzar, Renthy, 62, 63–64, 68–70, 72, 74
Kendall, Daniel, 96
Khasis, 64–65, 71, 141–42
Kuki, 65, 141–42

Lallawmzuala, K., 77
Lalpekhlua, L.H., 143–44
Laseto, Razouselie, 76
liberals, 19, 51, 67, 131, 154–55
Lightfoot, Joseph Barber, 37–40
local church, 2, 4, 110–15, 117, 119, 128, 135, 157–59, 166, 167, 169, 170

Longchar, Wat, 60, 62, 69–70, 130
Longkumer, Limatula, 79

Majority World, 1–5, 49, 62, 102, 106, 118–19, 122–24, 150–51, 153–54, 173–77
margins, 54, 71–72, 78, 123–24, 138, 157, 175
methods, 1, 12, 17–18, 30, 53, 55, 73, 76, 90, 98, 137, 149, 164, 173–75
Michaelis, Johann David, 25
Milbank, John, 102
mission, 57–58, 60–64, 67–68, 72, 116, 127–28, 134, 142–43, 147, 156, 160, 163, 174
Mizos, 63–66, 71, 141–42, 144–45

Nagas, xi, xii, 4, 62, 64, 66, 70, 142–43
naturalism, 8–10, 12–13, 32, 35
New Testament, 17–19, 24–25, 27–29, 37, 76, 91, 94–96, 102, 106, 108, 136, 152
norm, 14, 28, 82, 113, 127–30, 141, 153, 161, 163
North East India, v–vi, 3, 57–59, 62, 66–68, 70, 73–74, 78, 141–42

O'Collins, Gerald, 96

Pettigrew, William, 143, 147
Pietists, 23, 24, 25
postmodern, v, 1, 4, 44–46, 48–50, 54–55, 77, 81, 87–89, 108, 114–15, 121–22, 137, 149, 153, 173, 174

rationalist, 14, 16, 23, 25–26, 28, 35–36, 38, 40
reader-response, 46–47, 77
Reformation, 7, 22–23, 26, 129, 135, 164, 166–67, 171, 177
Reformers, 8, 18, 23, 166
revelation, 8–9, 16, 19, 24–26, 41, 43, 51, 66, 71, 97, 147, 159–61, 167
Roman Catholic Church, 18, 84

sacred, 20, 43, 70, 90, 130, 142, 155, 160, 164
Schleiermacher, Friedrich Daniel Ernst, 33, 34
secular, 26, 67, 83, 102, 131, 142, 155, 160, 164
Semler, Johann Salomo, 25
Senate of Serampore, 65, 67–68, 72
Shimray, Shimreingam, 69
Simon, Richard, 14, 18
Soares-Prabhu, George, 123
sociopolitical concern, 6, 64, 68, 124, 128, 130–31, 140, 150, 153, 155, 161, 163–64, 177
solas, 129, 164, 166–68, 170–71, 177
Spener, Philipp Jacob, 24, 25
Spinoza, Baruch, 12, 13, 16, 17
spiritual, 2, 13, 23, 26, 73, 84, 94, 118, 125, 138, 142, 155, 163, 164
Strauss, David, 34
Stuhlmacher, Peter, 84
supernaturalist, 8, 9–10, 23, 35, 36
Supreme Being, 141–42, 147
Syielieh, B. J., 76
syncretism, 45, 72
synthesis-praxis, 70, 73

Tangkhul Naga, 3–4, 141, 143, 147, 162
Thanzauva, K., 58, 60, 66–75

theodramatic, 106–7, 109–11, 116, 170, 175
theological interpretation of Scripture (also TIS), vi, 4–6, 81–85, 95, 100–1, 106–19, 121–39, 147–49, 155, 160, 165–66, 170–71, 173, 175–78
theological method, 3–4, 69, 73, 106–7, 117, 164, 171
Thumra, Jonathan H., 59, 62, 141, 142
tribal churches, 57, 62, 64, 72, 126, 128, 131, 138, 141, 145, 147, 162–63, 166
Tribal Study Centre, 68, 71
tribal theology, 71–74, 76, 79–80, 106, 119, 122–25, 127–31, 137–38, 147–48, 153–55, 160–62, 164, 170–71, 174–77
Tübingen, 38, 40

universities, 32, 87

Vanhoozer, Kevin J., vi, 1, 4–5, 28, 82, 85–86, 95, 103, 105, 106, 109–13, 164

Watson, Francis, 86, 88
west, v, xii, 1, 3, 5, 7–8, 10, 13, 30, 57, 70, 122, 124, 152–54, 159, 166, 168, 174, 175, 177
Westcott, Brooke Foss, 37–38, 40–42
Western missionaries, 57, 63–64, 71, 127, 128, 130, 141, 146–47, 162, 174
Whiston, William, 19, 20
women, 48, 78–79, 124, 157, 162
Word of God, 26, 50, 52, 54, 63, 69, 85, 89, 97, 107, 110, 113, 127, 138, 140, 147, 148, 156, 160–62, 168
Wrede, William, 25, 29

Zolawma, R., 145